Labour and Transnational Action in Times of Crisis

Studies in Social and Global Justice

Series Editors:

Ben Holland, Lecturer in International Relations, The University of Nottingham

Tony Burns, Associate Professor of Political Theory, The University of Nottingham

As transnational interactions become more prevalent and complex in our interconnected world, so do the questions of social justice that have always featured in political discourse. From new debates on human rights and global ethics to changing patterns of resistance and precarity in the global economy, Studies in Social and Global Justice features books that grapple with a broad array of critical issues faced in the world today.

In partnership with the Centre for the Study of Social and Global Justice at the University of Nottingham, the series comprises both empirical and theoretical studies that critically address issues of social justice using a wide array of approaches, providing a vital space for the interdisciplinary interrogation of such issues. The series draws upon diverse work from international relations, political theory and philosophy, as well as utopian studies, urban studies, gender studies, queer studies, postcolonialism, critical animal studies, disability studies, and theology, amongst other fields of study. It problematizes the dualisms between explanation and evaluation, theory and practice, the academy and activism, universities and the local communities in which they are situated, and between the Global North and Global South.

Labour and Transnational Action in Times of Crisis

Edited by Andreas Bieler, Roland Erne, Darragh Golden, Idar Helle, Knut Kjeldstadli, Tiago Manuel Matos and Sabina Stan

ROWMAN & LITTLEFIELD
INTERNATIONAL

London • New York

Published by Rowman & Littlefield International, Ltd.
Unit A, Whitacre Mews, 26-34 Stannary Street, London SE11 4AB
www.rowmaninternational.com

Rowman & Littlefield International, Ltd. is an affiliate of Rowman & Littlefield
4501 Forbes Boulevard, Suite 200, Lanham, Maryland 20706, USA
With additional offices in Boulder, New York, Toronto (Canada), and London (UK)
www.rowman.com

British Library Cataloguing in Publication Information Available
A catalogue record for this book is available from the British Library

ISBN: HB 978-1-7834-8277-1
ISBN: PB 978-1-7834-8278-8

Library of Congress Cataloging-in-Publication Data

Labour and transnational action in times of crisis / edited by Andreas Bieler, Roland Erne, Darragh
Golden, Idar Helle, Knut Kjeldstadli, Tiago Matos and Sabina Stan.
pages cm. -- (Studies in social and global justice)
Includes bibliographical references and index.
ISBN 978-1-78348-277-1 (cloth : alk. paper) -- ISBN 978-1-78348-278-8 (pbk. : alk. paper) -- ISBN
978-1-78348-279-5 (electronic)
1. International labor activities. 2. Labor unions. 3. Labor movement. 4. Crises. I. Bieler, Andreas,
1967-
HD6475.A1L35 2015
331.8--dc23
2015009806

Printed in the United States of America

Contents

Introduction

The Structuring Conditions of the Global Economy and Possibilities of Agency

Andreas Bieler, Roland Erne, Darragh Golden, Idar Helle, Knut Kjeldstadli, Tiago Matos, and Sabina Stan

Processes of neoliberal globalization have put national trade unions under pressure. As a result of the increasing transnational organization of production and the integration of the Chinese, Indian, and other new working classes into the global economy, national labour movements have been put in competition with each other. The global economic crisis has intensified these pressures further. And yet, these economic and political integration processes have also provided workers with new possibilities to organise resistance.

During 2013/2014, the editors of this book worked on the project *Globalisation and the Possibility of Transnational Actors — The Case of Trade Unions* at the Centre for Advanced Study in Oslo, Norway (see http://transnationallabour.wordpress.com/). Our objective was to elucidate the many facets of the possibilities and constraints that globalization puts on trade unions. A key moment in the project was our international workshop on *Labour and Transnational Action in Times of Crisis: From Case Studies to Theory* in February 2014. One special issue resulting from this workshop with the journal *Transfer: The European Journal for Labour and Research* is dedicated to analyzing contentious labour politics and collective action in Europe (Stan, Helle, and Erne 2015); another special issue from the workshop with the journal *Labor History* deals with the contribution of politicization to transnational trade union action (Erne et al. 2015). The main aims of the workshop were, however, twofold and are mirrored in the purposes of this publication.

The first purpose of this volume is to emphasize the importance of labour agency and to investigate what new weapons the labour movement may have in times of crisis, historically and now, and how it is conditioned by the current setting of transnational capitalist social relations of production. The book draws on a variety of fascinating cases,

1

across a range of formal and informal collectives. Key here is the way trade union action at the local and national level may be connected across borders in moments of transnational solidarity. 'Labour' refers to trade unions but also other, more informal forms of collective action by workers understood in a broad sense, including also women, migrants, and precarious workers. One particular form of transnational solidarity—analyzed in some of the contributions—is the willingness and ability of trade unions to reach out to labour migrants.

When assessing different instances of transnational agency, **the edited collection as its second purpose** intends to clarify conceptually which factors facilitate the formation of solidarity and which factors are likely to be an obstacle. To date, there has been a whole range of projects collecting various individual case studies of successful and failed efforts of transnational solidarity (e.g., Bieler, Lindberg, and Pillay 2008a; Bieler and Lindberg 2010; Bronfenbrenner 2007; Novelli and Ferus-Comelo 2009). By contrast, the ambition of this volume is to move beyond empirical description of cases to a conceptually informed understanding of collective action across borders by providing an insightful theorization of transnational action and the construction of transnational solidarity.

Global restructuring may prevent transnational solidarity, as national labour movements are put in competition with each other. At the same time, global restructuring may actually facilitate transnational solidarity by connecting production processes across borders and thereby bringing workers into direct connection with each other. In short, the structural setting neither prevents nor automatically results in transnational solidarity, which is why a focus on agency and its potential different strategies is so important. Nonetheless, agency can never be studied in isolation of the structural setting, within which it takes place. As Karl Marx famously stated:

> Men make their own history, but they do not make it as they please; they do not make it under self-selected circumstances, but under circumstances existing already, given and transmitted from the past. The tradition of all dead generations weighs like a nightmare on the brains of the living. (Marx 1852)

Thus, this introduction will first provide an overview of the structuring conditions in the global capitalist economy in terms of general structural tendencies as well as the more specific dynamics within the current epoch of globalization. Then, the agency of labour will be introduced at a conceptual level. Two main claims will be made. First, classes as collective actors are not given as a result of how people are located within the social relations of production. Class formation is a process in which class-consciousness is established as the result of concrete struggles. Second, when analyzing labour movements and their involvement in class struggle, it is important to define them in a broad sense going beyond the issues of the workplace and covering also struggles in the broader sphere of social reproduction. Finally, this introduction will provide an overview of the structure of the volume.

THE STRUCTURING CONDITIONS OF NEOLIBERAL GLOBALIZATION

When analyzing the structuring conditions of the global economy, we can distinguish between the general structural tendencies within the capitalist social relations of production and the more specific structural dynamics of the current epoch of globalization. In this section, the two areas will be discussed in turn.

The Structuring Conditions of Capitalism

As a result of the way the capitalist social relations of production are organized around wage labour and the private ownership of the means of production, both labour and capital have to re-produce themselves through the market. Workers have to sell their labour power and often compete with each other over finding the best jobs. Capitalists too, however, are in constant competition with each other over market share and, therefore, are driven generally though the introduction of new technology to produce new and better products in order to secure and increase their market share. Their rivals have to do everything possible in order to match and overtake them, in turn. Otherwise, they are in danger, first to lose market share, and then to go bankrupt. As Marx noted, 'under free competition, the immanent laws of capitalist production confront the individual capitalist as a coercive force external to him' (Marx 1867/1990: 381). The fate of Nokia, once dominating the mobile phone market, but now almost extinguished as a brand, is an interesting example in this respect. It is because of this inbuilt focus on competitiveness that capitalism is such a dynamic, as well as destructive production system.

And yet, this dynamism comes at a price. What is logical for the individual capitalist is problematic for capital as a whole. When every capitalist attempts to produce more goods with fewer workers through the application of new technology, there will be fewer and fewer people who can actually buy those goods. In other words, there are tensions between growth and technological progress, which are 'just too powerful to be contained within the confines of the circulation of capital' (Harvey 1985: 132). Hence, there will be a crisis of overproduction and, as a result, a declining rate of profit. 'We see here', Harvey argues, 'the necessary contradiction that arises when each capitalist strives to reduce the share of variable capital in value added within the enterprise while speculating on selling his output to workers employed by other capitalists' (Harvey

2006a: 134). Expressed differently, there is a situation of a surplus of both capital and labour, which can no longer be brought together in a productive way within the capitalist social relations of production, a 'state of overaccumulation' (Harvey 1985: 132). The current global financial crisis clearly demonstrates this dynamic. In order to overcome the crisis of overaccumulation in the early 1970s and the related decline in the rate of profit, a financial fix with a shift towards investing in financial markets to make profit took place (Harvey 1985: 137–39). More and more new, innovative financial instruments were set up in order to develop new areas for the accumulation of surplus value. This also included the highly risky subprime mortgages. What was, however, logical for one financial company due to the initially high profit rates in the subprime mortgage market turned out to be disastrous for the whole financial system. As soon as all financial institutions became involved in this risky area, the bubble burst revealing the fragile foundation of these financial instruments.

With accumulation opportunities exhausted within the existing capitalist social relations of production, the resulting structuring condition is a fundamental dynamic of capitalism towards outward expansion, incorporating ever more additional geographical areas into capitalism (Luxemburg 1913/2003: 332–38) or reorganizing already existing relationships between different geographical areas, between the core and the periphery in novel ways. Samir Amin, for example, illustrated how in the current phase of capitalism forms of production were established through foreign direct investment (FDI) in peripheral spaces enjoying the advantage of low-wage costs. Peripheral countries ceased to export only agricultural products and moved towards the export of low value-added, labour-intensive manufacturing products (Amin 1976: 185–86). More recently, rather than exporting low value-added manufacturing products, cheap labour locations such as China have become assembly platforms of information and communication technology products and electrical goods. Unsurprisingly, 'Chinese exports are Chinese only in the sense that they were assembled in China' (Hart-Landsberg 2013: 38), while 'foreign corporations are responsible for approximately 88 per cent of all Chinese high-technology exports' (Hart-Landsberg 2013: 94). This outward expansion of capitalism proceeds along lines of uneven and combined development, as first conceptualized by Leon Trotsky (1929/2007: 132–37). Development of peripheral countries is combined with the core, but in highly uneven ways (see also chapter 3 in this volume).

These structuring conditions apply to the capitalist social relations of production in general. As Robinson, however, noted, 'globalization represents an epochal shift; that is, fundamental worldwide changes in social structure that modify and even transform the very functioning of the system in which we live' (Robinson 2004: 4). The next section will look in more detail at the specific underlying dynamics of globalization.

The Structural Dynamics of Globalization

Structural change related to globalization since the early 1970s has further shaped the structuring conditions for agency by labour. In response to a crisis of overproduction, capital has abandoned the post–World War II class compromise embodied in the Keynesian welfare state in developed countries. The related restructuring was driven by neoliberalism, which has to be understood as a project by capital to restore class power (Harvey 2006b: 29). Several main developments can be related to neoliberal globalization from the perspective of labour movements (Bieler, Lindberg and Sauerborn 2010: 249–53).

First, globalization has led to an increasing transnationalization of production, with the production of many goods being organised across borders. Outflows of FDI rose from US$88 billion U.S. dollars in 1986 to US$1,187 billion in 2000 as peak year (Bieler 2006: 50). A period of recession caused a decline in FDI flows from 2001 to 2003, but four years of consecutive growth led to a new all-time high of FDI outflows of US$1996.5 billion in 2007 (United Nations Conference on Trade and Development [UNCTAD] 2008: 253). Overall, there were close to eighty thousand transnational corporations (TNCs) with roughly the same number of foreign affiliates in 2007 (UNCTAD 2008: 212). Unsurprisingly, FDI flows have again declined since the onset of the global financial crisis in 2008 (UNCTAD 2013: 213), but even slightly lower levels contribute to the continuing build-up of FDI stocks over time, indicating the ever more important role played by TNCs. While outward FDI stocks had been US$2,091,496 million in 1990, they were US$8,025,834 million in 2000 and US$23,592,739 million in 2012 (UNCTAD 2013: 217). Empirical indicators of the increasing organization of production across borders also include 'the phenomenal increase in cross-border mergers and acquisitions; the increasing transnational interlocking of boards of directorates; the increasingly transnational ownership of capital shares; the spread of cross-border strategic alliances of all sorts; and the increasing salience of transnational peak business associations' (Robinson 2008: 30). As a result, workers in different countries and varying national contexts, both in the North and in the South, have been thrust into unprecedented competition with each other in these transnational production sectors. All too often, unions, locally at the factory level and nationally in centralized negotiations, are confronted with the threat that unless they agree on concessions, employers will transfer production units and jobs to locations with lower labour costs (Bieler, Lindberg, and Pillay 2008b: 272).

Second, the increasing transnationalization of production, which implies a 'centralization of command and control of the global economy in transnational capital' (Robinson 2004: 15), has gone hand in hand with greater decentralization and fragmentation of the production process itself through processes of outsourcing along the production chain. Thus, transnational production, under the direction of TNCs, is increasingly organized in global commodity chains (GCCs) (Robinson 2008: 27). In this process, TNCs 'began dividing the production process into ever finer segments, both vertical and horizontal, and locating the separate stages in two or more countries, creating cross-border production networks' (Hart-Landsberg 2013: 91). In these networks, TNCs no longer own the various production sites along the GCC, but rely on 'independent contract manufacturers to procure the necessary parts and components and oversee their assembly into final products' (Hart-Landsberg 2013: 92). It is no surprise that bilateral and multilateral, regional free trade agreements have become ever more important for transnational capital, as these transnational production networks could not function without free trade. As a result, however, 'the complex nature of this strategy, which involves a variety of business relationships, means that trends in the international trade of components are a better measure of the importance of cross-border production networks than are changes in [FDI]' (Hart-Landsberg 2013: 92). In other words, TNCs are still in charge, but their strategy has significantly changed. From owning cross-border production structures, they have moved to coordinating GCCs. As confirmed by the United Nations, 'TNC-coordinated [GCCs] account for some 80 per cent of global trade. Patterns of value added trade in [GCCs] are shaped to a significant extent by the investment decisions of TNCs' (UNCTAD 2013: xxii).

These developments, however, could not have occurred without the dramatic increase in the global workforce (see also chapter 1 in this volume). Richard Freeman (2010) shows that the integration of China, India, and the former Soviet Union during the 1980s and 1990s doubled the global workforce to almost three billion by 2000. As David Coates correctly notes, 'the enhanced global mobility of capital in the last three decades has social rather than technical roots. Capital is more geographically mobile than it was in the past because it now has more proletariats on which to land' (Coates 2000: 255). This reorganization of the production process around transnational outsourcing and centralization of decision-making and the integration of new working classes, all part of globalization, has led to an increasing casualization and informalization of the economy in which permanent, full-time employment contracts have to a large extent become a thing of the past. This is especially the case in developing countries, which had never been in a position to establish a large industrial sector with permanent and secure employment. 'According to the most recent estimates, non-agricultural employment in the informal economy represents 82 per cent of total employment in South Asia, 66 per cent in sub-Saharan Africa, 65 per cent in East and South-East Asia (excluding China), 51 per cent in Latin America and 10 per cent in Eastern Europe and Central Asia' (International Labour Organization 2014: 6). Nevertheless, informalization more and more also affects developed countries in the North, where employers are on the offensive and demand a flexibilization of the labour market with the argument that it is necessary in order to retain competitiveness (Bieler, Lindberg and Pillay 2008b: 266–67; see also Standing 2011). Indeed 'it is no longer accurate today', Dan Gallin (2001: 228) rightly concludes, 'to describe the informal sector as "atypical"'.

It is at this point, however, that one has to be careful not to slide into a purely structuralist argument. First, restructuring within industrialized countries and the intensified exploitation of the existing workforce are always contested and never conflict free. And it is in this contestation that agency of resistance plays a crucial role. As Cleaver argues, capital's focus on increasing productivity is not only the result of competition with other employers, it is also a response to workers' struggles, establishing a new way of controlling labour (Cleaver 2000: 89). In other words, while the pressure for outward expansion results from capitalism's crisis tendency, the way this unfolds and the extent to which space is incorporated into capitalism is very much the result of class struggle. 'The production of economic landscapes is the result of political conflict, between labour and capital and between different segments of labour and of capital who might have quite different visions for how the landscape should be structured' (Herod 2006: 158). In the next section, this class agency will be conceptualized.

CLASS AGENCY IN THE GLOBAL POLITICAL ECONOMY

In this section, we will first discuss more generally how agency can be conceptualized, before providing several examples of concrete cases of transnational solidarity under conditions of globalization.

Conceptualizing Agency

Social class forces as key collective actors are engendered by the social relations of production. Thus, by class is meant 'a group of people who share a common relationship to the process of social production and reproduction and are constituted relationally on the basis of social power struggles' (Robinson 2004: 37). Capitalism in general leads to a division between capital, the owners of the means of production, on the one hand, and labour, those who are 'free' to sell their labour power on the market, on the other. If left on its own, however, this understanding collapses into a position of economic determinism, which explains workers' and trade unions' strategies simply as a straightforward result of their location in the production process. In reality, the relationship between the structural location and agency of labour is rather more complex. Of course, there is a tendential link between the objective class position of social forces and the particular strategies they adopt. Nevertheless, 'what the economic cannot do is (a) to provide the contents of the particular thoughts of particular social classes or groups at any specific time; or (b) to fix or guarantee for all time which ideas will be made use of by which classes' (Hall 1996: 44). In other words, within each given set of structuring conditions, agents are not completely free in their actions, but they nonetheless still have a range of strategies at their disposal, from which they can choose how to go forward.

Thompson warns against a static, structural definition of class. 'From a static model of capitalist productive relations there are derived the classes that ought to correspond to this, and the consciousness that ought to correspond to the classes and their relative positions' (Thompson 1978: 148). He does not 'see class as a "structure", nor even as a "category", but as something which in fact happens (and can be shown to have happened) in human relationships' (Thompson 1963: 8). Class is, therefore, for Thompson a historical category, an observed behaviour over time. 'We know about class because people have repeatedly behaved in class ways; these historical events disclose regularities of response to analogous situations, and at a certain stage (the "mature" formations of class) we observe the creation of institutions, and of a culture with class notations, which admits of trans-national comparisons' (Thompson 1978: 147). At the same time, Thompson was fully aware of the importance of the social relations of production in shaping people's agency. 'The class experience is largely determined by the productive relations into which men are born—or enter involuntarily. Class-consciousness is the way in which these experiences are handled in cultural terms: embodied in traditions, value systems, ideas, and institutional forms. If the experience appears as determined, class-consciousness does not' (Thompson 1963: 8–9). In short, rather than deducing specific ideas and strategies of workers from their location in the social relations of production, the analytical focus has to be on class struggle and the way workers' strategies are developing over time. Class struggle is the process in which labour identities are formed and transformed. It is the moment when structuring conditions are being confirmed or changed. Whether different labour movements engage in relations of transnational solidarity is, therefore, the outcome of open-ended class struggle. In his contribution to this volume, Ingo Schmidt draws explicitly on the work of Thompson in assessing the possibility for the formation of a European working class.

The analysis of class struggle is, however, often too narrowly focused on struggle between workers and employers at the workplace or trade unions and employers' associations at the national level. Unsurprisingly, a focus on class struggle is often accused of being reductionist. By contrast, when reflecting on the increasing number of struggles of the late 1960s and 1970s, Harry Cleaver asserts that 'the reproduction of the working class involves not only work in the factory but also work in the home and in the community of homes . . . ; the working class had to be redefined to include nonfactory analysis' (Cleaver 2000: 70). Hence, the analysis of class struggle has to cover the whole 'social factory', not just the workplace. This allowed Cleaver to take into account all the other forms of unwaged activities including childrearing and education, which are necessary for the reproduction of capital, but take place outside the workplace. Drawing on the work of the so-called Italian New Left around Mario Tronti and Antonio Negri, he concluded that 'the identification of the leading role of the unwaged in the struggles of the 1960s in Italy, and the extension of the concept to the peasantry, provided a theoretical framework within which the struggles of American and European students and housewives, the unemployed, ethnic and racial minorities, and Third World peasants could all be grasped as moments of an international cycle of working-class struggle' (Cleaver 2000: 73).

Another attempt to include struggles outside the workplace into class analysis is made by Kees van der Pijl. He argues that neoliberal capitalism is characterized by the fact that capitalist discipline has now also been further extended within the entire process of social reproduction, involving the exploitation of the social and natural substratum. In response to the commodification of social services, and the intensified destruction of the biosphere as well as the disruption of traditional life, a whole range of new, progressive but also nationalist right-wing social movements have emerged to defend the environment and sphere of social reproduction (van der Pijl 1998: 46–48; see also Bakker and Gill 2003). This has to be analyzed as class struggle as much as exploitation and resistance to it in the workplace. They become class projects in that moment, when they entail 'a direct challenge to the circulation and accumulation of capital' (Harvey 1996: 401). As a result, the struggle of social movements against neoliberal globalization, for example, can also be conceptualized as class struggle. In this volume, the contribution by Jenny Jungehüelsing (chapter 13) analyzing the potential for transnational solidarity in the organization of migrant workers clearly reaches into areas beyond the workplace and includes aspects of the sphere of wider social reproduction within the social factory.

Transnational Solidarity in Practice

In general, it is often assumed that areas of transnational production are those most easily susceptible to strategies of transnational solidarity. Unions in these sectors are the first to recognize that organisation at the national level is no longer enough to keep wages and working conditions outside capitalist competition. And there are positive examples of transnational solidarity. In 2001, European General Motors (GM) unions and works councils organised a successful one-day strike of forty thousand GM workers across Europe against the closure of the GM plant in Luton in the United Kingdom. This did not only lead to a pioneering European labour agreement that prevented forced redundancies in all European sites from 2001 to 2008, it also showed that competition for investments does not necessarily preempt transnational collective action (Erne 2008: 34). Nevertheless, transnational solidarity in transnational production structures is not automatic. When GM established a new production site in Poland in the late 1990s, this new site 'entered a competitive race with the German plant in Rüsselsheim over the distribution of new Opel Zafira capacities' (Bernaciak 2010: 37). Moreover, in view of GM's decision to close down the production of Opel in Bochum/Germany towards the end of 2014, the German chairman of the European Works Council, as well as chair of the works council at Opel in Bochum, tried to save local jobs by highlighting the higher quality and productivity of their production sites (Schaumberg 2014). Thus, in manufacturing, where often different production sites are played out against each other, the push for solidarity action is great, but competition is a strong counterforce at the same time.

To avoid that labour movements from different countries compete with each other by offering lower wages, the wider challenge is to coordinate union action across a whole sector, at least regionally. The European Metalworkers' Federation, which organizes workers in one of the most transnationalized sectors in Europe, including many TNCs in consumer electronics, car manufacturing, and machinery production, became aware of these dangers in the early 1990s. Plans for Economic and Monetary Union (EMU) implied the danger of social dumping through the undercutting of wage and working conditions between several national collective bargaining rounds (Erne 2008: 80–90). In response, the European Metalworkers' Federation approved the European-level coordination of national wage bargaining in 1998, and it tried to ensure that national unions pursued a common strategy of asking for wage increases along the formula of productivity increase plus inflation rate. And yet, the implementation of the coordination strategy was unsuccessful. In 2006, the European Trade Union Confederation published, for the last time, data on whether the various national collective bargaining rounds had been in line with the European Trade Union Confederation guidelines. The findings make clear that only Finland had achieved this target (Erne 2008: 97).

It is, however, important to remember that the challenges in manufacturing, characterized by transnational production, are not typical of the challenges for all kinds of workers all over the world. Perhaps it is actually the service sector in which solidarity across borders can be established more easily? In services, workers do not directly compete with each other over jobs. A hospital cannot be simply located in another country, for example. It has to remain where it is needed. Second, the service sector facilitates the cooperation between trade unions, representing workers in the sector, and social movements, organizing the service users. Such alliances potentially broaden the social basis of resistance against neoliberal restructuring. The European Citizens' Initiative 'Water is a Human Right' provides an example of solidarity at the transnational level between trade unions and social movements. Coordinated by the European Federation of Public Service Unions, a large alliance of trade unions, social movements, and environmental nongovernmental organizations was established at the European, but also various national levels of European Union member-states for the European Citizens' Initiative. On the one hand, there is the interest of trade unions in keeping water provision in public hands, as working conditions are generally better in the public than the private sector. On the other hand, user groups are supportive of universal access to affordable clean water. Three key objectives were stated at the launch in May 2012: '(1) The EU institutions and Member States be obliged to ensure that all inhabitants enjoy the right to water and sanitation; (2) water supply and management of water resources [will] not be subject to 'internal market rules' and that water services are excluded from liberalisation; and (3) the EU increases its efforts to achieve universal access to water and sanitation' (Water is a Human Right n.d.). Between May 2012 and September 2013, the initiative collected close to 1.9 million signatures and forced the Commission into an official position on water. While the campaign did not obtain all its objectives, it had managed to push the Commission into excluding water from the Concessions Directive and, thereby, ensured that water liberalisation and, thus, privatisation was off the agenda for some time (Bieler 2015). The struggle over access to water is clearly an example of struggle within the wider social factory, identified by Cleaver. It goes beyond concerns related directly to the workplace and yet every worker's daily life is affected by and depends on it.

In construction, the challenge is yet again different. The Berlin labour market for building and construction after 1990, with its huge influx of foreign posted workers, provides a striking example of competition at the workplace itself (Erne 2008: 90–94). In 2000, out of nearly ninety thousand construction workers in Berlin only twenty-three thousand had permanent residence there, while thirty thousand came from lower wage countries in Southern Europe and another thirty thousand from Central and Eastern Europe. Most of the temporary Berlin building workers were employed by foreign companies and posted in Germany. Several German firms even set up Portuguese daughter companies in order to bypass German collective agreements. Here, the aim of the construction workers' union was to ensure that all workers on the same site be regulated by the same collective agreement of the host country. The contributions by Knut Kjeldstadli and Tiago Matos to this volume (chapters 6 and 7), dealing with the organization of workers in the Norwegian construction industry, explore this scenario further.

OVERVIEW OF THE BOOK

The book is structured in four parts. Part I adopts a broader historical as well as conceptual dimension and is dedicated to the dynamics of class formation underlying the variety of strategic responses by labour movements within any given structural setting. This includes an assessment of class formation as a structural and 'objective' phenomenon by Marcel van der Linden as well as a focus on (European) class formation as the result of agency by Ingo Schmidt. Andreas Bieler investigates structural and agential tensions undermining transnational solidarity over free trade, whereas Jörg Nowak discusses contemporary instances of mass strikes in Brazil, India, and South Africa. Part I, thus, sets the stage for the volume's focus on the importance of labour agency understood in a broad sense. Part II assesses the historical trajectories of transnational action, investigating transnational solidarity in its historical and contemporary form in order to identify some of the obstacles to transnational solidarity, but also some of the positive conditions facilitating it. Especially Darragh Golden's contribution on Italian and Irish unions' internationalism vis-à-vis European integration captures the historical dimension. Knut Kjeldstadli and Tiago Matos, in turn, analyze contemporary attempts at transnational solidarity in the Norwegian construction industry. Importantly, while globalization has implied new obstacles to transnational solidarity, it has also provided workers with new weapons and new power resources. Part III addresses the potentially new weapons or power resources available to labour movements in times of globalization. Here, the focus on agency is combined with assessments of the new possibilities for workers to organize resistance against capitalist exploitation. All three authors, Eddie Webster, Marissa Brookes, and Jamie K. McCallum, explore different aspects of these new powers, before Bianca Föhrer completes this part with an assessment of the potential role of trade union education in transnational solidarity. Part IV, finally, is dedicated to the analysis of solidarity at and across different levels, conscious of the fact that transnational solidarity always combines actions at different levels into an overall strategy. In addition to Jenny Jungehüelsing's study of transnational solidarity in an era of transnational migration, Sabrina Zajak identifies multiple transnational pathways of influence and Charles Umney explores the differences between 'managerial' and 'mobilizing' transnationalism. The last chapter will systematize the positive conditions and obstacles to transnational solidarity in order to provide some conceptual conclusions. Unsurprisingly, the various contributors to this volume come from a variety of conceptual backgrounds. Nevertheless, their common focus on the possibilities of agency of transnational solidarity and how to conceptualize them ties the contributors together and allows this final exploration.

Part I

Class Formation

An Introduction

Andreas Bieler

Historical materialist approaches are often criticized for their alleged economic determinism, identifying classes and their interests purely through an identification of their location in the production system. What critics, however, overlook is the important distinction between a class-in-itself and a class-for-itself. Yes, the location within the production process is decisive when identifying social class forces. Within the capitalist social relations of production, organized around wage labour and the private ownership of the means of production, it is capital and labour, who are the main classes opposing each other. The definition of class is thereby relational in that classes are identified through their relations to each other as a result of their respective locations within production. Importantly, however, the location within production generates only classes-in-themselves. The location may shape the identities and interests of classes, but it does not determine them. Whether a class develops class-consciousness and transforms itself into a class-for-itself depends on its agency within processes of concrete class struggle. As E. P. Thompson argued, people, 'experience exploitation (or the need to maintain power over those whom they exploit), they identify points of antagonistic interest, they commence to struggle around these issues and in the process of struggling they discover themselves as classes, they come to know this discovery as class-consciousness' (Thompson 1978: 149).

All four contributions to the first part of this volume speak to this discussion about class formation. As Marcel van der Linden outlines, while the global working class has grown enormously since the early 1990s and especially China's entry into global capitalism, the organizational strength of labour as reflected in the power of trade unions and related social democratic and labour parties has declined. In other words, while labour as a class-in-itself has grown, as a class-for-itself there has been a decrease in power. And yet, the decline in power of organizational labour does not mean that there would be no labour unrest. As Jörg Nowak outlines, especially in so-called emerging economies we have experienced increasing levels of labour unrest in the form of mass strikes. In all three countries, be it the construction sector in Brazil, mining in South Africa, or the automobile industry in India, workers have been involved in large strike movements. These developments are closely in line with Beverly Silver's argument that where production moves, labour unrest will move too (Silver 2003: 41). Beyond occurring at the same time, there has been so far no solidarity across national borders between these movements, but the contemporary occurrence as such may indicate a new period of transnational solidarity, Nowak contests.

Ingo Schmidt develops this focus on class formation further. While he accepts that the European working classes have been to some extent unmade as a result of neoliberalism, drawing on the work of E. P. Thompson, he argues that the current struggles against austerity may already sow the seeds, which will ultimately facilitate the making of a European working class. Andreas Bieler adds to the discussion of class formation with his investigation of the possibility of transnational solidarity between different national labour movements over free trade policies. While they often find themselves in rather different locations in the global economy and could therefore be regarded as different class fractions-in-themselves, the example of the labour movements of the Americas and their successful struggle against the Free Trade Agreement of the Americas does suggest that transnational solidarity, and perhaps even transnational class-consciousness, may be possible as the result of joint struggles.

ONE

The Crisis of the World's Old Labour Movements[1]

Marcel van der Linden

Both the size and composition of the world working class have changed dramatically over the last four decades. But these massive shifts are not reflected in the strength of workers' organizations. In what was traditionally called 'the global South', capital accumulation has resulted in the fast growth of the number of wage earners in industry, building, services, and transport. A recent International Labour Organization study revealed that in the period 1980 to 2005, the labour force in the Middle East and North Africa region had grown by 149 per cent. In sub-Saharan Africa, Latin America, and the Caribbean, it had roughly doubled, in South Asia it had increased by 73 per cent, and in East and Southeast Asia by 60 per cent (Kapsos 2007). Simultaneously, enormous shifts are taking place *within* separate regions. A historic migration from the countryside to swelling megacities is under way. In 2000, the Chinese Ministry of Human Resources and Social Security estimated that there were 113 million migrant workers in the country. Ten years later, that number had more than doubled to 240 million, including 150 million working outside their home areas. Of those 150 million, about 72 per cent were employed in manufacturing, construction, food and beverage, wholesale and retail industries, and hospitality (China Labour Bulletin 2012: 4). In India, internal labour migration has exploded since the 1990s, the temporary and seasonal migration rate being highest in poor regions like Nagaland and Madya Pradesh (Bhagat and Mohanty 2009).

Such shifts are often accompanied by an intensification of social struggles. In Indonesia, the Konfederasi Serikat Pekerja Indonesia (Indonesian

Trade Union Confederation) organized a national strike on 3 October 2012, and a second one—demanding a 50 per cent increase of the minimum wage—on October 31. These were not truly general strikes, but they nevertheless were joined by many hundreds of thousands of workers, especially in the Jakarta region (*International Viewpoint*, 4 November 2013). In India, on 20 and 21 February 2013, over one hundred million workers across the country went on strike for a list of demands including a living wage indexed to inflation, universal food security, and equal pay for equal work (*International Viewpoint*, 2 March 2013). In China, the labour shortages that began to emerge from 2004 led to a rapid growth of workers' protests, which have 'not only increased in number but have shifted focus from a reactive response to labour rights violations towards more proactive demands for higher wages and improved working conditions' (China Labour Bulletin 2012: 5). The Chinese Academy of Social Sciences reported that there were more than sixty thousand so-called mass incidents (popular protests) in 2006 and over eighty thousand in 2007. Since then, official figures have no longer been published but experts believe that in recent years the number has further increased (China Labour Bulletin 2012: 9). Since the beginning of the economic crisis, more than thirty national strikes occurred in Greece, while Spain and Portugal saw several general strikes, including bi- and multinational ones. The dramatic overthrow of the Mubarak dictatorship in Egypt in 2011 could not have happened without the labour movement's strong support (Beinin 2011). And in South Africa, massive and often violent strikes follow one another rapidly.

There is, however, a fundamental problem. The militancy of the workers has not yet been consolidated in strong organizations. In fact, 'old-style' labour is in decline, and fundamental changes will be necessary before a vibrant transnational union movement can be built. Let me support this contention by having a closer look at trade unions and workers' parties.

UNIONS

The surest sign of organized working-class formation is the development of trade unions and similar interest groups. Independent mass trade unions had their origin in the nineteenth century, and exist today in large parts of the world—although there are also major regions where they have almost no influence. The most striking example of a fast-growing capitalist economy without independent trade unions is the People's Republic of China. It hosts the world's largest workers' organization, the All-China Federation of Trade Unions (ACFTU) with 230 million members. This is not an independent union, but rather a transmission belt for the Chinese Communist Party. Most of the numerous labour conflicts in the People's Republic take place not with the support of but despite the ACFTU (Bai 2012). The *China Labour Bulletin* calls the ACFTU 'something of a lost cause at present. In general, it lacks the tools and the strategies needed for a timely and effective response to workers' initiatives and is out of touch with the realities of labour relations in China today' (China Labour Bulletin 2014: 38).

In countries *with* independent workers' organizations, union density (union members as percentage of the total labour force) generally has been declining. Table 1.1 reconstructs the trends in thirteen countries for the period 1920 to 2010. In eleven cases, the high point lies in the past (between 1950 and 1990), although the situation is relatively stable in Canada and Norway. In nine cases, we can observe a clear downward trend. The table might give the impression that the situation is more promising in India or Indonesia. But we should remember that union density is calculated for the *formal* economy, which, for example, in the case of India, covers about eight percent of the labour force. A union density of 41 per cent thus boils down to 3.2 per cent.

On a global scale, union density is almost insignificant. Independent trade unions organize only a small percentage of their target group worldwide, and the majority of them live in the relatively wealthy North Atlantic region. By far, the most important global umbrella organization is the International Trade Union Confederation (ITUC), founded in 2006 as a merger of two older organizations, the secular reform-oriented International Confederation of Free Trade Unions and the Christian World Confederation of Labour. In 2014, the ITUC estimated that about 200 million workers worldwide belong to trade unions, and that 176 million of these are organized in the ITUC.[2] The ITUC also estimates that the total number of workers is roughly 2.9 billion (of whom 1.2 billion in the informal economy). Therefore, global union density currently amounts to no more than 7 per cent (ITUC 2014: 8).

There are quite a few factors that contribute to the weakness of the unions. First, the composition of the working class is changing. Unions find it difficult to organize employees in the service or financial sector. The rapidly growing informal economy is complicating things further, since workers change jobs frequently and have to earn their income under often very precarious conditions. Another important factor is what labour economist Richard Freeman has called the 'labor supply shock', which has manifested itself since the early 1990s. Through the entry of Chinese, Indian, Russian, and other workers into the global economy, there has been an effective doubling of the number of workers producing for international markets over the past two decades.

> A decline in the global capital/labor ratio shifts the balance of power in markets away from wages paid to workers and toward capital, as more workers compete for working with that capital. . . . Even considering

Table 1.1. Union Densities: Stability and Decline, 1920–2010

	1920	1930	1940	1950	1960	1970	1980	1990	2000	2010
Australia	51.6	45.0	49.0	60.0	50.2	44.2	49.6	45.4	24.5**	18.0**
Canada	16.0	13.9	16.3	28.4	29.2	31.0	34.0	34.0	30.8	29.4
France	7.2	7.4			19.6	21.7	18.3	10.0	8.0	7.9
Germany*		37.5		32.7	34.7	32.0	34.9	31.2	24.6	18.6
India									37.9 (2001)	41.1 (2008)
Indonesia								5.0 (1986)	5.0 (1997)	11.8 (2007)
Italy				46.5	24.7	37.0	49.6	38.8	34.8	35.5
Japan					32.9	35.1	31.1	26.1	21.5	18.4
South Korea					9.4 (1963)	12.6	14.7	17.2	11.4	9.7
Malaysia								16.5	11.0 (1999)	10.2 (2007)
Norway	20.3	19.0	36.7	50.6	60.0	56.8	58.3	58.5	54.4	54.8
UK	45.2	25.4	33.1	44.1	40.4	44.8	51.7	39.7	30.1	27.1
USA	17.6	12.7	22.5	31.7	30.9	27.4	22.3**	15.5**	12.8**	11.4**

* For 1950 to 1990: West Germany.

Source: ICTWSS Database, Amsterdam Instituut voor Arbeidsstudies (www.uva-aias.net/207), version 4, April 2013. All percentages indicate net union membership as a proportion of wage and salary earners in employment, unless these figures are not available. If data were missing, net union membership as a proportion of wage and salary earners in employment was used, as in national household or labour force surveys (indicated with **).

the high savings rate in the new entrants—the World Bank estimates that China has a savings rate of 40 [per cent] of GDP—it will take [thirty] or so years for the world to re-attain the capital/labor ratio among the countries that had previously made up the global economy. Having twice as many workers and nearly the same amount of capital places great pressure on labor markets throughout the world. This pressure will affect workers in the developing countries who had traditionally participated in the global economy, as well as workers in advanced countries. (Freeman 2010)

Secondly, significant economic shifts have taken place. The growth of foreign direct investment in the core countries and the semiperiphery of the world economy has been impressive, and transnational corporations and multistate trading blocs (European Union, North American Free Trade Agreement, Mercosur, etc.) have multiplied. Brazil, India, and especially China are important new players who change the rules of the game. This is accompanied by new supranational institutions, such as the World Trade Organization, established in 1995.

And thirdly, the old-style unions have to face more and more competition from alternative structures. In Brazil, South Africa, the Philippines, or South Korea, new, often militant, workers' movements (social movement unions) have emerged (Scipes 2014). New forms of rank-and-file trade unionism outside the established channels appeared since the 1970s, with international connections at the shop-floor level 'bypassing altogether the secretariats, which they see as too often beholden to the bureaucracies of their various national affiliates' (Herod 1997a: 184). A well-known example is the Transnational Information Exchange, a centre in which a substantial number of research and activist labour groups exchange information on transnational corporations (TNCs). Another example is the 'counter foreign policy' existing since the early 1980s in the American Federation of Labor and Congress of Industrial Organizations (Spalding 1992). I should also mention the increasing number of activities carried out by nongovernmental organizations that should, in theory, be the responsibility of the international trade union movement, such as the struggle to regulate and abolish child labour. The ineffectivity of old-style unions is underlined by the growing tendency on the part of global unions (formerly called international trade secretariats) to engage in the direct recruitment of members in the periphery. Think, for example, of the activities of the Union Network International (the global union for the service sector) relating to information technology specialists in India (*Süddeutsche Zeitung*, 8-9 September 2001).

WORKERS' PARTIES

Another expression of class formation is political in nature. Labour, Social Democratic, and Communist parties are generally considered to be
political representatives of the working class. Let me begin with the oldest parties, the Social Democratic and Labour parties. Electorally, these
parties are not doing very well. Table 1.2 indicates that of the fifteen
parties listed, twelve reached their apex between 1940 and 1989; Switzer-
land was earlier (1930s), while Portugal was later (early twenty-first century). The only exception is the Brazilian Partido dos Trabalhadores,
which seemingly is going from strength to strength.[3] More important,
though, is that this family of parties is struggling with a fundamental
identity problem. Social Democratic and Labour policies have since the
1930s/1940s been based on two pillars: social Keynesianism and a specific
'red' party subculture with its own sports associations, women's clubs,
organizations for nature lovers, consumer cooperatives, newspapers,
theatre groups, and the like.

The sociocultural and economic reversal since the 1960s/1970s toppled
both 'pillars' of the social Keynesian stage as the parties' subcultural
networks fell to pieces and social Keynesianism became less feasible. A
great many challenges had to be met more or less simultaneously. Traditional centralism had to be reconciled with basic democratic movements
and feminism with the conventional androcentric culture. Moreover, the
environmental movement needed to be taken seriously without abandoning the pursuit of economic growth (the condition for social redistribu-
tion in a capitalist context). Generalized confusion resulted in a tremen-
dous increase of floating voters, ageing and decreasing membership
numbers, and the virtual disappearance of active proletarian members.
Paradoxically, this loss of identity explains the explosive growth of the
umbrella organization, the Socialist International (SI), which has been
doing extremely well. Since the 1970s, the number of countries with SI
members has more than doubled. This tempestuous growth is especially
remarkable since the membership of the SI has been rather stable during
the preceding decades. In the years 1951 to 1976, the number of affiliated
parties had always fluctuated between thirty-four (at the foundation in
Frankfurt) and thirty-nine (van der Linden 2006).

Most of the parties that joined the SI after 1976 did not fit the organisation's old profile. Before the mid-1970s, nobody would have considered
ex-guerrilla movements like the Popular Movement for the Liberation of
Angola and the Sandinista National Liberation Front or the autocratic
Democratic Action in Venezuela as Social Democratic parties. Such organizations could find a home within the SI because its profile was fad-
ing. This dilution became official when the SI adopted a new 'Declaration
of Principles' at the 18th Congress in Stockholm in 1989, which acknowledges the existence of 'differences' in members' 'cultures and ideologies',

Table 1.2. Average Parliamentary Electoral Results of Social Democratic and Labour Parties, 1920–2013

	1920–29	1930–39	1940–49	1950–59	1960–69	1970–79	1980–89	1990–99	2000–09	2010–13
Australia	45.2	32.4	46.5	46.3	45.1	45.4	47.0	40.8	39.2	33.4*
Austria	39.3	41.1	41.7	43.3	50.0	45.4	47.6*	37.3	33.7	26.8*
Belgium	36.7	33.1	30.7	35.9	31.0	26.6	28.0	23.2	24.0	20.5*
Brazil	—	—	—	—	—	—	—	12.1	16.8	16.9*
Denmark	34.5	43.9	39.1	40.2	39.1	33.6	30.9	36.0	26.8	24.8*
France	19.1	20.2	20.9	15.1	15.9	21.0	35.3	34.6	38.8	29.4*
Germany	29.3	21.2	29.2	30.3	39.4	44.2	39.4	36.9‡	31.9‡	25.7*‡
Italy	24.7*	—	[20.7]	13.5	13.8	9.7	12.9	7.9†	—	—
Netherlands	22.0	21.7	27.0	30.7	25.8	28.6	31.0	26.5	21.2	19.6*
Norway	25.5	38.0	43.4	47.5	45.5	38.8	27.4	36.0	30.8	30.8*
Portugal	—	—	—	—	—	35.2	27.6	39.0	39.8	28.1*
Spain	—	23.1	—	—	—	30.4	44.1	38.2	40.2	28.8*
Sweden	36.0	43.8	48.8	45.6	48.4	43.7	44.5	39.8	37.5	30.7*
Switzerland	25.5	27.5	27.4	26.5	25.1	24.1	20.7	20.9	21.4	18.7*
United Kingdom	37.7	34.4	49.7*	46.3	46.1	39.1	29.2	38.7	38.0	29.0*
Average	31.3	31.7	36.8	35.1	32.7	33.3	33.3	31.2	31.4	25.9

*Only one election.
†Party disbanded in November 1994.
‡Including the former German Democratic Republic.

but emphasizes at the same time that the SI's core values (peace, freedom, justice, and solidarity) 'originate in the labour movement, popular liberation movements, cultural traditions of mutual assistance, and communal solidarity in many parts of the world'.[4] In short, the SI could only grow so dramatically *because* the classical Social Democratic parties were in a deep identity crisis.

Communist parties are the second major political form. The large majority of them was born or grew significantly in three waves: during the five years from mid-1918 to 1923, in the aftermath of the October Revolution; in the 1930s, as a response to the economic depression; and immediately after the Second World War. Some parties still have a rather solid, be it often small, base, such as the ones in Portugal, Spain, and Greece. These parties all developed under right-wing dictatorships and are characterized by their intransigence. Similarly, the influential South African Communist Party seems still to be going strong and has a significant influence on the politics of the African National Congress. But for most parties, the high point was in the 1940s. Now, many Communist parties are having a hard time. In quite a few countries, the parties have been dissolved after electoral decline, splits, or financial bankruptcy. This has for example been the case in Britain (dissolved 1991), Italy (disbanded 1991), Finland (bankrupt 1992), Brazil (internal coup and split 1992). Other parties have gone through mergers (e.g., in Mexico [founding of the Unified Socialist Party, 1981], Denmark [formation of the Red-Green Alliance in 1989] and in the Netherlands [founding of the Green Left Party in 1989]). Even the Communist Party of India Marxist in West Bengal, which got a majority of the votes in a whole series of elections (1971, 1980, 1989 to 2004), has now been reduced to a minor player (two out of forty-two seats!) because of its violent neoliberal policies. The rise and fall of the French Communist Party is illustrative (Figure 1.1).

The French example suggests that the problems of the Communist parties cannot be explained through the collapse of the Soviet Union. In many countries, the downward movement started earlier.

All in all, the foregoing seems to suggest two things: on a world scale, trade unions are not only a weak force, but their power is also decreasing; and in many countries trade unions have lost their natural allies, the workers' parties, either because these parties have disappeared or because they have adopted a variant of neoliberalism.

THE CAUSES OF TRADE UNIONISM'S CURRENT WEAKNESS

My hypothesis is that both old-style trade unionism and old-style workers' parties as described above can no longer cope with the challenges offered by the contemporary world. Globalization and neoliberal challenges require new policies and practices that they apparently cannot

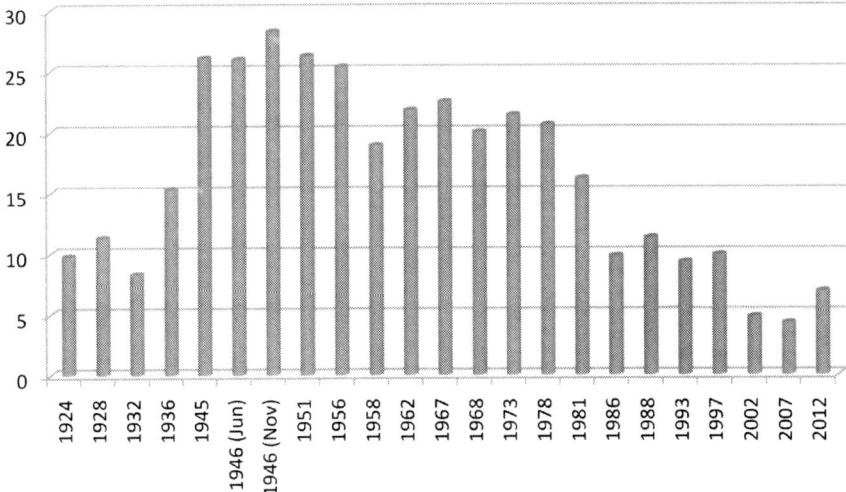

Figure 1.1.   French communist party: Electoral performance 1924-2012.
* In 2012 the PCF participated in the elections as part of a coalition, the Front de
Gauche. Source: own, adapted from official election results.

offer. They are in crisis. Here, I will only try to substantiate this critique for the unions, not for the parties (this I've partly done in van der Linden 2003: 95–116).[5]

I see at least two major difficulties. For a start, the historical trajectory of trade unions is, like that of other organizations, to a significant extent shaped by their founding moment. As Arthur Stinchcombe observed half a century ago:

> The organizational inventions that can be made at a particular time in history depend on the social technology available at the time. Organizations which have purposes that can be efficiently reached with the socially possible organizational forms tend to be founded during the period in which they become possible. Then, both because they can function effectively with these organizational forms, and because these forms tend to become institutionalized, the basic structure of the organization tends to remain relatively stable. (Stinchcombe 1965: 153; also Scoville 1973: 74)

Early trade unions in Europe and North America were mostly the creations of highly skilled male white workers, who had only one boss, yet at the same time, were relatively powerful on the shop floor and attempted to establish collective bargaining. This proved to be an exceptionally successful model that later on also inspired other sections of the working classes (women, blacks, low-skilled). It became the norm for trade unions across the globe. But the specific historic context in which this model had been constructed was forgotten, so that 'a naïve belief in the universal applicability of some form of collective bargaining' (Sturmthal 1973: 5) became more or less universal. Adolf Sturmthal (1973: 9) listed a series of conditions for 'a genuine collective bargaining system', including 'a legal and political system permitting the existence and functioning of reason-ably *free* labor organizations' and the requirement that 'unions be more or less stable, reasonably well organized, and fairly evenly matched with the employers in bargaining strength'. However:

> Effective unions have rarely if ever been organized by 'non-committed' workers, i.e. casual workers who change jobs frequently, return period-ically to their native village, and have no specific industrial skill, even of a very simple kind. Yet even fully committed industrial workers with little or no skill are capable of engaging in effective collective bargaining only under certain conditions which are rarely found. In most (though by no means all) newly industrializing countries, large excess supplies of common labor are available for nonagricultural work. Not only are unskilled workers rarely capable of forming unions of their own under such conditions; if they succeed in doing so, their unions have little or no bargaining power. (Sturmthal 1973: 10)

This is probably the crux of the matter. In the advanced capitalist coun-tries, standard employment relations which had become dominant in the 1940s to 1970s are gradually broken down, while casual and informal labour has 'always' been the norm in Africa, Asia, and Latin America (Breman and van der Linden 2014; van der Linden 2014).

Another difficulty is that old-style trade unions have also become, more or less, one with the nation-states where they originated. The trans-nationalization of capital is a trend they find very difficult to cope with. Globalization has stimulated new forms of cross-border organizing which challenge traditional organizational models. Already in the mid-1960s, the growing influence of TNCs stimulated the setting up of World Corporation Councils, notably in the chemical and automobile industries. Although many trade union militants had high expectations of these new bodies, their effectiveness has been rather less than anticipated, owing to the conflicting interests of employees in different countries (Bendiner 1987; Tudyka 1986; Olle and Schoeller 1987). The formation of trading blocs implied a certain equalization of legal and political parameters, so that the building of transnational trade union structures within each bloc was an obvious step. This collaboration is usually not evolving primarily at the top level of national trade union confederations, but at the subna-tional or branch level. In many cases, institutions other than trade unions (such as religious and human rights organizations) are also partners in projects of this kind. Examples include the 1980s Coalition for Justice in the Maquiladores, the Comité Frontizero de Obreras, and La Mujer Obre-ra (Armbruster 1995: 80–82; Borgers 1996: 81–85; Carr 1999). Equally worthy of note in this context is the Council of Ford Workers, founded by the United Auto Workers (Cyrus and Davis 1993: 165–66). Joint actions against TNCs by trade unions representing particular occupations in different countries (e.g., coal miners, electrical workers) have become much more frequent over the past two decades as well (Armbruster 1995; Herod 1995: 342). When the French car maker Renault announced the closure of its Belgian factory in February 1997, solidarity strikes and demonstrations were organized in France, Spain, Portugal, and Slovenia, giving birth to the new term 'Euro-strike' (Imig and Tarrow 2001). While trade unions support such actions, they frequently do not play a leading role in them.

According to Stinchcombe (1965: 154), 'an examination of the history of almost any type of organization shows that there are great spurts of foundation of organizations of the type, followed by periods of relatively slower growth, perhaps to be followed by new spurts, generally of a fundamentally different kind of organization in the same field.' It might well be that the great spurt of old-style unions has by now almost exhausted itself and that a next spurt with a new type of unionism is 'in the air'.[6]

PROSPECTS FOR A REVITALIZED AND TRANSNATIONAL UNIONISM

What are the challenges that a renewed trade unionism will have to face? First of all, it will have to develop a clear vision of where to go. Revitalization requires convincing policy proposals expressing solidarity between different segments of the working class within and between countries and continents. Second, there is the changing composition of the world working class. Until now workers' organizations of Organisation for Economic Co-operation and Development countries have dominated the ITUC. But their share in the world labor force is shrinking. More and more wage earners live in Asia, Africa, and Latin America. And an increasing part of these workers is female (Table 1.3). More than 40 percent of the world working class (1.2 of 2.9 billion employees) is active in the informal economy, and they have virtually no presence in the old-style union movements.

New forms of trade unionism will have to target this changing working class. The first-phase demarcation of the working classes was extremely narrow and Eurocentric, and needs to be revised and expanded (Antunes 2013: 80–95). There can be no doubt that the newly defined target group should no longer be dominated by white male workers in the North Atlantic region, but by women and people of color, many in forms of hidden wage labour, precarious jobs, or debt bondage. Trade unions in the periphery and semiperiphery are sometimes already now

Table 1.3.   Changing Shares of the World's Labour Force 1980–2005 (% of total)

	1980	2005
Female labor force	38.6	40.1
Youth labor force	27.8	20.8
OECD* countries	19.4	15.7
Eastern Europe and CIS*	10.1	6.4
East and Southeast Asia	35.5	35.9
South Asia	17.7	19.4
Latin America and Caribbean	6.5	8.4
Middle East and North Africa	2.6	4.0
Sub-Saharan Africa	8.2	10.2

*CIS = Commonwealth of Independent States; OECD = Organisation for Economic Co-operative and Development.

Source: Kapsos, S. (2007). *World and Regional Trends in Labour Force Participation: Methodologies and Key Results.* Geneva: International Labour Organisation, 13, 15.

abandoning the old demarcations, and have begun to recruit all kinds of 'nontraditional' workers.

A broadened definition of the target group will necessarily lead to a drastic change of unions' operational systems, in order to assist these 'new' workers to further their interests effectively. This also implies ending the strong emphasis on collective bargaining strategies (Hensman 2001). It is quite well possible that *mutualist* arrangements should be given priority in many cases, that is organizational forms focusing on mutual insurance against sickness, disability, and unemployment that were so prominent in eighteenth- and nineteenth-century European and North American labour movements (van der Linden 2008: 109–31). Much can probably be learned from the 'occupational unionism' which preceded the industrial unionism of the twentieth century (Cobble and Vosko 2000). Jeffrey Harrod sees 'the beginnings of collective organisations aimed at materially improving conditions but not based directly on work and production factors.' He mentions, for example, 'extra-economic' networks of unemployed Japanese youths whose social activity is centred on Internet cafes and Indian groups of casual workers pressuring the state for greater protection (Harrod 2014: 13–14). Some old-style unions already try to open up to such developments, be it hesitantly. In Italy, the trade union confederations CGIL and CISL have created special structures for the representation of 'atypical' workers, and the Austrian employees' union GPA now also enrolls 'dependent self-employed workers' (Cella 2012: 180).

A final necessary change concerns organizational structures and cultures. (1) The dual structure of the international trade union movement—collaboration of national confederations plus global unions—is a problematic relic of the past and likely to be discarded. Probably the best option would be a new unitary structure facilitating the inclusion of the 'new' target groups in the international trade secretariats. (2) The somewhat autocratic approach prevailing in the present-day international trade union movement will need to be replaced by a democratic approach, and greater participation of the rank-and-file workers. The possibilities offered by the Internet are a positive contribution to a renewed structure of this kind (Lee 1997). And third, and most importantly, new methods of collective action, especially across borders, have to be deployed. While lobbying governments and transnational organizations have to date been the principal activity of the international trade union movement (with the notable exception of the anti-apartheid campaign of the 1980s), and efforts are made to cultivate the good will of states (Greenfield 1988), effective action requires much greater effort in active measures, such as boycotts, strikes, and so on, which in turn demands a substantial strengthening of the internal structures. As Dimitris Stevis (1998: 66) has rightly observed, international labour organizations are 'not simply sleeping giants, but fundamentally weak intersocietal federations'.

The question is whether the existing international trade union movement can meet these challenges. It is likely that a new spurt in union development will be a difficult process, interspersed with failed experiments and moments of deep crisis. Organizational structures and patterns of behaviour that have existed for over a century are not easily changed. Moreover, it is highly unlikely that new structures and patterns will be shaped through reforms from above, through the central leadership. If there is one thing that history has taught us, it is that trade union structures almost never develop smoothly by means of piecemeal engineering. They are generally the outcome of conflicts and risky experiments. Pressure from below through competitive networks, alternative action models, etc., will be a highly important factor in deciding that outcome. What forms those pressures will take, and whether they will be sufficient to bring about major changes, no one can say yet with any certainty.

NOTES

1. I am grateful to Peter Waterman for the many discussions we have had over the years; they have helped me enormously to clarify my thoughts on international trade unionism. Earlier drafts received very useful comments from Andreas Bieler, Hans Boot, Matthias van Rossum, and two anonymous referees.

2. This calculation is probably misleading. A significant, but unknown, part of the union membership consists of pensioners.

3. Seemingly, because this could be a statistical artifact. Between 2000 and 2009, there have been two elections for the Brazilian Chamber of Deputies. In 2002, the Partido dos Trabalhadores achieved its highest result ever (18.4 per cent), but the average for the decennium was lowered by the bad result of 2006 (15.0 per cent). Thereafter, there was a certain recovery and the Partido dos Trabalhadores gained 16.9 per cent in 2010.

4. www.socialistinternational.org/4Principles.

5. The chances that successful new workers' parties will be established soon seem rather slim. Eric Hobsbawm once famously pointed out that workers' parties with a mass following emerged mainly in one specific historical period, namely between the 1880s and the 1930s. 'These parties, or their lineal successors, are still in being and often influential, but where they did not already exist, or the influence of socialists/ communists was significant in labor movements before World War II, hardly any such parties have emerged out of the working classes since then, notably in the so-called "Third World"' (Hobsbawm 1984: 60). The most important exception to this rule was the founding of the Workers' Party in Brazil in 1980, which gained a significant following. It is not possible to exclude the possibility that the Brazilian experience will be repeated in other places, but at the moment there are no grounds for assuming that this will happen. For now, it seems that trade unions will have to rely entirely on their own strength.

6. Perhaps we could consider this whole process as an example of 'the handicap of a headstart' or of uneven and combined development (see van der Linden 2007).

TWO

Farewell to Europe's Working Classes

Welcome the Making of the European Working Class?

Ingo Schmidt

In his 1978 Marx Memorial Lecture, Eric Hobsbawm (1978) speculated about the end of the forward march of labour. In the midst of the high tide of social unrest that marked the 1970s, this speculation seemed out of touch with reality. With hindsight, it turned out to be prophetic. The election of Margaret Thatcher the following year signalled the rise of neoliberalism and with it the long downward march of labour and other social movements in Europe and elsewhere. However, these retreats were punctuated by recurrent outbursts of protests, strikes and riots. Whether the capitalist offensive against workers', women's, student, and environmental movements would have gone even further without the latter's recurrent mobilizations is impossible to know. What is quite obvious, though, is that they were unable to stop the offensive. The fact that social unrest pops up, despite the string of defeats progressive movements suffered since neoliberalism first reared its head, poses the question why activists start over and over again. Are they possibly inspired by collective memories of past struggles? Do these struggles leave subterranean traces in the fabric of today's society? Do they point to alternatives that allegedly do not exist?

The retreat of progressive movements has sometimes been explained as the result of class struggle from above. It is interpreted as a response to the challenges of economic crises and the upsurge of social unrest from the late 1960s to the end of the 1970s (Harvey 2005; Duménil and Levy 2011). This capital offensive included the reorganization of labour processes, relocations, automation, privatisations, and a lowering of social standards. It undermined workers' bargaining power by tearing apart the social fabric on which working class identities and organisations had rested since these classes were first formed in the nineteenth century (Katznelson and Zolberg 1986). This line of reasoning explains the downward march of labour quite well, but it doesn't help to understand the recurrence of social unrest and its effects (Schmidt 2011, 2014). In the following pages, I will argue that the unmaking of working classes is actually complemented by first steps towards the making of a new European working class. The latter goes back to the upsurge of labour and other social movements in the 1970s. Though it is true that these movements were defeated by capital's counteroffensive, they also left collective memories, which, together with memories of social protections during the welfare state era, frame the ways in which everyday experiences, under the reign of neoliberal capitalism, are interpreted. These interpretations, in turn, impact the articulation of discontent with neoliberalism. Articulations of discontent range from protest votes to demonstrations, riots, and strikes. Though rarely having an immediate effect, they are an indispensable part of the making of a new European working class. This argument will be developed by analogy with E. P. Thompson's (1963) seminal work on the 'original' making of the English working class.

Thompson reconstructs the making of the English working class through the three main parts of his book. Part one, 'The Liberty Tree', looks at the coalescence of ideas of liberation, inspired by the French revolution and articulated through the agitation for political reform in England, with efforts to defend the moral economies of a faltering feudal society against the impositions of emergent industrial capitalism. Part two, 'The Curse of Adam', describes the effects of enclosures and the industrial revolution, respectively, on field labourers, artisans, and weavers, and how these groups of workers developed a commonly shared class consciousness, despite the differences in their occupational status, incomes, and working conditions. In part three, 'The Working-Class Presence', Thompson analyses the radical culture that had developed alongside the struggles of labour movements from the Luddites to the Chartists and the Owenites. This culture was crucial for the emergence and reproduction of the consciousness of, and debates about strategies for labour within, the English working class. The key to Thompson's concept of the working class is that it has to be understood in relation to other classes, chiefly, of course, the capitalist class. Equally important is the idea that the experiences that workers have in their daily lives, as much as in economic and political struggles, led to the development of class consciousness, despite differences in occupational status, incomes, and working conditions. In his words, 'class happens when some men, as a result of common experiences (inherited or shared), feel and articulate the identity of their interests as between themselves, and as against other men whose interests are different from (and usually opposed to) theirs'. This 'class experience', he goes on, 'is largely determined by the productive relations into which men are born or enter involuntarily' and concludes that this experience is translated into 'class consciousness' by 'the way these experiences are handled in cultural terms: embodied in traditions, value systems, ideas, and institutional forms' (Thompson 1963: 8–9). This consciousness represents 'an identity of interests as between all the diverse groups of the working people and as against the interests of others' (Thompson 1963: 212).

Thompson drew these conclusions from his analysis of workers' efforts 'to re-impose the older moral economy as against the economy of the free market' (Thompson 1963: 73). These efforts created a situation in which 'the legal code and the unwritten popular code . . . have been sharply distinguished from each other' (Thompson 1963: 64). The latter, informed by the moral economy of the past, gave legitimacy to opposition against the new capitalist order, be it food riots, resistance against enclosures, or acts of machine breaking. The distinction between legal and popular codes was further accentuated by the notion that the working people who opposed the free market were 'Free-born Englishman' (Thompson 1963: chapter 4). These notions, which harkened back to the English revolution of 1688, were brought back to life by the French and American revolutions of 1789 and 1776, respectively, and adopted by the English Jacobins who spread the ideas Thomas Paine had outlined in his Rights of Man. None of the oppositional movements mentioned above achieved their goals. What they left, despite their failures, was a collective memory of struggles for a better world. Later in the nineteenth century, this memory turned out to be the soil from which unions, and eventually the Labour Party as political expression of the organized working class in England, would sprout.

The following discussion of the unmaking and remaking of working classes from the 1970s until today adopts Thompson's three-step framework. The next section, 'Reclaiming the Liberty Tree', focuses on protest movements from the late 1960s to the early 1980s. These movements, often inspired by the anticolonial revolutions in Cuba and Vietnam, reinvented ideas of liberation in Western European welfare states but also the communist regimes of Eastern Europe. These movements that fought for liberty in and against the administered worlds East and West were either crushed or marginalized. Rather than enhancing the liberties of the common people, they contributed, against their intentions, to the liberation of capital from political fetters in the West and paved the way for the reintegration of Eastern Europe into world capitalism. Another section, 'The Curse of Hayek', looks at effects of privatizations and industrial restructuring on European societies since the 1980s and shows how these changes led to an unmaking of the old European working classes. The final section, 'The Working-Class Future', argues that the discontent with neoliberal capitalism, and recurrent struggles against it, prepared the ground for the making of the European working class similar to the original making of the English working class. Organizing an analysis of contemporary reconfigurations of classes and class-relations around Thompson's work requires awareness of the differences between the times he was scrutinizing and ours. Thompson understood the making of the English working class in the context of the unmaking of precapitalist popular classes and the emergence of industrial capitalism in England. What we are looking at is the unmaking of working classes shaped by industrial capitalism and integrated into welfare states following World War II. We are also looking at the unmaking of working classes shaped by Soviet communism and, following the end of the Cold War, the making of a transnational working class within the institutional confines of European integration.

RECLAIMING THE LIBERTY TREE

The liberation from Nazi rule produced further reaching hopes for an end to economic exploitation and social injustices (Horn and Kenney 2004: chapters 1 and 2). Hopes that were soon buried under the Cold War order and the administered worlds East and West (Marcuse 1964). Workers living standards rose significantly during the long boom following World War II, and inequalities were reduced while income and employment security improved significantly. At the same time, the social engineering that administered these material gratifications, through tripartism between capitalists, state bureaucrats, and union leaders in the West, or state and party officials in the East, disempowered workers who had been active in their unions and political and cultural organizations ever since they came to see themselves as working classes. This disempowerment was furthered by the colonization of workers' life worlds through mass consumption and mass culture. Working class integration was supplemented by the marginalization of radicalism, signified by the 'containment' of French or Italian communists or the outlawing of the West German communist party. The Stalinization of Eastern Europe had similar effects. Where revolts occurred, despite the combination of mass integration and marginalization of dissent, as in East Germany in 1953 and Poland and Hungary in 1956, repression was swift and ruthless. However, the end of Stalinist terror, first steps towards détente, and the anticolonial revolutions in the Global South brought new life to the idea of liberation. New sprouts on the liberty tree manifested themselves in a transnational moment signified by the Prague Spring and the May general strike in France in 1968 and Italy's Hot Autumn in 1969 (Horn and Kenney 2004: chapters 5–8; Suri 2003). Workers and students, a little later joined by women, immigrants, and environmentalists, were on the march in those days; on their own, sometimes together and sometimes clashing with each other. A fair number of activists who took part in protests, teach-ins, occupations, and strikes of those days thought that the ideas that had been discussed in the small circles of the New Left since the late 1950s had gripped the masses and were becoming a material force.

Some of the activists and intellectuals involved read the unexpected labour militancy that was part of '68' as a sign of the return of the class politics of the 1920s and 1930s and turned to neocommunist organizing. Others saw this militancy as workers' last stand in the face of the transition to postindustrial societies and dissociated their politics, soon lumped together as new social movements, from references to class. With hindsight, it is easy to see that both currents had it half right and half wrong. When mass unemployment returned in the wake of the world recession 1974/1975, labour struggles became much more defensive. The second slump from 1980 to 1982 effectively ended the wave of militancy that had begun during the boom and full employment years of the late 1960s. Most of the workers who had been active in these struggles had been socialized under the economic conditions of full employment and prosperity; they were not the tough guys who had survived depression and war and were prepared to keep up the struggle despite the economic hardships of the 1920s and 1930s. Marcuse (1964) was right in declaring that kind of class dead while the long boom was still going strong.

Yet, this did not mean that class had become irrelevant as new social movement builders thought it did. For the most part, these movements fought against the capitalist enclosures of private households, education, culture, and nature (Habermas 1987: 332–73). However, the autonomy that these movements, ranging from women demanding wages for housework and an expansion of public services to squatters and radical environmentalists, tried to defend or conquer was highly fragile (Katsiaficas 2006). Many of their claims aimed at public funding, which is ultimately tied to state capacities to collect taxes or sell bonds to private investors, and was thus susceptible to the imperatives of capital accumulation. Attempts to build an alternative economy outside such imperatives never reached the critical mass necessary to ensure their survival in the face of capitalist competition. As a result, most of the self-managed and collectively owned firms in this alternative economy were pushed into bankruptcy while a few turned out to be seeds for new capitalist enterprises. Moreover, capitalist enclosures of the spheres of reproduction, education, and the environment also meant an expansion of capitalist employment relationships. Thus, an increasing share of the entire population had to come to terms with their direct subjugation to capitalist rule, one way or another.

The activist exuberance that revived labour movements and gave rise to the new social movements around 1968 did not last long but the ideas that had inspired them survived in a confusing variety of miniscule acti-

vist and discussion groups, connected through cultural centres and publications; a 'scene' that looked like a twentieth-century update of the
corresponding societies in late-eighteenth-century England. Ideas of liberation from the rule of capital and its injustices and exploitation went
into survival mode while the exact opposite idea of liberty, capital investments unlimited by political or moral barriers, occupied more and more
social and economic spaces.

THE CURSE OF HAYEK

In 'The Making', Thompson (1963: chapters 7–9) explores the ways in
which field labourers, artisans, and weavers experienced the effects of
industrialization and enclosures. This analysis offers a few leads for the
understanding of working class experiences in Europe from the 1970s
until today. The first is that he shows that labour-saving technology and
the replacement of complex labour processes by simple and repetitive
tasks were not the only factor responsible for the creation of the supply of
cheap labour for emerging industries. Equally important were political
interventions, notably the enclosure and poor laws. More recently, workers were downgraded by the combined effects of new technologies, notably computer-based production and distribution systems, and the deregulation of labour markets, social spending cuts, and the privatization of
public services and enterprises (Doogan 2009; Eurofound 2006). Welfare
state expansion during the post–World War II boom had led to a, however partial, decommodification of labour power, but the transformation of
welfare into workfare states led to its recommodification akin to the effects of the enclosures in England during the industrial revolution. During both eras, recommodification led to a deterioration of living standards for many workers and was experienced as discomforting even by
others whose jobs and incomes were not negatively affected. Even this
latter group of workers felt under pressure to maintain their social position and was increasingly anxious of being unable to do so. Containing
the discontent produced by the commodification of labour required ideological justification. Thompson discusses the contradictory role Christian
theology played in this respect. As the dominant ideological framework
of feudalism it also delivered the 'languages' to express support of, or
opposition to, the transformation to capitalism. Christian dissenters from
the time of the Glorious Revolution to the enclosures gave legitimacy to
common people's efforts to defend their moral economies against free
market challenges before such opposition could be articulated in the secular language of the working class that would develop later (Thompson
1963: chapter 2). On the other hand, precapitalist theology could also be
transformed in such a way, Thompson (1963: chapter 11) highlights
Methodism in this respect, that it would justify capitalist work discipline.

In the twentieth century, liberalism, including its radical offspring in the forms of socialism and national liberation, had replaced Christianity as the dominant ideology in the centres of the capitalist world system (Wallerstein 1995: particularly 72–93). Not surprisingly, then, discontent with welfare capitalism, and Soviet communism, was expressed by quests for a more libertarian socialism beyond the alienation experienced in the administered worlds of the East and West. When Western capitalists went on a counteroffensive against old and new social movements, they did so in the name of market liberalism, an ideology that was able to pick up the libertarianism of the New Left and the new social movements and turned them into a justification for the unlimited rule and expansion of capital. Ironically, though, the transformation of the embedded liberalism, with its Keynesian and welfare state ingredients, into neoliberalism also included the reinvention of Christian ideas about work discipline. Kalecki had foreseen the capitalist turn against Keynes accompanied by references to Christian values prophetically, even before the rise of the Keynesian welfare state. Commenting on capitalists' and procapitalist economists' views on full employment and social expenditure, he mockingly argued, 'a "moral" principle of the highest importance is at stake. The fundamentals of capitalist ethics require that "[Y]ou shall earn your bread in sweat"—unless you happen to have private means' (Kalecki 1943: 326).

The rise of a new spirit of capitalism (Boltanski and Chiapello 2007; Harvey 2005: chapter 1) that transcended the social liberalism of the postwar era by incorporating some of the libertarian ideas of the New Left marks only the ideological side of the neoliberal turn and its project of unmaking working classes and their institutionalized power. The material side of this turn is about lowering social standards, fostering capital mobility and privatizations, and reorganizing labour processes. The overarching goal of these efforts was bypassing workers' bargaining power and the welfare state that capitalists saw as a threat to their power and profits (Harvey 2005: chapter 3; Silver 2003). Rolling back labour was seen as a way to restore profit rates that had come under pressure during the postwar prosperity due to rising capital costs and growing overcapacities. Workers and welfare states were not responsible for either of these but were expected to pay the price of restoring profitability anyways. Technological and organizational changes were also implemented under the reign of welfare capitalism (Mandel 1975: chapters 5–8). In those days, their goal was not necessarily to bypass unions but to increase labour productivity sufficiently so that real wage increases would not lead to falling profit rates. These changes included deskilling, speedups, and intensified management control, factors that did more to trigger labour militancy in the late 1960s than claims for higher wages. The same changes also caused capital costs, or, in Marxist terminology, the organic composition of capital to rise. In this light, profit rates were under pressure due to rising costs of capital more than they were from labour costs.

Industrial restructuring from the late 1970s onwards can be seen as an effort to lower both types of costs (Husson 1999). Significantly, these changes, more or less, continued along already existing paths of innovation through the 1980s; a major shift towards the establishment of international production networks occurred only in the 1990s when Eastern European countries and China became available for capitalist investment (Zysman, Doherty, and Schwartz 1996). At that point, labour militancy had already decreased to levels that were even lower than those before the strike wave from the late-1960s until the late 1970s (Glyn 2006: 3–8). If the new social movements ever had been a challenge to capital rule, they certainly were not one by the time the Berlin Wall came down, a world historical turning point brought about by protest movements in the East. Echoing Gorbachev's attempts to reform the Soviet Union from above, these movements were demanding democratisation from below in other communist countries (Horn and Kenney 2004: chapters 9 and 12). If the new social movements in the West had paved the way for piecemeal neoliberalism against their intentions, democracy movements in the East did the same for a fast-track invasion of Western capital paired with a large-scale accumulation of dispossession. For old capitalists from the West and the new rich in the East, these were welcome investment opportunities rather than attempts to get around assertive working classes. The continued unmaking of these classes, and the boost respective measures gave to profitability, were positive side effects but not the cause for action, as it has been when this unmaking started in the early 1980s. Needless to say, there were also negative effects. As Silver (2003: 20–25) predicted, the dismantling of workers' protections leads to crises of legitimacy. These crises were lingering in Europe for a long time, discussed in terms of a democratic deficit in the public sphere and erupting politically in no-votes on the European Union constitution in France, the Netherlands, and Ireland. Yet, only the aftermath of the Great Recession and the euro crisis propelled the lack of legitimacy into a major factor determining the future of European integration. Euro critics left and right advocate not only changes within the institutional confines of the European Union, some of them are also quite successful in campaigning for exit from the European Union or its total dissolution (Schmidt 2013).

It took Keynesian measures to stop the Great Recession from turning into another Great Depression but the Euro crisis dashed any hopes that these measures had been the beginning of the end of neoliberalism. While the political responses to the latter crisis ushered in a new age of austerity, they also triggered social unrest that was much broader in scope than anything since the last major wave of unrest in the 1970s. Despite its diversity and fragmentation, this recent outburst may be another step on the way to the making of a European working class.

THE WORKING CLASS FUTURE

Against defeatist views that see working classes and their struggles evaporating in the thin air of neoliberal globalization with its fully computerized world economy, Silver (2003: 74) argues, 'where capital goes, conflict goes'. Conflict does not necessarily mean that one of the contending forces is a collective agent named working class. Yet, as Thompson has shown, the experiences different groups of workers made in scattered conflicts with their employers and the state can be translated into a common class consciousness by 'the way these experiences are handled in cultural terms: embodied in traditions, value systems, ideas, and institutional forms' (Thompson 1963: 8–9). The question, then, is whether the cultural terms Thompson mentions exist on the European level and whether they foster the making of a European working class despite the very real dangers of racist and nationalist divisions within Europe, and between European and non-European countries.

A rising tide of right-wing populism and extremism is one expression of the crisis of legitimacy of the European Union (Langenbacher and Schellenberg 2011), but that does not mean that the populist or far right is unstoppable on the rise (Mudde 2013). At the other end of the political spectrum, we see a rising tide of protests and strikes against neoliberal austerity and some efforts to build new left parties after social democracy took the Third Way to neoliberalism (Daiber, Hildebrandt, and Streithorst 2010; Evans and Schmidt 2012). Political reorientation towards the left and right goes hand in hand with a significant drop of trust in political institutions on the European Union and nation-state levels. At the same time, though, core principles of the welfare state, such as jobs creation and protection and the provision of public health care and education, enjoy continued popularity (European Commission 2013). The downgrading of individuals to reference numbers in an administered world, which helped the new social movements of the 1970s to get off the ground, has turned into even nastier treatments of anyone applying for state services since welfare states were transformed into workfare states. The ironic result of this transformation is that memories of welfare states are much more positive than the views contemporaries held about it before the neoliberal counter-reforms began. These memories are one of the inspirations that lead workers, students, and unemployed youth to struggle against austerity; they are also the reason why many, who do not actively participate, see such struggles with sympathy.

Memories of the welfare state, it seems, are an important part of the traditions and value systems with which workers and other subordinated groups handle their daily life experiences in cultural terms. This, it should be noted, is not only true for the West but also the formerly communist East (Haggard and Kaufman 2008: chapters 4 and 8). Part of this experience is, of course, that protests, strikes, or protest votes did not stop the neoliberal counter-reform. Paraphrasing Thompson (1963: 73) one could say that efforts to 'reimpose the older moral economy (of the welfare state) against the economy of the free market (European Union)' are futile because the national institutions in which this moral economy has been, and to some degree still is, embedded are powerless in the face of global capital and its political supporters in national governments and supranational institutions.

This was a widespread sentiment in the 1990s prompting efforts to Europeanize unions through the coordination of bargaining across countries, the establishment of European Works Councils, and support for efforts of embedding the European Single Market in institutions that could provide social protections (Bieler 2006; Erne 2008). These efforts aimed at transposing welfare state institutions from nation-states to the European Union level. They raised difficult questions concerning the effectiveness and legitimacy of multilevel governance (Scharpf 2007). Their technocratic design made it difficult to garner grassroots support despite repeated union participation at European-wide protests. Rather than relying on protestors, social Europe architects were hoping for the support from social democratic governments that had been elected in increasing numbers during the 1990s. Like national welfare states in the post–World War II era, social Europe was designed as a framework to negotiate class compromises on the basis of strong economic growth. Yet, while the 1950s and 1960s saw unprecedented economic prosperity, hopes for an equally prosperous New Economy in the 1990s were as inflated as information technology stocks. The bursting of the dot.com bubble and the world recession that accompanied it in the early 2000s led to a social democratic turn from vague Third Way-New-Economy-Social-Europe notions to very real austerity measures that sent their electoral approval plummeting almost like information technology stocks. While stocks recovered from the 2001/2002 crash and even from the much deeper fall in 2008/2009, social democratic approval rates remain for the most part at levels lower than at any other time since World War II (Bailey et al. 2014). The turn from the New Economy to economic stagnation and social democratic decline buried hopes for a social Europe (Schmidt 2009).

Efforts to build a social Europe from above were accompanied by grassroots movements, such as the European Marches Against Unemployment, the European Social Forum, and the Association for the Taxation of Financial Transactions. These movements struggled against the commodification of public and private spheres of life (Birchfield and Freyberg-Inan 2004; Mathers 1999). Organizing practices and political outlook, notably its libertarianism and diversity, of these movements resembled those of the new social movements of the 1970s. Not surprisingly, 1990s activists had similar conflicts with the top-down approach of most unions and parties of the left. At the same time, grassroots activists and technocratic social Europe builders shared the neglect of macroeconomic developments in general and the effects of economic crises on social movements of all sorts. The quest to regulate financial markets—the Tobin-tax served as common denominator for the European branches of the altermondialistas—was meant to limit the power of global capital but not as a means of Keynesian moderation of cyclical crises or, more radically, a step towards overcoming capitalism altogether. The rising tide of demonstrations for another Europe, which protestors claimed to be possible against the one-dimensionality of neoliberalism, reached its high mark just around the time the dot.com bubble burst. Demonstrations against the war on Iraq, headily praised by Habermas and Derrida (2003) as the birth of a social and peaceful Europe, distinguished from America's market radicalism and imperialism, did not signal the transformation of the altermondialista movements into a movement that would confront capitalist crises and imperialism head on. Rather, these demonstrations were the beginning of the end of altermondialista mobilizations.

Yet, the new wave of austerity measures following the Euro crisis brought labour and other social movements back to life in many European countries. The new wave of unrest that was triggered by the Euro crisis includes mass protests of educated but unemployed youth from the Indignados in Spain to Gezi Park occupiers (Karaagac and Yilmaz 2013; Morell 2012). It further includes the riots of marginalised youth, for example in England and Sweden (Kings, Ålund, and Schierup 2013; Murji and Neal 2012). And it includes a series of political strikes (Gall 2012; Gallas, Nowak, and Wilde et al. 2012) and the already mentioned party-building efforts. The social basis of this unrest is as diverse as the motley crew of field labourers, artisans, and weavers that Thompson wrote about. And the same is true about the diversity of tactics. Where Thompson saw Luddites, Owenites, and Chartists, we see protestors, rioters, and strikers. Today's attempts of moving from protest to the building of new political formations and electoral politics are similar to Chartists' efforts of rallying in the streets to democratize existing political institutions. Even if today's efforts fail like the Chartists did, they may still represent a collective experience crucial to the emergence of new class identities and the building of more effective political formations in the future.

The return of neoliberalism after the Keynesian interlude, which contained the Great Recession, destroyed illusions anyone might still have had about the possibility of transforming existing national or European Union institutions into a social Europe worthy of the name. At the same time, altermondialistas' widespread ignorance of state power has been rendered obsolete by the massive use of that power to shift the burden of the crisis from the haves to the have-nots. Not surprisingly, then, struggles against austerity are very much struggles against states and supranational institutions that are pushing the neoliberal agenda. This state-cen-

teredness of social conflicts carries the risk of transforming social demands into nationalist protections and thus interstate conflict and mobilizations against immigrants within each state. The European Union's division between debtor and creditor states could also be translated, and to
some degree has already done so, into attempts to pit workers in debt-
ridden peripheries against workers in the credit-issuing centres. But the
policies with which governments and supranational institutions are con-
fronting workers are the same in all European countries, articulated with
national accents and prescribed in different doses, but qualitatively are
the same. The fact that states lead the neoliberal charge also has coalesc-
ing effects in affecting workers who might see themselves, and be seen as
such by others, as distinct groups if confronted by their respective employers. Cutting public services affects not only public sector workers
negatively but also workers in the private sector who cannot afford private services. Cutting unemployment benefits and minimum wages affects not only those workers negatively who receive these benefits and
wages, respectively, but also those better-paid workers who feel the
downward pull on their wages and working conditions. Experiences
with the short-lived New Economy euphoria of the 1990s, continuing
economic stagnation today, and the ecological crisis make clear there is
little hope for future class compromise built on prosperity. Struggles
against austerity bear the potential of making a European working class.
The dream of another Europe that inspired activist groups in the later
1990s could become true if this class lends its hands, brains, and minds,
and their numbers and their diversity to this cause.

THREE

Free Trade and Transnational Labour Solidarity

Structural and Agential Challenges for the Twenty-First Century

Andreas Bieler[1]

INTRODUCTION

Since the completion of the General Agreement on Tariffs and Trade Uruguay Round in 1993, the global free trade regime has been fundamentally transformed. While the postwar free trade regime of General Agreement on Tariffs and Trade was part of the compromise of embedded liberalism, which combined an openness to the international economy with the right for individual governments to intervene into their own economies in order to ensure domestic stability (Ruggie 1982), the post-1993 regime governed by the newly established World Trade Organization (WTO) has significantly undermined national sovereignty through its dispute settlement mechanism. Moreover, the free trade agenda was expanded from its focus on facilitating trade in goods through lowering tariff barriers to new areas including now also trade in services, public procurement, trade-related investment measures, intellectual property rights, as well as the highly controversial investor-state dispute settlement provisions. With China's accession to the WTO in 2001, the vast majority of countries are now members and, therefore, subject to its rules and limitations. It is this expanded free trade agenda, which is one of the key issues, over which tensions have developed between Northern trade

41

unions and labour movements from the Global South (Bieler, Hilary, and Lindberg 2014).

During the talks over the revival of the WTO Doha round in 2008, these tensions developed into an open confrontation. The European Metalworkers' Federation co-operated with the European Automobile Manufacturers' Association in the publication of two joint press releases, demanding reciprocal market access in the Global South (European Automobile Manufacturers' Association–European Metalworkers' Federation 2008a, 2008b). These joint statements led to an angry response by the Congress of South African Trade Unions. The European Metalworkers' Federation was accused of undermining workers' solidarity, since their cooperation with European employers in demanding equal market access would imply job losses in the Global South and undermine the internal unity of the International Trade Union Confederation (Congress of South African Trade Unions 2008). The WTO Doha round, intended to deepen the expanded free trade agenda further, has stalled. Nevertheless, especially the United States and European Union have pushed the expanded free trade agenda further in bilateral negotiations with other countries or groups of countries, exposing again the divisions within the global labour movement. This currently includes the negotiations of the Comprehensive Economic and Trade Agreement between Canada and the European Union, the Transatlantic Trade and Investment Partnership as well as the Trans-Pacific Partnership Agreement. In particular, the European Union's Global Europe free trade agenda has raised concerns by labour movements in the Global South. While European trade unions, and here especially those organizing workers in the export-oriented, manufacturing industries, support the opening up of new markets elsewhere, as they regard this as a way to secure the workplaces of their members, labour movements in the Global South vehemently reject it, as they are concerned about the related deindustrialization and loss of jobs in their countries, unable to compete with high-productivity products manufactured in the North (Bieler 2013; Hilary 2014).

The purpose of this chapter is to analyse the underlying reasons for this division within the global labour movement. Is it inevitable that trade unions from the North and South oppose each other, and, if so, how can this be explained? Or how could it be possible to form relations of transnational solidarity despite different economic interests? The argument is structured in three parts. First, I will discuss the structural explanation of this division based on uneven development. Second, I will look at the argument of 'labour aristocracy', before turning towards a discussion of the notion of 'false consciousness'. Third, the conclusion will summarize the findings of the chapter and argue that ultimately the analytical focus has to be on open-ended class struggle. Transnational solidarity is neither impossible nor automatic, but can only be the result of concrete struggles.

UNEVEN AND COMBINED DEVELOPMENT AND THE DIFFERENT INTERESTS OF TRADE UNIONS

Organized around wage labour and the private ownership of the means of production, capitalist social relations of production are enormously dynamic, since both labour and capital have to reproduce themselves through the market. While workers compete with each other to sell their labour 'freely', capitalists are in constant competition with each other over profitability and market share. As Marx argued, 'the development of capitalist production makes it necessary constantly to increase the amount of capital laid out in a given industrial undertaking, and competition subordinates every individual capitalist to the immanent laws of capitalist production, as external and coercive laws' (Marx 1867/1990: 739). Hence, capitalism is characterized by a constant drive towards further innovation in order to outcompete one's competitors. While capitalism is very dynamic, however, it is also crisis prone. The more goods are produced, the more profits are generated, looking for further profitable investment opportunities, the more difficult it becomes to bring together excess labour and excess capital in a fruitful way. Expressed differently, there is a situation of a surplus of both capital and labour, which can no longer be brought together in a productive way within the capitalist social relations of production, a 'state of overaccumulation' in David Harvey's understanding (Harvey 1985: 132). Thus, Marx identified the following economic cycle: 'feverish production, a consequent glut on the market, then a contraction of the market, which causes production to be crippled. The life of industry becomes a series of periods of moderate activity, prosperity, over-production, crisis and stagnation' (Marx 1867/1990: 580). Hence, periodically and inevitably capitalism experiences crises of overaccumulation.

Rosa Luxemburg had already pointed to 'the inherent contradiction between the unlimited expansive capacity of the productive forces and the limited expansive capacity of social consumption under conditions of capitalist distribution' (Luxemburg 1913/2003: 323). These crises, she argued, cannot be solved within capitalism itself. Instead, new markets have to be opened up elsewhere. 'The decisive fact is that the surplus value cannot be realised by sale either to workers or to capitalists, but only if it is sold to such social organisations or strata whose own mode of production is not capitalistic' (Luxemburg 1913/2003: 332). In short, capitalism depends on the constant possibility of outward expansion, creating hothouse conditions for capital accumulation in noncapitalist environments (Luxemburg 1913/2003: 338). Ray Kiely engages critically with Luxemburg's analysis of the outward dynamic of the capitalist mode of production. Historically, capitalist accumulation did not functionally depend on absorbing ever more noncapitalist space. Before World War I, for example, most capital was invested in, and trade took place between, industrialised countries (Kiely 2010: 79–81). And yet, at the same time, it is a fact that capitalism did expand outwardly in encompassing the whole globe. Expressed differently, 'outward expansion' can take place in an extensive, geographical way, when new regions are incorporated into the capitalist social relations of production, as well as in an intensive way through, for example, the re-commodification of public services or the commodification of household activities (Robinson 2008: 6–7). Already in 1848, Marx and Engels wrote about how capital overcomes periodic crises 'on the one hand through the enforced destruction of a mass of productive forces; on the other through the capture of new markets and a more thoroughgoing exploitation of old ones' (Marx and Engels 1848/1998: 18). The enforced destruction of productive forces and a more intensive exploitation of existing capitalist social relations of production are linked to Kiely's emphasis on developments internal to industrialized countries. The capture of new markets, however, refers to Luxemburg's focus on outward expansion. In other words, we can summarize that while outward expansion is not the only way capital attempts to overcome crises, it is clearly one significant aspect to it. The notion of uneven and combined development becomes relevant especially in relation to outward geographical expansion of capitalist accumulation.

It was Leon Trotsky who introduced the notion of uneven and combined development, when analyzing the particular location of Russia within the world economy. While Russia was economically backward based on a large sector of inefficient agriculture indicating the unevenness of development in relation to advanced Western countries, a number of small pockets of highly developed industries, especially in military-related production, were established as a result of foreign pressure by more developed neighbours in the West. 'The Russian State, erected on the basis of Russian economic conditions, was being pushed forward by the friendly, and even more by the hostile, pressure of the neighbouring State organizations, which had grown up on a higher economic basis' (Trotsky 1906/2007: 27). Hence, capitalist expansion is also 'combined' as a result of 'the sociological outcome of international capitalist pressures on the internal development of non-capitalist societies' (Rosenberg 2006: 319). In short, in response to the crisis tendency of the capitalist social relations of production, there is an inherent dynamic of outward expansion along uneven and combined lines. There is some discussion to what extent Trotsky envisaged that countries could catch up and overtake already developed countries due to the 'privilege' of their historical backwardness, allowing them to skip stages of development, other countries before them had to go through (Trotsky 1932/2008: 4; see also Selwyn 2011a). While Trotsky considered this to be possible indeed, it is also clear that this has been rather an exception based on specific historical circumstances (Bieler 2013: 175–77). While development clearly results from uneven and combined development processes, the gap between advanced industrialized countries and developing countries tends to increase. As Samir Amin has noted,

> historical capitalism, as it has really existed, has always been imperialist in the very precise sense that the mechanisms inherent to its worldwide spread, far from progressively 'homogenizing' economic conditions on a planetary scale, have, on the contrary, reproduced and deepened the contrast, counterposing the dominant (imperialist) centers to the dominated peripheries. (Amin 2010: 84)

Importantly, 'this unevenness is not seen as a result of market imperfections, but is in fact a product of the way competitive markets work in the real world' (Kiely 2007: 18). As a result of these processes of uneven and combined development, however, it is clear that different national labour movements are in very different positions within the global economy. German or Swedish trade unions, for example, organizing workers in high-productivity export sectors, are differently located in global production than African trade unions, organizing workers in relatively low-productivity manufacturing sectors. Hence, transnational solidarity is anything but automatic.

The answer to the question of why European trade unions and labour movements of the Global South disagree over free trade agreements could, therefore, be that this is simply the inevitable result of different positions within the global capitalist social relations of production. As Harvey has noted, 'in so far as class struggle yields a terrain of compromise between capital and labour within a region, organized labour may rally in support of such alliances in order to protect jobs and privileges already won' (Harvey 2006a: 441). The support by European trade unions for Global Europe is clearly an example in this respect. The conclusion, however, that this cooperation with employers, at the expense of labour in the Global South, is inevitable due the particular location of European labour in the global economy, is problematic on two accounts. First, conceptually it collapses into a structuralist, economic determinism, an analysis which reads trade unions' strategies simply off the economic structure. It completely denies room for agency. Second, empirically it is incorrect. When the North American Free Trade Agreement came into force on 1 January 1994, there was no common trade union position. While the Canadian Labour Congress had been opposed, the main Mexican trade union confederation supported the agreement. The US trade unions presented a mixed picture (Ciccaglione 2009: 2–3). As a result of experiences with the North American Free Trade Agreement, however, a learning process had taken place and a common position between trade unions from the Global South and North could be established over time (Kay 2011). While workers felt to have different interests in the short term, experiences and joint struggles allowed them in the medium to long term to acknowledge the common threat posed to them by the more extensive

Free Trade Area of the Americas, as well as their common interest in working together on the basis of transnational solidarity to defeat this threat. This new position does not only include a rejection of neoliberal free trade agreements, such as the defeated Free Trade Area of the Americas initiative, but as Bruno Ciccaglione makes clear, it also 'seeks to design a model of integration that is an alternative to free trade, not only because it proposes alternative trade rules, but because it aims at moving away from neoliberalism by giving a new centrality to the State, and to a new democratic and participatory process' (Ciccaglione 2009: 30). Hence, transnational solidarity by trade unions in the resistance to free trade agreements is possible, even if these trade unions are in rather different locations in the capitalist social relations of production.

Nevertheless, if it is not structure which explains European trade unions' support for the European Union free trade strategy, how can we then understand the fact that some trade unions have decided to cooperate with capital, albeit at the expense of workers elsewhere? In the next section, I will assess the arguments that workers in developed countries have become transformed into a 'labour aristocracy', intent on securing its own privileged position among the global working class, and that trade unions would operate under conditions of 'false consciousness'.

CLASS BETRAYAL? THE NOTIONS OF 'LABOUR ARISTOCRACY' AND 'FALSE CONSCIOUSNESS'

When Lenin explained the reasons for the split within the European working classes into revolutionary communists and reformist social democrats in the wake of the Bolshevik Revolution in Russia in 1917, he argued that opportunists, a small section of the working class, had been bribed by capital to maintain the capitalist social relations. They had established labour parties with a reformist focus, which do not question capitalism as such. 'Economically, the desertion of a stratum of the labour aristocracy to the bourgeoisie has matured and become an accomplished fact; and this economic fact, this shift in class relations, will find political form, in one shape or another, without any particular "difficulty"' (Lenin 1916: 10). The money to bribe the labour aristocracy comes from super profits of the colonial empires. In the words of Bukharin, a close associate of Lenin, 'the colonial policy yields a colossal income to the great powers, i.e., to their ruling classes, to the "state capitalist trust". This is why the bourgeoisie pursues a colonial policy. This being the case, there is a possibility for raising the workers' wages at the expense of the exploited colonial savages and conquered peoples' (Bukharin 1915/1929: 164). As a result, 'a privileged upper stratum of the proletariat in the imperialist countries lives partly at the expense of hundreds of millions in the uncivilised nations' (Lenin 1916: 2). Clearly, this argument can be extended to

European labour's support for the European Union's free trade strategy, Global Europe. Trade unions and their members operate like this purely out of self-interest. They have become used to their benefits as part of a labour aristocracy and are determined to maintain these benefits at all costs, be it at the expense of labour in the Global South. Some would even go one step further and maintain that trade unions do not only represent a labour aristocracy internationally, but even within a country at times, when they focus on the interests of their members on full-time contracts, thereby forgetting others in informal working conditions (e.g., Pillay 2008).

And yet, such an evaluation would be a gross misrepresentation of workers' situation in the Global North. Unemployment is in many European countries at a record high. 'The EU-28 unemployment rate was 10.1 [per cent] in August 2014' (Eurostat 2014). Moreover, atypical work contracts and flexibilized labour have increasingly become the norm. While work pressure is constantly increased, employment itself has become ever more insecure. The current crisis is used across the European Union to undermine European welfare states. Trade unions supporting free trade agreements are not securing privileges of luxury for their members. Rather, they are involved in protecting their members' very basis of existence. Trade union work in the North, against the background of the global financial crisis and constant pressures of restructuring, is a defensive struggle for survival, not a struggle to secure imaginary riches. As Hart-Landsberg illustrates when discussing the US experience of globalization characterized by the increasing transnationalization of production, it is not only Chinese workers who find themselves in low paid jobs and poor working conditions. US workers too have suffered from the intensification of free trade. While household debt increased drastically and the wage share declined, there was an additional negative impact on employment and wages. 'The loss of manufacturing work reduced the demand for local non-traded services and thus non-manufacturing employment. At the same time, the loss of manufacturing work swelled the supply of non-manufacturing workers, putting downward pressure on non-manufacturing wages' (Hart-Landsberg 2013: 58). Of course, workers in the Global North are still better off than workers in the Global South. Nevertheless, understanding that trade unions' activities are of a defensive nature, and not consciously exploitative of workers elsewhere indicates that transnational solidarity is at least not excluded from the outset. At least, they are not a 'labour aristocracy'.

Moreover, as Moorhouse argues, divisions within the labour movement are normal and have always existed. They are not the result of bribes, nor necessarily linked to imperialism (Moorhouse 1978: 68–69). There are no specific mechanisms that direct the benefits of imperialism to sections of the working class. In any case, the gains made by workers, Moorhouse argues, were made at the expense of employers, not of exploited people elsewhere (Moorhouse 1978: 76). Historically, according to Michael Barratt Brown, imperialism has not benefitted working people. First, because the cost of lives of imperialist adventures has generally been paid by the working class and second, because intensive investments overseas in the colonies caused higher levels of unemployment back home. 'The high levels of unemployment in the developed countries [have resulted] both from this export of capital and—more importantly—from the impoverishment of markets in the countries overseas, whose economies were distorted by economic dependence on the developed countries' (Barratt Brown 1972: 80). Eric Hobsbawm, in turn, acknowledges the existence of a labour aristocracy in nineteenth-century Britain, a nucleus of skilled workers on higher wages (Hobsbawm 1984: 220, 234). Nevertheless, this does not imply that there was a less privileged section of the working class, which was more revolutionary, while the labour aristocracy demonstrated moderation and reformism. On the contrary, 'the bulk of organized working class activism in the later Victorian and Edwardian periods, leaving aside special cases like mining, came from among this stratum. If anything, the labour aristocracy was therefore the nursery of the left' (Hobsbawm 1984: 243–44). Along this line, Callinicos further points out that it had been the well-organized, relatively well-paid metalworkers who were behind struggles after the First World War and joined Communist parties (Callinicos 2009: 50), that is, precisely those sections of the working class we would expect to be part of the labour aristocracy and reformist social democratic parties. In short, it would be wrong to accuse trade unions, who cooperate with employers in certain circumstances, of class betrayal. Rather, such issues are a matter of strategy for trade unions. 'They would strike and support wider class action when they considered this appropriate, and they sought change in what was the only feasible way: by making real gains via gradual reform' (Moorhouse 1978: 58).

In sum, trade unions in the Global North find themselves in a defensive position. They do not defend a situation of luxury. If they do manage to secure a larger share of income for workers, and this has increasingly been less the case, then it is at the expense of profits for capital, not of workers elsewhere. Nevertheless, if trade unions are in a defensive position and if they have actually not benefitted from expanded free trade as Hart-Landsberg's example of American workers shows (see above), why do trade unions in the Global North, in Europe, continue to support free trade negotiations?

If we accept that strategies of cooperation with capital are consciously chosen as the best way forward even if they do not result in concrete benefits for workers, would we then not have to conclude that these trade unions operated under conditions of 'false consciousness', that is, not realizing their true interests as the result of an incorrect analysis of the situation?[2] The late Stuart Hall has engaged with the role of ideology from a historical materialist perspective and looked at the issue of 'false consciousness' more closely. He convincingly makes clear that it would be wrong to argue that 'false consciousness' results from an incorrect analysis of economic reality. The problem is not that the analysis is incorrect; the problem is that the analysis is only partial. 'In a world where markets exist and market exchange dominates economic life, it would be distinctly odd if there were no category allowing us to think, speak and act in relation to it. In that sense, all economic categories—bourgeois or Marxist—express existing social relations' (Hall 1996: 36). Because bourgeois economic understanding is so widespread and has become common sense including within many trade unions, their assessment of the situation is based on this market understanding. Especially the (neo-)liberal idea of free trade being beneficial for everyone involved, the understanding that it would be best if countries concentrated on their comparative advantage in production and trade for all other goods, are firmly established within the dominant common sense of how to understand today's global economy. And on the basis of this partial understanding it makes perfect sense to cooperate with employers in support of further free trade. 'The falseness therefore arises, not from the fact that the market is an illusion, a trick, a sleight-of-hand, but only in the sense that it is an inadequate explanation of a process' (Hall 1996: 37). Parts of reality are invisible, given the concepts and categories used. And that this is the case should not come as a surprise.

> In a world saturated by money exchange, and everywhere mediated by money, the 'market' experience is the most immediate, daily and universal experience of the economic system for everyone. It is therefore not surprising that we take the market for granted, do not question what makes it possible, what it is founded or premised on. It should not surprise us if the mass of working people don't possess the concepts with which to cut into the process at another point, form another set of questions, and bring to the surface or reveal what the overwhelming facticity of the market constantly renders invisible. (Hall 1996: 38)

What is overlooked in many partial analyses are the implications of the 'hidden abode of production' including private property, wage labour, and the expropriation of surplus value and all the relations of inequality and exploitation which come with it. In short, the decision of cooperating with employers is perfectly logical within dominant bourgeois ideology.

CONCLUSION

As the example of the struggle against the Free Trade Area of the Americas has demonstrated, transnational labour solidarity against free trade agreements is possible. Importantly, as Chandra Talpade Mohanty makes clear, 'solidarity is always an achievement, the result of active struggle to construct the universal on the basis of particulars/differences' (Mohanty 2003: 7). This understanding has conceptual implications. Rather than regarding solidarity as the automatic or impossible result of structural conditions and specific trade union strategies, the focus has to be on class struggle, which is inevitably open-ended. When analyzing class struggle and the possibility of transnational labour solidarity, the distinction between class-in-itself and class-for-itself is relevant. A class-in-itself can be identified due to the way production is organized, but it may not yet have developed a class consciousness in struggle and, thus, become a class-for-itself. Robinson, for example, argues that transnational labour so far has only developed into a class-in-itself resulting from the organization of production at the transnational level. 'But this emerging global proletariat is not yet a class-for-itself; that is, it has not necessarily developed a consciousness of itself as a class, or organized itself as such' (Robinson 2004: 43). The transition from a class-in-itself to a class-for-itself is made in class struggle. People 'experience exploitation (or the need to maintain power over those whom they exploit), they identify points of antagonistic interest, they commence to struggle around these issues and in the process of struggling they discover themselves as classes, they come to know this discovery as class-consciousness' (Thompson 1978: 149). Hence, although classes-in-themselves can be identified through a focus on the social relations of production, the analytical emphasis then has to turn towards the analysis of class struggle and the potential of forming class consciousness. In short, class struggle is the moment when agency meets structure, when labour meets the structural contradictions of the capitalist social relations of production. Class struggle is the process in which labour identities and interests are formed and transformed. It is the moment when structural constraints are being confirmed or changed. Hence, it is through the prism of class struggle that we can best analyse trade unions' responses to global restructuring. Whether different labour movements engage in relations of transnational solidarity is not predetermined by their structural location in the capitalist social relations of production or any given and firm understanding of their interests, but ultimately depends on the outcome of class struggle.

When Gramsci analysed the dynamics of class struggle, he emphasized the importance of the realm of ideas, since 'it is on the level of ideologies that men become conscious of conflicts in the world of the economy' (Gramsci 1971: 162). As it was outlined above, the decision of cooperating with employers is perfectly logical within the common sense of bourgeois ideology. The task then has to be to expand beyond this ideology and employ concepts, which allow a fuller assessment of reality. In other words, the task is to challenge the very formation of dominant common sense (Robinson 2006). For Gramsci, 'revolutionary theory is born in opposition to existing common sense. What is at stake is the conception of the world of the subalterns, a world view that needs to be transformed or replaced' (Liguori 2009: 129). However, Gramsci did not only ask to attack the hegemonic bourgeois common sense in the struggle for hegemony. As Green and Ives make clear, 'Gramsci is interested in transforming common sense and developing a "new common sense" and, by extension, a truly transformed language founded upon a critical awareness that will provide the masses with a foundation to transform their conditions' (Green and Ives 2009: 12). Common sense is, thus, not simply a negative set of ideas. Rather, it is something to transform into a progressive outlook through class struggle. As Liguori argues, 'the historical-materialist world view, in Gramsci's view, is established by superseding existing common sense in order to create another common sense' (Liguori 2009: 133).

According to Gramsci, it is the task of 'organic intellectuals', the true representatives of the social group of the working class, the subaltern (Gramsci 1971: 5), to work towards 'radicalising common sense and providing subaltern groups with the intellectual tools necessary to confront dominant hegemony, philosophy and power' (Green and Ives 2009: 13). For Gramsci, organic intellectuals are engaged in active participation in everyday life, acting as agents or constructors, organizers, and 'permanent persuaders' in forming social class hegemony, or by performing a valuable supporting role to subaltern groups engaged in promoting social change, that is then '"mediated" by the whole fabric of society' (Gramsci 1971: 12, 52–55). Thus, organic intellectuals do not simply produce ideas; they also concretize and articulate strategies in complex and often contradictory ways, which is possible because of their proximity to the most powerful forces in society. It is their task to develop the 'gastric juices' to digest competing conceptions of social order in conformity with a hegemonic project (Gramsci 1971: 128n.6). Put differently, it is their social function to transcend the particular interests of their own social group which brings 'the interests of the leading class into harmony with those of subordinate classes and incorporates these other interests into an ideology expressed in universal terms' (Cox 1983: 168). When ideas are thus accepted as common sense—or 'diffuse, uncoordinated features of a generic mode of thought' (Gramsci 1971: 330)—they become naturalized in the form of intersubjective meanings, potentially providing the basis for an alternative order of society.

The demonstrations against the WTO meeting in Seattle in 1999 heralded for many the start of successful resistance against neoliberal capitalism by a so-called global movement of movements. The attacks on the United States of 11 September 2001 and the subsequent global war against terror, however, undermined this progressive resistance movement. Analyzing the disintegration of the movement of movements in Australia, Elizabeth Humphrys concludes that 'the process of crystallisation had not progressed far enough for a minority within the movement to come together to develop a collective intellectual' (Humphrys 2013: 375). And yet, especially in response to the global financial crisis and related austerity new movements of resistance have emerged since 2007/ 2008. Occupy in the Global North and the increasing militancy by Chinese workers in the Global South are only two examples. As demonstrated in this chapter, transnational solidarity over free trade agreements is neither impossible nor automatic. It depends on the outcome of open-ended class struggle. Could this be the moment to establish a Gramscian type of 'organic intellectual', able to overcome the dominant bourgeois common sense and replacing it with an alternative, new common sense on trade? Interestingly, within Europe the Alternative Trade Mandate alliance (http://www.alternativetrademandate.org/) published in November 2013 its proposal for an alternative trade mandate for the European Union entitled *Trade: Time for a New Vision* (Alternative Trade Mandate Alliance 2013). Consisting of trade unions and other social movements, perhaps this Alternative Trade Mandate alliance could provide this kind of 'organic intellectual'? The European AlterSummit movement (http://www.altersummit.eu/) may provide the institutional framework within and through which such a collective organic intellectual operates.

NOTES

1. Many thanks to my colleagues from the Oslo Transnational Labour project (see http://transnationallabour.wordpress.com/) and two anonymous reviewers for comments on earlier drafts.

2. The concept 'false consciousness' was first used by Engels in a letter to Mehring (1893). It was later Lukács, who developed it further in *History and Class Consciousness* (1968/1971: 46–82). Many thanks to Jörg Nowak for drawing my attention to this.

FOUR

Mass Strikes in Brazil, South Africa, and India after 2008

Separate Battles, but a United Struggle?

Jörg Nowak

The years since the onset of the global financial crisis saw a wave of protests all over the world, and among them were a series of mass strikes in the Global South that have not yet been investigated extensively, with the exception of the mass strikes in China (Butollo and Brink 2012; Chan and Hui 2012; Chen 2013; Friedman 2012; Kan 2011) and the strikes in South African mining in 2012 (Alexander 2013; Bond and Mottiar 2013; Chinguno 2013a, 2013b). My current research on mass strikes in Brazil, South Africa, and India has revealed that there are enormous similarities despite very different local, regional, and national contexts and path dependencies: The strike waves in the construction sector between 2011 and 2014 in Brazil, the strikes in South African mining in 2012 and 2014, and the strikes in the Indian automobile sector are examples of strikes in central sectors of the national economies. These sectors have witnessed continual growth over the past fifteen years, and at the same time workers experienced deteriorating working conditions, such as lower wages, an increase in contract work, and/or a higher work speed. The focus in the initial phase of the strikes was on wage demands and working conditions, but during the course of the struggles a political dimension emerged quite quickly. In a number of cases, workers organized illegal strikes or developed activities that could not be controlled by the trade unions (e.g., setting fire to workplace premises, expelling union representatives with violent means, or killing managers). And many of these strikes were met with repression, such as the police massacre in Marikana in South Africa, the repeated deployment of the national guard and military police to break strikes in Brazil, or the arbitrary arrest and long-term imprisonment of workers in India.

Despite these obvious similarities, there has been almost no communication between the workers involved in these strikes across national borders, nor any significant transnational solidarity during the mass strikes. Due to these contradictions between the transnational similarities of these strikes and their largely national political context, I pose the following question: Is transnational solidarity overrated, at least at this point in time, or would it make a difference if there had been a significant degree of transnational solidarity during such strikes? In order to assess this question, I will describe the organizational and political dynamics that facilitated the mass strikes in the three countries. According to a categorical assessment of mass strikes, inspired by the seminal work of Rosa Luxemburg (1906/2008), the defining characteristics with which one can distinguish mass strikes from any strike that includes a lot of workers, will be discussed (see also Nowak and Gallas 2014). Beyond general characteristics, mass strikes may have different forms of how they unfold on an organizational and geographical scale. In order to assess these specific dynamics, I will refer to the approach of labour geography that includes the notion of space into research on the prerequisites of labour struggles (Herod 1997b).

I take the following steps in this contribution: First, I will give a description of the scope of the mass strikes mentioned. In doing so, I will provide some ideas about which kind of solidarity was effective for which reasons and outline the limits for solidarity that exist. Second, I assess the specific dynamics of the mass strikes in question. Finally, I will draw conclusions for a future perspective of transnational solidarity for mass strikes in the age of austerity and global slump.

MASS STRIKES AFTER 2008 IN BRAZIL, SOUTH AFRICA, AND INDIA

The years after 2008 saw a wave of mass strikes in the Global South, with many of these strikes going beyond the established patterns of trade union action. Focusing on the strikes in the South African mining sector in 2012, the strikes in the construction industry in Brazil between 2011 and 2013, and strikes in the automobile sector in India in 2011/2012, important structural and political similarities are obvious: All three sectors are central sectors of the respective economies and they saw constant growth rates in the past fifteen years. In the following, I will briefly describe the dynamics of the strikes mentioned and the role of transnational solidarity in these strikes.

Construction Sector in Brazil

The Brazilian construction sector saw continual growth rates, increasing by 49.6 per cent between 2004 and 2012 (Blanford and Cummings 2013; Departamento Intersindical de Estatística e Estudos Socioeconômicos 2013). In 2011, 7.8 million workers join the construction sector, 8.4 per cent of the total workforce. Between 1998 and 2008, the construction sector saw an influx of two hundred thousand workers. In 2011 and 2012, the strikes of construction workers saw a peak: 580,000 construction workers went on strike in 2011, and 500,000 construction workers in nineteen regional states went on strike in 2012. The major grievances were wage differences between and within regions and workplaces, and harsh restrictions on holidays: Many workers work away from their families and were only allowed to leave the workplace every three to six months. Helpers were not allowed any leave in some places. In addition, housing facilities, transport, and food for workers were regularly suboptimal.

The first big and hitherto unprecedented strike wave, the biggest since the strikes in 1980 in the Sao Paulo area, occurred in February and March 2011 when 170,000 construction workers went on strike. The strike wave started in a number of smaller construction sites in the state of Bahia in February, including eighty thousand workers. In the middle of March, the strike wave extended to the whole country, predominantly to the big construction sites of the government program Programa de Aceleração do Crescimento: The biggest mobilization occurred at two industrial complexes, a refinery and a petrochemical complex, in Suape, in the state of Pernambuco, involving thirty-five thousand workers (Véras 2013, 2014). The hydroelectric plants in Jirau and Santo Antontio in the state of Rodonia saw huge mobilisations as well with twenty thousand and sixteen thousand workers and another focal point in March 2011 was in the state of Ceará at the construction site of a thermoelectric plant in Pecém with six thousand workers on strike. The special feature of the strikes on the sites that belong to Programa de Aceleração do Crescimento was the absence of trade unions in the initial phase of the mobilizations and the practice of burning the housing facilities and other parts of premises by the striking workers. As their protest was directed against the miserable conditions of housing, the demand for better housing was put into practice by setting the former facilities ablaze. The different strikes did not start based on a common call, but broke out more or less independently from each other, though media reports might have had a role in triggering more conflicts after the first strikes started. In the area of Jirau, the federal government ordered the national guard (Força Nacional) to break the strike immediately after it broke out.

The first strike wave also led to many more strikes in the same year, often in the same sites, because employers did not keep the promises made in various collective agreements after the conflicts. During 2011, the conflicts were largely centred on the Northern and Northeastern regions of Brazil. In the course of the next year, the strikes also extended to various other places with a high number of workers, such as the Comperj industrial complex under construction close to Rio de Janeiro and the Belo Monte Dam in the state of Pará, ran in the North of Brazil. The strikes did not only spread to other states and regions—the state of Rio de Janeiro is part of the Southeast of Brazil—but there was also a diffusion of protest dynamics, since the workers at Belo Monte Dam set fire to the premises and sent away both management and the trade union in November 2012, pelting stones at them in order to protest against a wage settlement of the trade union Sindicato dos Trabalhadores nas Industrias da Construção Pesada do Estado do Pará (affiliated to the right-wing trade union Força Sindical) that did not meet their approval. The federal government used the army again to break the strike and installed a permanent five hundred–strong unit of Força Nacional at the site in June 2012. The stay of the national guard has been prolonged for another six months in summer 2014.

Although these strikes saw a historical participation of workers and had major importance for the public debate on workers' rights, there were no significant international responses nor were there any acts of transnational solidarity. The solidarity during the strikes in March 2011 did take place mainly between the workers of different plants—it was the sheer mass of strikers and the destruction of property of the companies that built up enough pressure to arrange for settlements. The companies that are responsible for the construction works were mainly the 'big five' in Brazilian construction: Odebrecht (120,000 employees in thirty countries), Andrade Gutierrez (223,000 employees in forty countries), Suez (236,120 employees), Camargo Correa (61,000 employees in twenty countries), and the Grupo OAS (a civil engineering company with 55,000 employees in twenty countries).

Mining in South Africa

The mining industry is one of the central sectors of the South African economy. While gold mining remained stable in the past fifteen to twenty years, platinum mining saw a 67 per cent increase in output between 1994 and 2009 (Capps 2012: 64). The illegal strike of several thousand workers at the Karee mine in South Africa, owned by Lonmin company, led to the massacre that became known worldwide as 'Marikana' that left thirty-four workers shot by the police, and it was followed by an enormous strike movement that covered the entire mining sector, which lasted until the end of October 2012 in some of the mines. Wage settlements led to wage hikes between 11 and 22 per cent. The exodus of mine workers from the National Union of Mineworkers (NUM), affiliated to the federation Congress of South African Trade Unions, after the strike and the police massacre deepened the political divisions in Congress of South African Trade Unions and undermined the legitimacy of the ANC. About a third of the workforce in South African platinum mines is employed by contractors (Bezuidenhout and Buhlungu 2011; Chinguno 2013b); a huge number are migrant workers that have to feed two families (at Lonmin, 82 per cent are migrant workers). Lonmin is the third largest platinum producer worldwide, and the mining in Rustenburg (Marikana is a hill area close to Rustenburg) accounts for 80 per cent of its output.

The first of these huge illegal strikes started in January 2012 at the Impala mine in Rustenburg: the strikers demanded a 200 per cent increase of their wages (from 3,000 Rand to 9,000 Rand), and they did not cooperate with their trade union NUM, but relied on independent strike committees. The strike lasted for six weeks, was started by five thousand rock drill operators, and extended to all seventeen thousand employees of the mine. The company offered an 18 per cent wage hike but it was refused by the workers. They finally went back to work without any change to their work conditions (Chinguno 2013a). At least two thousand contract workers were terminated after the strike.

The strike at the Karee mine at Lonmin in Rustenburg in late July 2012 followed the same pattern: It was started by rock drill operators (Chinguno 2013b) and led by an independent strike committee, and their wage demand of 12,500 Rand was triple their current income. Almost within one day most of the twenty-eight thousand workers at Lonmin went on strike. Reasons for the strikes were primarily low wages, but also problems with health and safety issues due to lung problems. Work shifts beyond 12 hours and harassment by managers were additional reasons for the strikes (Alexander 2013). The first deadly casualties were two workers who were killed by trade union officials of NUM, and one can assume that the police massacre a few days later was supposed to discourage similar strike movements—which proved to be ineffective. Subsequently, the strikes at Implat and Lonmin prompted strikes at two Gold Fields mines with twelve thousand and fifteen thousand workers in late August and early September 2012 that took up the demand of 12,500 Rand, and in late September thirty-two thousand workers at AngloGold Ashanti demanded the same wage. Finally, the world's biggest platinum producer, Amplat, was hit by several strikes since September 2012, and the wage demand extended to 16,000 Rand there. In all of these conflicts, wage hikes around 10 per cent were attained (Alexander 2013). Again, similar to the Brazilian construction strike wave, the strikes at the South African sites 'inspired' each other, sometimes one mine from a company started a strike that was joined by another mine from the same company, like in Gold Fields, or a strike at one company, like in Lonmin, was inspired by a preceding one in the same area and in the same industry.

Three out of the four big mining companies that were hit by strikes are multinational companies: Lonmin, Gold Fields, and AngloGold Ashanti.

Car Production in India

Car production in India is one of many sectors that is expanding and driving the economy. Passenger car sales grew at 15.2 per cent per year between 2005/2006 and 2010/2011. Growth in the industry fell after 2011 and collapsed in 2013. At the same time, the real wages of auto workers dropped since 2000 from 80,000 rupees a year in 2000/2001 to 65,000 rupees in 2009/2010 (People's Union for Democratic Rights 2013), while the output of cars tripled and the inflation of food prices was way above the average rate of inflation.

In India, one out of two factories of the biggest car passenger producer Maruti Suzuki saw two illegal strikes and occupations in June and October 2011 and labour unrest in July 2012. The Maruti company was a state enterprise in the past but is controlled at present by the Japanese multinational Suzuki. The factory at Manesar was seen as a model factory—it opened in 2007 and recruited young workers, and was set up in a new industrial area with only a small village nearby. The management thought that these young workers without experiences in labour organizing, located in a remote area, could be handled more easily and employed at lower wages. Permanent workers only accounted for about 30 per cent of the workforce, while the remaining employees were contract workers from sixty different contractors, trainees, and apprentices that earn much lower wages. In 2011, contract workers earned about half of the wage of a permanent worker (9,000 rupees versus 17,000 rupees/month). Only 1,054 workers were permanent in summer 2012, and there were 416 technical trainees, 225 apprentices, and 2,700 contract workers (People's Union for Democratic Rights 2013).

The conflict in the Manesar factory that has unfolded since has gained significance over the strikes at Honda in Gurgaon in 2005/2006; these were followed by many smaller strike movements. The workers in the Manesar factory aimed to set up their own trade union, the Maruti Suzuki Workers' Union, while the company wanted them to join the trade union in the mother plant, Maruti Udyog Kamgar Union. The workers in Manesar saw Maruti Udyog Kamgar Union as a management-led trade union and insisted on their right to choose their own trade union. The reasons behind wanting to establish their own union were wage issues, the huge extent of contract labour, high work speed, harassment by supervisors, and the lack of breaks that would enable workers to go to the toilet and have food or drinks.

After the company tried to force the permanent workers in Manesar to join Maruti Udyog Kamgar Union, they went on a two-week-long illegal strike in June 2011 during which all categories of workers participated.

The workers stayed inside of the factory during the strike. The company did not recognize the Maruti Suzuki Workers' Union and resorted to a lock-out of all contract workers in late September. The response to this company move was the blockade of the gates and a second illegal strike, and occupation by the permanent workers for another two weeks in October 2011. This time, three neighbouring Suzuki factories, which produce engines for Maruti Suzuki and motorcycles, also went out on strike and occupation, as well as another fourteen factories in the area, some of which are suppliers to Maruti Suzuki. The striking feature of the Honda case, a few years before, was that a joint strike of contract and permanent workers in 2005 led to better conditions for permanent workers, and a subsequent strike of Honda contract workers in 2006 remained isolated and unsuccessful. In contrast to these events, it remained a feature of the strike at the Manesar factory that contract and permanent workers acted in solidarity—a fact that caused widespread fear among employers. The second strike in October 2011 ended with an agreement between workers and the company that did not include substantial changes of work conditions. In the course of 2012, the independent trade union could finally register under the name Maruti Suzuki Employees Union, but none of its demands were met and talks with the management collapsed in the summer of 2012. In this already tense situation, a worker was slapped by a supervisor and subsequently sacked after he filed a complaint. That led to negotiations between the trade union and management, and during the course of that day, 18 July 2012, violence broke out in the factory that left fifty managers injured and one dead. After the unrest, the workers fled from the premises and the factory remained closed for one month. The company fired 2,300 (1,800 contract and 500 permanent) workers arbitrarily, and 148 workers were arrested with the charge of murder. These workers have remained in jail until today (30 September 2014) without bail being granted and without a sentence.

Two months after the unrest, the company increased the wages of permanent workers, and the contract system has now been modified: Instead of contract workers, the company employs similar numbers of casual workers for the same wages. The difference is that these workers are on the payroll of the company but they continue to get sacked after six months, and are eventually employed again after a break of six months. In the case of the conflict at the Manesar factory, in a number of interviews all workers have emphasized that the unity between the workers in the factory and the solidarity strikes at other factories has been the most important mechanism of support.[1] Other important sources of solidarity were workers from other factories, people from the neighbourhood, and families of the workers that provided food and water during the occupation of the plant in June 2011. There have been a number of solidarity demonstrations in several cities of India, some of which were heavily attacked by the police, both during and after the

strikes. International support has not been significant, but since the conflict there has been some contact to the minority trade union, Zenroren, at
the Suzuki plant in Japan and to a trade union of a Suzuki plant in
Thailand. The office of Industriall in New Delhi arranged for contacts to
be made to the officially recognized trade union at the Suzuki company
in Japan and urged them to exercise pressure on the headquarters of
Suzuki company, but without any significant results thus far.[2]

Obviously, the strike at Maruti Suzuki lacked the strength of the mass
strikes in Brazil and South Africa, and could only attain some changes in
wages and working conditions at a high price for the employees that face
prison, court charges, and unemployment. Although the second strike
extended to three other factories of the same company and fourteen others in the same industrial district, it did not lead to a strike wave in the
industry as such, as was the case in Brazil and South Africa. And, the
second plant of Maruti Suzuki in Gurgaon remained unaffected by labour unrest. The Suzuki motor corporation is the tenth largest automobile company worldwide and the second biggest in Japan by production.
It employs fifty-five thousand employees worldwide with production
facilities in twenty-three countries. Although the metal unions, and the
automobile unions specifically, claim to be organized well on an international level, there was no significant or efficient international trade union
action that could be compared to the strong support the striking workers
received at the local level.

TRANSNATIONAL SOLIDARITY

With regard to the relevance of transnational solidarity, there have been
countless accounts of the topic. The classical notion of 'international solidarity' underlined the character of the labour movement as transcending
national boundaries. In the era of globalization, in which competition of
national economies has gained significance, transnational solidarity of
labour movements has often been highlighted as the difficult-to-reach
solution to all problems of national competition between workers. Since
the late 1990s, many observers have emphasized the interdependence of
local and global struggles, underlining the necessity of a local basis for
transnational struggles. In order to assess a new form of international
solidarity that emerges from the mass strikes, I will combine Luxemburg's insights into the special features of mass strikes (1906/2008) with
Herod's insights (1997b) into the specific spatial limits and dynamics of
labour mobilization. Rosa Luxemburg puts emphasis on the fact that
mass strikes do not follow a ready-made path, thereby distancing herself
both from the anarchist myth of 'the general strike as a means of inaugu-
rating the revolution' (1906/2008: 112) and the bureaucratic engineers of
the workers movement in German social democracy 'who would, in the

manner of a board of directors, put the mass strike in Germany on the calendar on an appointed day, and those who, like the participants in the trade-union congress at Cologne, would by a prohibition of "propaganda" eliminate the problem of the mass strike from the face of the earth' (1906/2008: 116). Instead, Rosa Luxemburg describes the mass strike as an outcome of specific social and political conditions, as a mass action that cannot be directed by political leaders: 'If, therefore, the Russian Revolution teaches us anything, it teaches above all that the mass strike is not artificially "made", not "decided" at random, not "propagated", but that it is a historical phenomenon, which, at a given moment, results from social conditions with historical inevitability' (1906/2008: 117). Luxemburg describes the mass strike as a tactic of the workers movement with five features: (1) Its forms are constantly changing, sometimes mass strikes start with a political programme and end with purely economic demands, or they begin with demands related to the work situation and evolve into full-fledged political struggles (Luxemburg 1906/2008: 127ff, 144). (2) Mass strikes disrupt political life and enter into the public debate (Luxemburg 1906/2008: 140f). (3) They have a mobilizing aspect for the working class as a whole, as workers experience their collective power and receive a quick political education during these strikes (1906/2008: 140). (4) Mass strikes flow from one part of the country to other parts without a proper central organization (1906/2008: 120–29). (5) Mass strikes are not the final solution in the ultimate quest for political power, for mass strikes have to be transformed into another political strategy: 'The role of the political mass strike alone is exhausted but at the same time, the transition of the mass strike into a general popular rising is not yet accomplished' (1906/2008: 140). It is quite obvious that the strike movements I have described in the first part all match with the criteria developed by Luxemburg with reference to the mass strikes in Russia between 1896 and 1905. But in order to catch their specificities, I aim to grasp the spatial dynamics of mobilization, because these are relevant to the issue of international solidarity. Andrew Herod developed his approach of labour geography in order to provide attention to 'workers as active geographical agents' (1997b: 2) that 'shape economic landscapes and uneven development' (1997b: 1). As it is the case for capital, the agency of workers is restricted due to preexisting social and political conditions (1997: 16), but labour is like capital establishing spatial fixes as a part of the overall dynamic of capitalist accumulation (1997b: 17). Thus, solidarity is conceived by Herod as a successful effort to establish a certain spatial fix (1997b: 20). And most relevant to my account of international solidarity is Herod's claim that workers are also producing the geographical scales on which the conflict with capital is fought out (1997b: 18).

All the three different national waves of mass strikes exhibit the characteristics stated by Luxemburg, most of all a quick diffusion of practices and organizational learning on a mass scale, contradicting widespread romanticizing and/or conservative notions that describe mass strikes as 'wild' or 'spontaneous'. Nevertheless, these strike waves meet spatial limits and patterns of mobilization that differ to some extent and can be understood as national and regional specificities. So, what are the organizational and spatial dynamics of the mass strikes that I described in the previous section? Basically, three kinds of dynamics can be found in these three waves of mass strikes: (1) a first pattern is diffusion of a certain form of strike within one sector, copycat strikes; (2) a second pattern is the diffusion of strikes, although not necessarily in the same form, to other sectors in the same national framework; and (3) the third pattern is the establishment of certain forms of strikes and the diffusion of experiences in one industrial region, at times across sectors.

The South African strike wave in mining is an example of pattern 1 combined with pattern 2. The characteristics of the first strike in January 2012 were copied in July 2012: Opposition and hostility to the trade union NUM and the establishment of independent strike committees, as well as the demand of a 200 per cent wage increase. The massacre by the police in August 2012 triggered a wave of strikes across the whole mining sector, transforming an economic strike into a political event which then transforms into a series of economic strikes (see Luxemburg 1906/2008: 121, on the strikes in the textile sector in 1896). The strikes in mining were followed by strikes of truckers and farmers that were obviously inspired by the miners' strikes (see Luxemburg 1906/2008: 123, on the general strike of 1902). This pattern also repeated over time: In January 2014, the miners in the Rustenburg area, where the massacre had happened in 2012, went on strike again for the same demands as in 2012, but this time with a new trade union and for the time of five months, until June 2014. The strike remained in the Rustenburg area but triggered a strike of the metal union National Union of Metalworkers of South Africa in the automobile sector that lasted about one month.

The strikes in Brazilian construction also fit into pattern 1, but with a stronger presence of pattern 2 and another temporal pattern: The first wave of construction strikes started in one regional state, Bahia (eighty thousand strikers), and extended within two months (February and March 2011) to quite distant areas in the North and Northeast of Brazil (one hundred thousand strikers), and it continued throughout the year (four hundred thousand strikers after March 2011). The diffusion of the forms of strikes started in March 2011, but continued into the next year with a revolt of workers at Suape against the trade union in August 2012, and a similar action, in November 2012, at the Belo Monte Dam. It was also in 2012 that the strike wave reached other construction sites in different parts of the country, and the momentum continued with five hundred thousand strikers in 2012, and most probably four hundred thousand in 2013. A diffusion of strikes to other spheres, which happened after the street protests in June 2013, galvanized union activities, and strikes of street cleaners and bus drivers in Rio de Janeiro in spring 2014, combined with other forms of street protests, were led against the official right-wing trade unions in the sectors. Thus, in Brazil there was another temporal pattern since the wave that begun in February 2011 did not lose momentum, and the street protests in June 2013 added another actor to strikes that took place inside of big cities. Here, again the politicization of economic strikes was occurring when the government sent the national guard to break strikes in March 2011, August 2012, and November 2012, and the diffusion of strikes into the political movement of street protests in 2013 encouraged urban workers to engage in strikes thereafter (see Luxemburg 1906/2008: 140, 144).

The strike activities in the Indian automobile industry resemble pattern 3: The industrial belt around Gurgaon South of New Delhi saw a series of strikes in 2005 to 2007, predominantly in the automobile industry, accompanied by conflicts in the pharmaceutical and the textile industry. The struggles circulate in the wider industrial region that increasingly stretches southward. After the Industrial Model Town in Manesar, twenty-two kilometres south of Gurgaon, saw the conflict at Maruti in 2011 and 2012, many factories have been located further to the South. But it was exactly there, in Pathredi, forty kilometres South of Manesar that workers occupied their plant at the auto parts producer Shiram Pistons and Rings in April and May 2014. In the Gurgaon region, the practice of factory occupation has been increasingly copied by workers, while the practice of widespread solidarity strikes remained limited to the conflict at Maruti Suzuki in Manesar. The strike activities in the Gurgaon region are also embedded in a national scenario of industrial unrest with bigger conflicts at motorcycle producer Bajaj Auto in June to August 2013 in Pune, close to Mumbai, and a month-long conflict at Toyota Kirloskar, close to Bangalore, in March and April 2014, but they exhibit strong regional differences. Labour conflicts in the Pune belt, for example, remain more in the control of trade unions and do not see occupations. The conflict at Bajaj Auto was one of the few bigger conflicts in the last ten years, and it was quickly compared to the conflict at Maruti by many commentators.

So far, we have identified three different patterns. The similarity of these patterns lie in the fact that in one sector in each country the mass strikes that disrupt political life are accumulating, but with important spillover effects to other sectors—this aspect is most vibrant in South Africa where the trade union leaders of the National Union of Metalworkers of South Africa explicitly stated that they feel inspired by the strike of the miners. Another crucial difference is the strong regional focus of the struggles of auto workers in the Gurgaon region South of New Delhi. If we look at these strikes with the categories created by Herod, one can state that workers used sectoral identities to create a culture of struggle and a common identification of workers, but also national and regional spaces. Thus, existing spatial patterns were used and transformed by the workers participating in mass strikes. Nevertheless, as preexisting spaces, they proved to be a limit to the mobilization of workers as well. Especially the national space seemed to be a limit that was not transgressed by the strikes, but only in the aftermath of the strikes when consequences of violent repression had to be dealt with. Thus, the spatial fix of labour is subject to the circumstances of the structural limits given in the organization of space and political conjuncture.

CONCLUSION

The mass strikes since 2008 are part of a global conjuncture of struggles that emerged in the years after the global financial meltdown. If we translate the way strikes referenced each other in the strike waves on the national or regional level, we might have a blueprint to rethink international solidarity. Street protests copied each other without any organic links: The Tahrir Square movement inspired the Spanish indignados that inspired Occupy in the United States, all during 2011. These street protests were seen as a (vaguely) connected movement by a number of commentators that compared the protests since 2011 with the protests around the year 1968 (Castells 2012; Kraushaar 2012; Mason 2013; Stiglitz 2012). The connection between these movements were, first, the modes of action (e.g., occupation of squares); second, the crucial role of educated young people; and third that they happened more or less at the same time within the year 2011. The transnational mass strikes since 2011 were a parallel development to the street protests, starting with mass strikes in Egypt and China in 2010, and expanding into other countries since 2011. I contend that the global wave of mass strikes has to be seen in a similar light as the street protests: A transnational wave, but characterized by national patterns of mobilization. These mass strikes were mainly based on informal networks between workers. In the case of South African mining and the Brazilian construction sector, there have been no tight organizational structures that organized the strike wave, but many informal contacts between workers (see Luxemburg 1906/2008: 120–29, on mass strikes in Russia). The same goes for the strikes in the Gurgaon region. The circulation of struggles is based on a circulation of experiences, enhanced by quick rotation between workplaces and a high amount of labour migration inside of national states. The solidarity during the strike waves was not based on a unified commando, but on an uncontrolled proliferation of strike movements, although there have been some organized kernels. This is not at all meant to celebrate the strikes as 'spontaneous'. The strikes have been well organized and well prepared in most of the cases. Thus, the question remains: Can common action during a strike wave can be seen as 'solidarity' or as a unified movement? Given that the strike waves have not been connected to national structures of organization in the cases presented here, one could ask if this can be conceived as 'solidarity' even within the national framework. Is solidarity only given if protest action is organized 'on behalf' of others in struggle, or could it include a common struggle with common effects, but separate organization?

At the international level, there have been almost no connections between the different strike movements. Almost all of the around forty workers I talked to in India and Brazil in 2013 and 2014 knew about the massacre against South African miners in 2012. Some of the Maruti workers in Delhi had been part of the organizing committee of two demonstrations taking place in New Delhi in solidarity with the South African miners in August 2012 and 2013. But beyond any organic connections between the strike waves, it was the sheer fact of their contemporaneity over two years which is astonishing: Revolts in Brazilian construction in February/March 2011, occupations at Maruti Suzuki in June and October 2011, uprising at Maruti Suzuki in July 2012, revolt in Suape in August 2012, strike and massacre in Marikana in August 2012, and revolt at Belo Monte in November 2012. Thus, the international solidarity in these cases just consisted in doing the same thing at (almost) the same time, often without knowing about each other. Similar trends of investment and restructuring of work, of the global economic downturn, of new expectations of workers and of new means of communication between workers led to an explosion of unrest in the workplaces—in the same way that street protests were emerging around different continents in the years after 2011. There were spatial limits of the strike waves in terms of mobilization (Herod 1997b). In Brazil and South Africa, these spatial limits coincided with national borders. Given the transnational organization of domination, this confinement to the national public is a decisive weakness—but it can be the sheer contemporaneity of struggles that becomes a mobilizing factor on its own, and it is this effect and its dynamics that remain to be understood better in research on mass strikes.

NOTES

1. Interviews with worker A at Maruti Suzuki on December 4, 2013, and worker B, C, D, and E on December 6, 2013.
2. Interview with Sudersan Rao Sarde, Industriall, on December 9, 2013.

Part II

Transnational Action—Past and Present

Introduction

Darragh Golden

Trade unions have organized workers and structured workers' movements since the middle of the nineteenth century, albeit in a variety of forms. Typically, unions 'have a hierarchy of levels from the workplace to the enterprise, from regional groupings to national federations and from national federations to international groupings' (Harrod and O'Brien 2002: 4). Thus, *formal* trade union internationalism preceded the execution of transnational action. Arguably, the greatest threat to the spirit of internationalism has been irredentist chauvinism, which reached fever pitch with outbreak of the two World Wars when 'national identities assumed overriding precedence' (Hyman 2005: 140). After each period of bellicosity, attempts were made to rekindle the spirit of labour internationalism.

This section is concerned with the post–World War period which stretches seven decades from 1945 to the present day. Here we can subdivide this timeframe into two separate periods: (1) the Cold War period, and (2) the post–Cold War period. Notwithstanding these periodizations, it would be an egregious error to assume that historical processes came to an abrupt end with the conclusion of the Cold War, or that the post–Cold War era represents a clean break with past legacies. Present and future transnational actions remain contingent on the past, which were shaped by tensions resulting from the Cold War. All too often, these tensions created constraints for trade unions, both national and international.

The quote 'the past is a foreign country' is well known amongst historians. Therefore, in the spirit of transnational action, we must cross that border in a bid to comprehend the constraints and contradictions that developed within postwar international trade unionism. The obstacles that union internationalism encounters today derive from institutional struggles for control in the immediate postwar period. This struggle, between a socialist and a liberal brand of internationalism, resulted in the creation of competing internationalisms, resulting in representational bias (see Gentile 2015). The legacy of this bias continues to affect international trade union campaigns today. Golden's focus is on the regional level where the divisions that emerged in the Cold War context are highlighted. Here, the positions of Italian and Irish unions on the question of European integration are critically evaluated through the lens of trade union internationalism. The bridging of divisions and the creation of a unified European structure was not only important for the representation of European labour's interests in supranational institutions, but also in terms of defusing a potential division in Irish trade union circles.

The other two contributions are rooted more firmly in the post–Cold War era, characterized by neoliberal globalization. While much of the focus regarding globalization has been on the growing impact of multinational companies, as demonstrated in the introductory chapter; there is another expression of globalization which is more ubiquitous than any other: transnational labour migration. Kjeldstadli and Matos' contributions are concerned with this phenomenon. In an era defined by 'free movement', unions have had to deal with the real threat of 'social dumping' whilst, at the same time, be sure so as not to betray the ethos of worker solidarity.

Transnational labour migration creates integrated social spaces that follow a logic different to that of a more 'homogenous', for want of a better term, space. The construction sector aptly acts as the backdrop for Kjeldstadli and Matos' study of Norwegian unions and migrant labour. Taken together, both chapters assess trade unions' strategies in an increasingly mobile era and its implications for national industrial relations systems. How might unions engender a spirit of solidarity between native and migrant workers? In many ways, this, as Kjeldstadli notes, is a learning experience for unions. Kjeldstadli argues that when it comes to organizing migrant workers the temporal dimension is important. It would appear that Matos' contribution corroborates this point. This raises further dilemmas for unions when dealing with short-term or 'posted workers'. Here unions have to devise different, less traditional, strategies. In the case examined by Matos, the media had an important role to play. The long reach of the media is a useful tool for publicizing and politicizing cases of social dumping thereby boosting the campaign's symbolic capital.

FIVE

Trade Union Internationalism and European Integration

A Critical Evaluation

Darragh Golden[1]

INTRODUCTION

Trade union internationalism has been an integral component of the labour movement, at least rhetorically. The underpinning principle being that workers' interest overrides the so-called national interest. This idea is of utmost relevance in today's setting of regional integration and globalization. Moreover, this idea needs to be more than aspirational if labour is to remain a relevant social force in the twenty-first century. However, there are different starting points and trade unions are products of their own environments. At its simplest, however, trade union internationalism is about unity and a willingness to act on the basis of such unity. This is by no means an easy task, especially if we consider that within certain national contexts establishing and maintaining unity within the national trade union movement is a difficult task. Questions of a political nature have the potential to divide the trade union community. European integration is one such question which has divided trade unions in the past and could potentially expose fault lines which exist both within and between trade union movements today.

Within Italy, the question of European integration consolidated a split in the Italian trade union movement. From the outset the communist union the *Confederazione Generale Italiana del Lavoro* (CGIL) and its sister party the *Partitio Comunista Italiano*, virulently opposed European economic integration. When the question of membership to the European Economic Community (EEC) was put before the Irish people, the Irish Congress of Trade Unions (ICTU) and its sister party the Irish Labour Party, also had serious concerns regarding the project. Did trade union internationalism play any role in defining the position of the European trade unions on the question of European integration? And if so, to what extent does it help us explain the position of the Irish trade union federation on internationalism and European integration? Also, how did European integration influence trade union internationalism?

This research is part of a doctoral project which assesses the changing positions of Irish and Italian trade unions on the question of European integration across time. This chapter has a historical focus and assesses the position of Irish and Italian unions on European integration through the lens of trade union internationalism. Naturally, there are other factors considered by unions when adopting a position on such questions, which cannot be covered here for reasons of space limitation. The role of trade union internationalism, which interacts and is entwined with class solidarity, as well as with national and religious loyalties, became more complex as a result of regionalism. This contribution is based on trade union archival research in Dublin and Rome.

This chapter will proceed as follows: first, I will outline the genesis of the international trade union movement in the post–World War II context, with particular attention being paid to the process of European integration. Then I will focus on the case of the Italian unions and the CGIL in particular. I will then turn my attention to the Irish case, and in particular the ICTU. Finally, the chapter will offer some conclusions on the relationship between trade union internationalism and European economic integration.

TRADE UNION INTERNATIONALISM IN THE POSTWAR PERIOD

As World War II began to conclude, international trade unionism began to re-emerge. The World Federation of Trade Unions (WFTU) was established in 1945 in Paris, on an antifascist programme of cooperation and pacifism thereby replacing the International Federation of Trade Unions. The number of unions affiliated to the WFTU was greater than that of any previous labour organization with one notable abstention: the American Federation of Labour (AFL). The AFL[2] refused to associate itself with the trade union confederation of the USSR or the other American union, Congress of Industrial Organizations (CIO). From the start, the incipient organization was plagued with divisions, in particular the Russians were suspicious of the British Trades Union Congress (TUC) and the American CIO (Carew 1987: chapter 5) and hopes that ideological differences could be bridged proved optimistic and were short-lived.

The emerging Cold War between the victorious superpowers was the source of tensions both within the WFTU and national labour movements. Regarding the WFTU, opinions were divided as to whether the organization was being used by the Russians as an instrument to propagate anticapitalist revolutionary ideals. The TUC and CIO struggled to keep Russian dominance at bay while defending the existence of the federation to their sceptical compatriots. It was also in the interest of the Russians that the federation survived for it extended the influence of the Russian labour movement into countries that might have been beyond their scope. The introduction of the Marshall Plan went beyond whatever compromise the Soviet leadership was prepared to make for the sake of trade union unity.

Although the WFTU never *officially* denounced the Marshall Plan, it was as Carew (2000: 175) writes, 'the symbolic issue over which communists and non-communists divided'. The question of Marshall Aid dominated discussion within trade union circles. Unable to arrange a meeting of the executive committee of the WFTU to discuss the implications of the Marshall Plan, the TUC organized an international labour conference in London in early March[3] (1948) to discuss the European Recovery Programme. Invitations were sent out to the trade unions of fifteen European states as well as the AFL and CIO. 'The conference forced wavering labour centres to choose sides' (Carew 1987: 77). As we discover below, the question of attending international conferences proved divisive for both Italian and Irish unions.

In January 1949, the TUC and the CIO quit the WFTU, despite last ditch attempts made by the Russians to save the organization. Over the following year and a half, most Western European federations followed the Anglo-American example. This, however, was not the case for the Irish federation. The idea of international trade union unity had collapsed under the manifestation of Cold War tensions; had it been that the Cold War had never transpired, the thought that the unity between the communist and anticommunist factions could have continued long-term seems unlikely. Notwithstanding this, the question of Marshall Aid had undone the semblance of trade union unity by exposing the ideological differences between the affiliate unions. Upon exiting the WFTU, trade unions with a social-democratic leaning set up the International Confederation of Free[4] Trade Unions (ICFTU). Meanwhile, the Christian trade unions were organized in a separate international body called the International Confederation of Christian Trade Unions (CISC). Communist-oriented unions, however, remained affiliated to the WFTU. Just as Marshall Aid had split the trade union community, the question of European integration too became a burning issue for European trade unions.

The idea of trade union representation and European integration were considered two sides of the same coin. This was evident in the institutional structure of the European Coal and Steel Community, however, less so in its successor, the EEC. Nevertheless, the national trade unions were prepared to define a role for themselves at the European level. European (noncommunist) unions from the six member-states were active at the European level through European-level branches. The ICFTU and CISC created European Regional Organisations, which met for preparatory talks on the implications of widening the scope of economic integration to encompass the free movement of goods, capital, labour, and services. Some communist federations (CGIL, General Confederation of Labour, Dutch De eenheidsvakcentrale, and Luxembourgeois Frei Lëtzebuerger Arbechterverband) established a Common Market Action Committee, which was largely ineffective.

In particular, the unions were keen to secure a voice in the supranational institutions. The prointegration stance of the unions in the European Coal and Steel Community was acknowledged by Monnet when he invited labour representatives to participate in the Action Committee of the United States of Europe (Duchene 1994). Trade unions were seen as playing a key role in convincing social democratic parties of the virtues of European integration (Suzuki 2008). There was also a sense of pride that unions were chosen as representatives over employers partly because the latter were 'incapable of distinguishing the general interest from their own' (Duchene 1994: 285). Nevertheless, the division of Europe into three trading blocs (EEC, European Free Trade Association, and Comecon) provided an obstacle to the emergence of a cohesive strategy vis-à-vis European integration.

Towards the end of the 1960s, attempts were made to consolidate the structure of the socialist and Christian unions. Hitherto, the ICFTU, which had affiliates in both EEC and European Free Trade Association member-states, had two European structures representing the two trading blocs in Western Europe. By now, the EEC had grown in importance as had the challenges associated with membership, and it was becoming increasingly clear that divisions within the trade union movement 'helped to create an almost permanent climate of conflict' and were doing little to enhance labour's European effort (Degryse 2013: 17).

A greater appetite for operating outside the constraints imposed by the ICFTU was developing. This became possible after the withdrawal of the AFL-CIO from the ICFTU in 1968 (Carew 2000: 333–34). The 1969 European Summit in The Hague announced the leap from a customs union to an economic and monetary union while proclaiming plans for greater political integration. Also, membership negotiations with Great Britain, Ireland, Norway, and Denmark were under way. In addition, by now the European employers' organization had adopted a more hardline position at the European level than at the national level. Divisions only served to weaken labour's broad interests in a deepening European community (Buschak 2003: 12). In late 1969, the ICFTU European Regional Organisations adopted a new organizational structure and eventually became the European Trade Union Confederation (ETUC).[5] Two meetings in Frankfurt and Oslo in 1971 settled the debate on the need for comprehensive and coordinated trade union representation at the European level. In 1974, affiliates of the EO-CISC[6] were incorporated into the ETUC which now represented thirty trade union organizations based in seventeen European countries (Degryse 2013: 23). A cohesive voice was necessary if a social Europe was to become attainable, or even adequately struggled for. However, there remained the question of the communist unions. We will return to this below.

ITALIAN LABOUR AND EUROPEAN INTEGRATION

The defeat of nazi-fascism presented Italian trade unionism with an opportunity to re-establish the labour movement. United in their defeat of fascism, the socialists, Christian democrats, and communists founded one trade union confederation. The *Confederazione Generale Italiana del Lavoro* was created under the 'Pact of Rome' signed on 3 June 1944. The objective of the united CGIL was to unify all the Italian workers under one union and consolidate an antifascist front. Representing over five million workers, the CGIL had three general secretaries[7] representing the different political strands; however, strictly speaking the union was free of political affiliation. The CGIL affiliated to the WFTU and played an active role within the nascent organization.

As Cold War tensions intensified, further stress was placed on the preexisting fault lines in the CGIL. The presence of the communists within the CGIL increased between 1945 and 1947 (Carew 1987: 28) and nominal parity between the factions ended when Di Vittorio became head of the CGIL in June 1947.[8] American policymakers were very much aware of the importance of European labour movements to the attainment of its broad economic and political goals, which were twofold: Create an international economic environment conducive to capitalism, and put a halt to the advent of communism in Western Europe. To that end, support was offered to noncommunists inside the CGIL. This support raised the status of noncommunist factions and boosted their influence well beyond that warranted by the size of their trade union following. The American administration was keen to manufacture a split in the CGIL, and the creation of an anticommunist, independent, nonconfessional trade union was central to their broader international vision. From an American perspective, it was paramount that the breakaway Catholic faction did not create a 'white' union federation. Here, the funds would most likely have come from a Vatican source (e.g., *Associazioni Cristiane Lavoratori Italiani*), which could have compromised the independence and aconfessional nature of the nascent union.

As mentioned in the section above, the question of Marshall Aid and attending the London conference was a divisive issue. This was no different for the CGIL. Officially, the CGIL boycotted the aforementioned London meeting; however, individuals such as Pastore,[9] on behalf of the Catholic faction, Canini, on behalf of the social democrats, and Parri, on behalf of the republicans, did attend. Just as the conference marked the beginning of the end for the WFTU, it did too for the CGIL as '[E]veryone had to choose, and the choice carried with it political, economic, social and strategic implications' (Filippelli 1989: 126). In April 1950, the *Confederazione Italiana Sindacato Lavoratori* (CISL) was founded and adopted a less ideological style of trade unionism. Instead, the emphasis was to be on productivity and collective bargaining.

By 1950, both the Italian and the international trade union movement were split into three clear camps: the communist unions in the WFTU, the so-called 'free' trade unions in the ICFTU, and the Christian unions in the CISC (later renamed the World Confederation of Labour). The CGIL remained afilliated to the WFTU, while CISL affiliated to the newly established ICFTU. As noted above, the question of European economic cooperation was widely discussed in each of the international federations. This was also the case in the Italian federations where the nature and *finalité* of European integration was broadly discussed (Ciampani 2000; del Biondo 2007; Pistone 1988). CISL (1955, 1956) was a clear champion of furthering economic integration and advocated an upward harmonization of social policies, especially those governing workers' lives such as working hours, holidays and wages (various CISL documents).

From the outset, the CGIL was extremely critical of the European integration process.[10] Once the EEC came into being, the national congresses of the union generally featured a debate on the nature of the Common Market and potential response strategies (various CGIL documents). As far as the Italian communists were concerned, the European project was capitalist, Atlanticist, imperialistic, and anticommunist. The CGIL joined Western communist parties, the Soviet communist party, and other communist trade unions 'in condemning the Community as a tool of imperialism that had the two-fold objective of subjugating Western Europe economically and politically to American capital, and strengthening imperialisms offensive against the socialist countries led by the Soviet Union' (Dunphy 2004: 72). In other words, hostility towards European integration was done so on filo-soviet and ideological grounds.

There was a notable shift in policy by the CGIL (1960) towards European integration at the V National Congress. An emphasis was placed on the need for the representation of workers' interests at the European level (i.e., internationalism) or a form thereof. However, a number of national federations were unresponsive to the CGIL's aperture. This policy of polycentrism also proved to be a source of tension within the WFTU, which played out in the WFTU conferences of 1961 and 1962 (Maggiorani

1998: 62). Notwithstanding this, the CGIL adopted an autonomous path thereby breaking with the directions of Moscow. Thus, internationalism had hindered the CGIL and consequently the Italian union was criticised for the type of internationalism that it espoused. The CGIL remained committed to establishing a regional liaison office. Realising the reluctance of the French or the Russians to change their position on representation within the EEC, the CGIL, acting on its own initiative, set up its own office in Brussels in 1963.

The office's objective 'was to break down the barriers between the communist and non-communist unions and establish a common front in EEC labour affairs' (Feld 1968: 253; see also Pernot 2001: 310–27). Attempts were made to create contacts with the European Commission as well as with unions of a 'free' and Christian orientation in the hope of creating a united front on labour issues. Here limited success was had; however, ideological pluralism became a reality when the CGIL became an affiliated member of the ETUC in 1974.[11] Such a move became possible after the CGIL had weakened its links with the WFTU by downgrading to associate member and support from the other Italian confederations was fundamental.[12]

IRISH LABOUR AND EUROPEAN INTEGRATION

Unlike the Italian political system, which is organized along a right-left ideological spectrum, the Irish case is quite unique. Instead, the Irish political system is more tribal and is divided along civil war lines.[13] Writing on the Irish political system, Inglehart and Klingemann (1976: 270) note that the 'left-right dimension is seen to have a relatively unclear meaning for the Irish public. Both the ideological components are weak in Ireland, our persistent deviant case'. Since the creation of the Irish Free State, the Irish political system has been obsessed with the question of partition. This has prevented Ireland from being integrated into the international system of states, resulting, ultimately, in splendid socioeconomic isolation. That does not imply that commonalities were not shared with other nations.

Nationalism and Roman Catholicism were the dominant integrative ideologies of the Irish Free State. 'The inspiration for party policy was regularly located in papal encyclicals [such as *Rerum Novarum*[14] and *Quadragessimo Anno*[15]] rather than socialist theory' (Bew, Hazelkorn, and Patterson 1989: 145). Therefore, any other type of ideology was considered 'foreign' and inapplicable to Irish circumstances and/or incompatible with the Church. The Labour party and other left-wing organizations, such as trade unions, failed, for a variety of reasons, to create a strong class consciousness, opting instead to engage in a campaign that viewed democratic socialism as being 'principally one of "social unity" not "class solidarity"' (Bew, Hazelkorn, and Patterson 1989: 144). Thus, these papal encyclicals had greater resonance with the Irish trade union movement than the works of Marx or Lenin (Lee 1979).

The postindependence trade union movement was (and continues to be) afflicted with a number of tensions. For starters, the unions 'had to operate under two distinct and mutually hostile regimes' (Henderman 1983: 123). Secondly, there was a strong nationalist wing within the movement. Thirdly, British unions continued to operate on the island, both North and South, and were constituent members of the national confederation. These tensions continue today, and although the situation may not be as hostile as it was in the formative years, the presence of British unions, as well as operating in two religiously defined jurisdictions, has impeded the political role of Irish unions in engendering a class consiousness. As Hardiman notes (1989: 125)

> class consciousness did not provide the primary political identity of the great majority of workers in the formative years of the political system, and socioeconomic issues were overshadowed by the constitutional issue of independence. But the trade union movement could not take up an unequivocally nationalist position either, because its membership spanned the sectarian and nationalist divide in the north. The trade union movement, as a result, stood apart from the party political system.

Arguably, this is the greatest difference between Ireland and Italy in the postwar years. As noted above, the Italian trade union movement was highly politicized and seen as an agent of broad working class interests. There were, however, a number of commonalities shared by the two countries in the postwar period. Economically speaking, both countries were stagnant and had underdeveloped regions. Unemployment and underemployment plagued both countries. The Catholic Church played an important political role in both contexts. Also in terms of foreign policy, both countries pursued a policy of nonalignment, albeit for different reasons and in the Italian case for much less time. In addition, the outcome of the historical 1948 election in Italy was also seen to have implications for Ireland (and Christian civilization) and considerable Irish energies and finance were covertly invested in the anticommunist campaign (see Keogh 1991).

Notwithstanding these commonalities, when it comes to the question of trade union internationalism, there is considerable divergence between the Italian and Irish unions. Just as the question of Marshall Aid and European integration caused tensions in the Italian and international labour movements, so too were such questions divisive in the Irish context, albeit for different reasons. To understand this context, however, requires greater background knowledge.

The turn of the twentieth century was characterized by a degree of trade union radicalism; however, this radicalism was not convivial with the nationalist ethos and eventually led to the radical wing of the largest union, Irish Transport and General Workers Union, splitting to create the Workers' Union of Ireland (WUI) in 1923. The agitator, Jim Larkin, became the leader of the latter while the more conservative William O'Brien headed the former (as well as being a Labour party deputy and an official of the ITUC!). Both men became bitter rivals, but the Irish Transport and General Workers Union remained the largest union in Ireland. Larkin was more internationalist in his outlook and the WUI affiliated itself to the procommunist Red International of Labour Unions also known as the Profintern. Consequently, the WUI came under constant fire for its membership of the Profintern and the WUI was not admitted to the Irish confederation until 1945, and only after the confederation had split (O'Connor 2002: 92).

Trade union nationalism implied a number of things and these ultimately impeded an internationalist perspective. As stated above, class-oriented trade unionism, such as the idea of 'One Big Union', was incompatible with the nationalist movement. 'Virulent opposition became a significant strand in Southern nationalism . . . [and] . . . labour organisations were called to account for any trace of communist influence in their midst' (Allen 1997: 55). Divisions were abhorred: 'To divide this united people, and especially to promote a politics which would pit class against class, was both anti-national and irrelevant, for there could only be common enemies, and these all lay outside the boundaries of the state' (Mair 1993: 404). This is not to say that such a position did not come in for severe criticism. McCarthy (1974: 63) was critical of what he called 'national separatism of a strikingly xenophobic kind which almost overwhelmed the broader based, more international character of the Irish trade union movement'.

Therefore, in order for internationalism to be incorporated into the trade union strategy, it had to be compatible with the strategy of national unity. International organizations were seen not only as an extension of solidarity but also as an opportunity to raise awareness of the Irish predicament (see Kennedy and O'Halpin 2000). Whether attended by representatives of Irish labour or by delegates of the newly established Free State, the presence of British forces on Irish soil was inevitably raised and support sought for the Irish cause (Keane 2006: 131–35). Such was the case when an Irish delegation attended Council of Europe and Organisation for European Economic Co-operation meetings in postwar years. Moreover, there was an expectation on delegates to raise the question of partition in international fora. Republicans were very supportive of the efforts made by Irish labour representatives to achieve recognition of the Irish cause through international organizations, provided of course the issue of self-determination was raised. Hence, the labour movements' connection with the broader international movement was shaped by the 'national question'. In theory, the Irish cause would have resonated within expressions of labour internationalism, such as the WFTU or the Third International where imperialism was admonished and national self-determination promoted, provided, of course, that it was of a socialist variant (Munck 2002: 139). This proviso was problematic for the conservative strand of Irish trade unionists who were not prepared to subordinate their interests to a socialist end.

Consequently, the trade union movement maintained an isolationist and insular outlook by declining invitations to join the International Federation of Trade Unions, the predecessor of the WFTU. As a result of self-imposed isolation, the Irish labour movement was disengaged from the broader international movement. As Lane (2008: 58) notes,

> Very little of European thought or experience has ever been directly tapped or assimilated by the Irish . . . Because of the irredentist obsession of political leaders with the problem of the six Ulster counties, and consequently neutrality in and after the Second World War, Ireland was cut off to an extraordinary degree from the mainstream of Western European life.

At most, linkages extended to sister organizations in the United Kingdom or participation in the meetings of the British Commonwealth Labour Conference, where the assemblies were, again, used as a platform to promote self-determination and denounce partition.

The tension between nationalism or self-determination and internationalism resulted in a division of the labour movement. Unlike in the Italian case, there was no external interference here. When Irish union delegates were invited to attend a World Trade Union Conference, in London, on the war economy and reconstruction, an argument developed. The war economy had provided the British-based unions in Northern Ireland with increased bargaining power. This was also reflected in their membership which increased from 68,000 in 1937 to 108,000 in 1944. This increase translated into influence within the ITUC and for the first time since 1918, the British unions secured a majority within the Congress executive (O'Connor 2011: 166). A large number of Irish unions strongly supported neutrality as a foreign policy. Nevertheless, neutrality was an expression and a result of partition. It was not an ideologically motivated policy, but just so happened to be in harmony with the Irish nationalist left.

The motion to attend the postwar London conference divided the Congress, and the decision to send two delegates to the London conference resulted in fifteen Irish unions[16] seceding from the ITUC on the grounds that the opinions and aspirations of Irish labour cannot be expressed by the ITUC which is controlled by British trade unions. This led to the creation of the Congress of Irish Unions which was nationalistic,

Catholic, and anticommunist in its outlook and distinguished itself from the left-wing internationalist outlook of the British unions, which remained affiliated to the ITUC.

Although Ireland was officially neutral during the war, the American administration was keen on Ireland's participation in the Marshall programme. This was the case despite the fact that a communist threat was absent, save a handful of individuals who did oppose the Marshall Plan (Whelan 2006). At the time, opinion on Marshall Aid was coloured more by the ideal of self-sufficiency, which was as critical of American materialism as it was of communism. Garvin (2004: 235) argues that this 'anti-intellectualism' was responsible for much of Ireland's economic underdevelopment. For many others though, Marshall Aid was seen as a means for lessening dependence on Britain (Geiger 2000; O'Hearn 2001: 126).

The two Congresses were reunited in 1959 under the banner of the current day ICTU. Henceforth, however, the cohesion of ICTU was paramount and was not going to be undermined or threatened by questions of an international nature. Internal or quasinational solidarity was favoured over international solidarity. One interpretation might be that the former had a functional logic whereas the latter was more symbolic in nature. Union leaders realized that the split had weakened their hand vis-à-vis the state. But the spilt epitomized the contradictions of Irish Labour: secular trade unioninsm operating in two different religious and legally defined jurisdictions. Inevitably, a more internationally inspired idealism and Irish idealism clashed.

Once the rift was healed with the creation of ICTU, questions which might undermine the cohesion of the cross-border union movement were, where possible, avoided. 'The trade union movement was deeply involved in trying to heal the wounds which had divided it and was not prepared to add another factor which would inevitably be divisive' (Hederman 1988: 768). In other words, all-Ireland trade unionism cohesion trumped labour internationalism. For this reason, ICTU did not affiliate itself with any of the international trade union organizations (e.g., ICFTU, WFTU, CISC) after 1950. Although, during the brief lifetime of the Congress of Irish Unions, the federation, at the behest of the Church, sought to affiliate itself to the International Christian Confederation, for one reason or another this never materialised (Pasture 2005: 23).

Although Ireland did not join the EEC until 1973, the question of European integration was on the trade unions' radar since the late 1950s (Murphy 1993). When the question of EEC membership was put before the Irish people, the vast majority of Irish trade unions were against Ireland joining. We have seen above that in the Italian case, a union's international affiliation is a good indicator in explaining the position a union adopted on European integration. In brief, unless affiliated to the WFTU in the 1950s, a union was most likely a strong advocate of economic integration. However, in the Irish case we do not have this luxury as the question of international affiliation had the potential to weaken union strength at home. Therefore, additional explanations are required; however, this is beyond the scope of this contribution. Instead, we will briefly focus on the creation of the ETUC and the logic underpinning ICTU's decision to affiliate to an international trade union organization.

Once the popular decision to join was taken, ICTU made no hesitation whatsoever in joining the ETUC. How is it that such a move did not threaten the internal cohesion of the movement? Arguably, the answer lies in the developments, outlined above, between the competing union ideologies in the 1960s and early 1970s. Had these divisions not been bridged, the ICTU would have faced the dilemma of choosing a regional representative body of the communists, socialist or Christian strand. Such a decision could well have undermined the associational monopoly of ICTU. Nevertheless, the leadership of ICTU was prompt, unlike their British counterparts, in pursuing an active role in the European labour movment. Fully aware of the paralyzing ability of divisions, ICTU favoured a united front at the European level. This was evident when ICTU argued in favour of the admission of the CGIL to the ETUC in 1974.

CONCLUSION

To conclude, it appears that ideological orientation and international affiliation had a bearing on the position of trade unions vis-à-vis the position of trade unions on European integration. This is certainly the case when we look at the Italian trade unions. In particular, the CGIL had to struggle within the WFTU to moderate its stance and engage with the process at the European level, which, until the 1970s, remained characterized by a divided and weakened European labour movement. Had these divisions persisted once Ireland joined, it is possible that the ICTU might not have engaged with the process as it would have had to choose one affiliation over another, which would have placed internal cohesion in jeopardy. The Irish trade union movement understood the importance of unity not only when it came to dealing with employers or the state but also for the sake of the movement. This approach was also promoted at the European level. Thus, domestic desires for trade union unity were projected onto the European level.

The cases presented above demonstrate that trade union internationalism is complicated and coloured by the national context. In the Irish case, the union movement developed independently of the debates which characterized and shaped Continental union movements, arguably to the detriment of the Irish labour movement.[17] Although partition was never the sole obsession, it inevitably featured in international questions. In that sense, joining the ETUC is significant and represented a learning process for the leadership of ICTU, an initiation of sorts. The American influence, which we have documented in the Italian case, would eventually commence the 'slow strangulation' of Irish unions, albeit in a different way and through different actors.

NOTES

1. A special thanks to the members of the CAS group and to Peter Waterman, Till Geiger, Tiago Matos, Marcel Van der Linden, and Antonina Gentile for help, comments, and observations.

2. As the WFTU was being founded, the AFL was creating its own European base with the objective of stemming the communist threat and undermining the nascent international organisation. For more on this see van Goethem and Waters (2013).

3. Another conference was held in July of the same year.

4. The term 'free' was an AFL initiative and it implied free from domination by political parties, employer, government or church.

5. There was a proviso, however, as the country had to be democratic. This meant that Greek, Spanish, and Portuguese unions were inadmissible. The Spanish UGT was an exception as it was operating clandestinely while in exile. These countries remained the responsibility of the ICFTU.

6. The Christian unions were admitted provided that 'by becoming members of the ETUC, [they] undertake to work for unity of the free and democratic trade union movement at all levels' (Gumbrell-McCormick 2000:372).

7. Giuseppe di Vittorio on behalf of the Communist party, Achille Grandi on behalf of the Christian Democrats, and Emilio Canavari on behalf of the Socialists.

8. The Democrazia Cristiana (DC) organized the Catholic faction through the *Associazioni Cristiane Lavoratori Italiani*, which criticized the CGIL for allowing the union to become an instrument for the political end of the *Partitio Comunista Italiano*. The *Associazioni Cristiane Lavoratori Italiani* received massive funding from the Church and it had offices all over Italy, as well as thirteen offices in cities abroad (Filippelli 1989: 143).

9. Future leader of *Confederazione Italiana Sindacato Lavoratori*.

10. Hostility towards the process was done so explicitly through the various channels of expression available to the party and the union. These included the daily paper *Unita'* originally founded by Gramsci and the journal *Notizario CGIL* later renamed *Rassengna Sindacale*. It was in the pages of these publications, and others such as *Critica Economia*, that opinions were expressed on the creation of the Common Market.

11. The CGIL also applied to join the ICFTU in 1974; however, bizarrely this application was rejected on the grounds that it was a communist union (Gumbrell-McCormick 2000: 356).

12. Thanks to Antonina Gentile for pointing this out to me.

13. The Irish Civil War took place between 1922 and 1923. The war was fought over the Anglo-Irish Treaty which accepted the partition of the island into two jurisdictions, known today as Northern Ireland, consisting of six counties and the Republic of Ireland, consisting of twenty-six counties. On the one side, there were those who were pro-Treaty and saw the acceptance of partition as a gradual step towards independence. On the other side, there were those who opposed any such division. The two main political parties in Ireland today are direct descendants of the conflict with Fine Gael representing the former and Fianna Fáil the latter.

14. This encyclical warned against the dangers of socialism and secularism.

15. This encyclical encouraged the creation of occupational organizations as an alternative to class conflict.

16. For a list of the unions see McCarthy (1973: 615–21).

17. This does not suggest that the Irish trade union movement did not have its own spiritual leaders.

SIX

A Closed Nation or an Open Working Class?

When Do Unions Opt for Including Labour Migrants?

Knut Kjeldstadli

OPTING FOR INCLUSION: OSLO CONSTRUCTION WORKERS AND LABOUR MIGRANTS

The logic of unions is the cartel: to sell labour power collectively and minimize competition between individual sellers. Throughout their history, trade unions have faced a strategic choice: Should they try to fence in a segment of the labour market, thereby making the sale of labour power an exclusive right and reducing the supply, in principle secure a monopoly of supply (Nielsen 2013: 48)? Or should they try to organize all possible sellers in the market? This insider-outsider division has rested on gender, age, skill, ethnicity, and on nationals versus foreigners.

Perhaps this dilemma has manifested itself most clearly with respect to transnational migration, from late nineteenth century onwards (Hamamovitch 2003; Strikwerda 1999), in particular labour migrants or 'transnational workers' (Ness 2005: 1). In 2003/2004, the Construction Workers' Union in Oslo developed their position, expressed in the slogan 'we are a union for workers in Norway, not only for Norwegian workers' (Rodal 2013: 47).[1] Later, this was also adopted by their nationwide trade union *Fellesforbundet*, a dominant union within *Landsorganisasjonen i Norge*, the Norwegian Trades Union Congress. Serious efforts were made by the construction workers to organize and represent migrant immigrant workers. From 2004, this meant mostly workers from Poland, Latvia, and Lithuania. The Construction Workers' Union succeeded to such a degree that it was nicknamed *Polakkforeningen* — the Poles' union.

This was not self-evident. Examples of unions choosing a strategy of enclosure against immigration, and also towards immigrant or migrant workers, are many. During the transatlantic proletarian mass migrations in the nineteenth and twentieth centuries, this became a major issue. American unions, such as the Knights of Labour, were restrictive, even outright hostile. Chinese workers in particular were targeted and barred from entering by the Chinese Exclusion Act in 1882. The American Federation of Labor swung into a prorestriction stance from 1897. It defended 'American' skilled craft workers against 'foreigners', and even came to argue in terms of 'racial purity' (Higham 1998: 162ff). Only in 2000 did the American trade union movement reverse its restrictive stance and endorse the rights of work migrants, including *sans papiers* (Ness 2005: 43).

German unions hesitated to include the *Ruhr-Polen* in the coal mines in the late nineteenth century. So Poles founded their own separate union in 1908 (Klessmann 1985: 264). From 2004, German *IG Bau* organized a parallel union for migrant and seasonal workers in construction and agriculture, *Europäischen Verband der Wanderarbeiter*. This was chosen as an alternative to inviting them into the existing *IG Bau* organization.[2]

The Norwegian Trades Union Congress supported, in 1975, a law on a temporary stop to inward migration. The argument ran: Those who came should enjoy the same economic and social standard as the resident population. But to obtain this goal, few might be let in (Brochmann and Kjeldstadli 2008: 201ff).

So, choosing closure, for instance on a national basis, happens frequently. Therefore we shall ask: *How and why did the open union policy develop in Oslo?* Through this case study, more general insights may be derived.

The approach here is actor orientated, aiming to identify micromechanisms. Without understanding the minutiae of quotidian organizing, one does not understand the unions' choice of strategies. The primary material for this article consists of interviews with Norwegian unionists. This approach may be reproached for being union centered; ideally, a relational approach should have been chosen, including also the experiences of the migrant workers and the rank and file of Norwegians. There is a possible bias in the material, stemming from people belonging more or less to the same circles. Yet this has the benefit of rendering their more or less unanimous version; understanding the 'group think', the collective opinion, is an aim.

BACKGROUND: RECENT WORK MIGRATION TO NORWAY

In 2004, and then again in 2007, the European Union expanded with several new countries in Eastern Europe joining. Norway is not a European Union member, but cooperates with the European Union with the European Economic Area (EEA); this includes the so-called Four Freedoms. Consequently, Norway too got its share of *Polonia*, the Polish name for those more than two millions Poles abroad. In particular, this refers to the Polish men that worked in the construction industry. For the labour migrants, the primary interest was to accumulate an amount of money in a limited time. Even if a Pole earned less than the Norwegians, the wages doubled Polish wages (Naperiala and Trevena 2007). Only when he stayed for a longer period, might his interest might become similar to the resident population. To some degree, migrants were able to get into segments of the labour market with secure and well-paid work. Among the Polish construction workers, 15 per cent had a permanent job in 2006; in 2010, around 20 per cent (Friberg 2013).

For the resident workers, be it Norwegians or former immigrants, labour migrants represented a possible downward pressure on wages and work conditions. 'Social dumping' became a well-known phenomenon. The danger of producing an underclass was very real. A survey from Oslo in 2006 showed that many worked illegally; one third did not pay taxes neither in Norway, nor in Poland (Friberg and Tyldum 2007).

The conflicts were sharpened as the tendency went from the 'standard worker', being someone with a permanent employment, to an increasing share of temporarily employed workers. Some entrepreneurs, and some of the big temporary work agencies, offered permanent employment and paid collectively agreed wage rates. However, several varieties of firms existed, and at the other end of the scale there were bizarre and criminal firms. Despite these differences, the 'normal' construction worker was well on his way to becoming someone who was not directly employed in the firm where he actually worked.

POLICY DEVELOPMENT THROUGH LEARNING PROCESSES

Now, how did the unions respond to this situation? In 2009, the leader of the Construction Workers' Union summed up their position: 'The policy of the Oslo building workers' union takes solidarity among workers as its point of departure, we cannot see foreigners as enemies. The union has a class perspective on these matters. This is the best way of avoiding workers standing on opposite sides' (interview with P. Vellesen, leader of the Construction Workers' Union, 2009).

How did the issue of work migrants come within the horizon of the union? The possible answers were discussed and developed along the road. The answers from the unionists were not a predetermined given, to be picked out from some kind of ideological storage. There were internal debates with sharply opposing opinions. However, these debates led to policy conclusions, which have been followed for roughly ten years. A *collective learning process* took place, collective in the sense of shared learning, as opposed to a learning process taking place in a mysterious supraindividual entity 'above' men: An issue appeared within the horizon; by and by, union officials, and members, realized that the question was not likely to go away. Dominant activists developed analyses—often interpretations opposing one another. The analyses led to suggestions advocating action. Eventually, a strategic line was decided upon and implemented. Subsequently, the successes and failures of this action program were noted. The experiences were interpreted and came to guide union policy in the years to come.

This learning process recalls the concepts of *fight cycles* and *learning cycles*, as developed by Michael Vester (1970) with respect to the English labour movements in the nineteenth century and Marco Guigni (2001) on the broader European development. In such a cycle, an action program is articulated. These ideas may find resonance with people, other than those who implement them. A cycle seldom lasts for a long, sustained period, and a fight and learning cycle often leads to defeat. Yet, according to the theory, a defeat may be productive, as it is used to formulate a new program. Some cycles may lead to a systemic change, such as the transitions in Eastern Europe after 1989; some cycles become slack or exhausted. Activists may be coopted, while some withdraw from the public into the private sphere. The system where the cycle takes place may be modified, but is, most of the time, not dissolved.

Notwithstanding this, the learning process among the Oslo Construction Workers' Union differs from this pattern, insofar as they have maintained their political line since 2004. We may thus supplement the cycle theory with an idea about a *formative period* of time followed by momentum as a 'system' becomes settled. A policy is made in a certain situation and becomes routine. This policy is then followed until new factors transpire and erode the policy. In such a situation of crisis, new learning and reformulation takes place.

The unionists learned *by* approaching the new comers. Learning *from* newcomers, in the sense of implementing new union traditions, or injecting a new social militancy into the Norwegian movement, seems to have been hitherto rare or nonexisting (Stang 2008: 19). There was a subject-object relation more than a subject-subject relation. In this respect, the Norwegian scene lacks, for instance, the kind of innovative social movement unionism combining top-down and bottom-up strategies which developed within the Latino community in Los Angeles from 1990 (Milkman 2006).

We shall return to the question of agency and who reformulated the policy. Drawing on Antonio Gramsci's concept of the party as '*a collective intellectual*', we shall argue that the Oslo Construction Workers' Union themselves filled this role.

There were in particular three questions which, by and by, lead to new insights. The first of these lessons contained the first of the, by now, classical union dilemmas on migration expressed by Rinus Penninx and Judith Roosblad (2000: 4ff): Should unions be restrictive or more liberal towards migration? In this case, should there be transitory arrangements after the expansion of European Union with East European members in 2004?

The second question corresponded to Pennix and Roosblad's second dilemma: Should there be special demands for migrant workers? More precisely, should the unions opt for general application of collective agreements, for an *erga omnes* clause (i.e., rights stated in an agreement are applied to all workers in the same field)?

This same dilemma was also present in the third, and final, issue to be tackled by the construction workers: Should a statutory minimum wage be introduced?[3]

These three issues—transitory arrangements, *erga omnes* clause, and minimum wage—were met separately, as they presented themselves at different points of time. Nevertheless, they came to form a whole, but represented phases in the local learning cycle.

In addition, three rounds of legislative measures against social dumping were implemented by the Red-Green governments in 2006, 2008, and 2013 (Støstad 2013). On these measures, there has been full agreement among unionists. Yet, also in light of these legislative measures learning took place; this is because the first measures taken were not effective, leading to a demand for new legal means.[4] Unionists opine that although these measures were positive, they were not really effective and would not suffice as long as the labour market had been conquered by temporary work agencies, foreign firms with posted workers, and entrepreneurs conducting business on the margins of or outside legality.

LESSON ONE: TRANSITORY MEASURES?

When did the migrant worker question appear within the horizon of the unions? Since the 1990s, the unions had faced migrant workers, many from Nordic countries, whose immediate interests differed from those of the local workers. Yet, the work migration issue was put clearly on the agenda when the European Union in 2004, and then again in 2007, expanded with new member-states joining. Norway expected a large inward migration of new workers. And by 2007 about 35 per cent of the firms, with more than ten employees, in the Norwegian construction industry had made use of foreign labour from the new European Union countries (Stang 2008: 15).[5]

No unionist spoke openly of radical restrictions to the Norwegian labour market. However, within *Fellesforbundet* two opposite stances materialized—fencing in or general organizing. The first faction feared that a rapid swell of immigration might drastically alter the relations between supply and demand, and possibly lead to social dumping.[6] Therefore, they argued for *transitory arrangements*, in order to sluice newcomers into the labour market gradually. The idea was to buy time, gather experiences, and then introduce necessary regulatory measures. At the congress of *Fellesforbundet*, in 2003, this faction managed to swing the opinion, leading to the congress unanimously adopting a line advocating protransitory measures. Later on, the *Landsorganisasjonen i Norge* followed suit.[7] The government responded to the demand for control by prolonging the existing rules—such as a residence permit in order to stay more than ninety days and a work permit. Also, having a full-time job was necessary, and wage levels were to correspond to collectively agreed rates, or where there was no collective agreement, the local customary rate was to be paid. Employers had to apply to the Norwegian Directorate of Immigration for a permit to import labour.[8]

The counterarguments were launched by other trade union officials.[9] Their reasoning against introducing transitory arrangements may be summed up in three points.

1. Labour migration is here to stay; migration is not a transitory, but a permanent state. Therefore, temporary limitations do not matter much. Problems with social dumping were obvious, before the European Union expansion.

2. If migrants had to have a job in order to be allowed to enter and stay, they would be dependent on one employer and unable to change job or move. The migrants then were 'locked in', thereby producing insecurity and extra potential for exploitation.[10] Possibly, they would try to avoid the unions, fearing that contact with them could lead to loss of job and risk of deportation. Some cases of underpayment actually turned out this way. So, the argument went, the transitory measures would not encourage unionization and collective agreements. These unionists framed the theme in terms of 'feudalism' and 'serfdom', pointing to the dependent and subservient position relative to the one employer. A 'capitalist' model implied, after all, the free sale of labour power in a market with more than one buyer.

3. This faction claimed that restricting labour migration was not a task for trade unions. According to one spokesman, Kjell Skjærvø, 'the task for the unions was to organise those who were here, not decide who ought to be here' (Skjærvø 2011). This did not necessar-

ily mean that this faction was in favour of a completely open labour market, EEA and non-EEA citizens alike. But this was a matter for the political parties and authorities. If the unions took on a task of limiting migration, they would alienate newcomers, they claimed, pointing to the problematic experiences of German *IG Bau*. Unions should not be a 'police reserve'. By 2004, this faction had the upper hand in the local union. The open union option, to go for general organizing, had been chosen.

Yet, the transitory measures were renewed by the authorities in 2005 (and expired in 2009 and 2012). The critics pointed out that the measures did not cover posted workers, nor those workers who formally worked as small independent firms (Skjærvø 2011: 5). And despite the transitory measures, labour migrants did come. Due to a change in the supply/demand balance, employers could pay labour migrants lower wages. The phrase 'social dumping' was now commonplace. Yet, there was no generally accepted definition of this concept. The employers claimed that paying foreign workers less than Norwegians did not amount to social dumping, as they earned lower wages at home. The unions needed to find another definition and chose as their starting point: 'What did Norwegians find acceptable?' This had to be operationalized. One suggestion was to take the average wages in the union branch as the measure.[11] However, the unionists came to argue that wages for foreign workers should not be below the minimum wage level in the collective agreement.[12]

LESSON TWO: *ERGA OMNES*?

The next issue for the unionists was: How do we work with the East Europeans, at the time Poles, against social dumping? One possible strategy was to activate a sleeping law from 1993 on the *general application of collective agreements*, the *erga omnes* principle. A publicly appointed committee may decide that the rules in a collective agreement shall apply to all in the same branch, sometimes within one area. The law had been passed in connection with Norwegian entry into the EEA in 1994, in order to reassure trade unionists against the fear of pressure on wages. The law might be used if foreigners had 'demonstrably' inferior wages and working conditions.

Initially, there was considerable scepticism towards the *erga omnes* principle in the union ranks. There was a fear that workers might become too passive if they were 'given' the benefits of collective agreements without having to organize. There was also indignation towards 'free riders', but it was combined with the insight that the fight against free riders actually sent an implicit signal to existing members who might consider opting out of the union. More generally, there was the general strategic choice between the legislation road and the collective agreement road, between relying on state measures or on collective union strength.

When it came to activity, the principle of general application actually turned out to be one of the most effective ways of conveying, to immigrant workers, the value of organizing. The migrants saw that they had rights, which were not necessarily honored by the employers. When the *erga omnes* clause was activated, many foreign workers discovered that much higher wages were due to them and could be fetched through the force of the union. Most of those who chose to enter into such cases experienced an immediate and substantial rise in wages and other benefits. Although they were still paid below the mean in the branch, their wage might be quadrupled.[13] Contrary to the fears about the possible effects of general application, the percentage of workers covered by collective agreements did not decline. And there was no tendency towards minimum wages becoming standard wages. Wages have been kept at the same level.[14] And last, but not least: The contacts established in this process opened a dialogue between migrants and unionists, leading to a breakthrough and a fairly high union density.

As the influential Oslo union, traditionally a centre for disseminating ideas and norms, opted for general application in 2003 (Rodal 2013: 56), this strategy was introduced to the construction business throughout the Oslo fjord region in 2005, then in the Western county of Hordaland in 2006—a strategy called 'patchwork erga omnes', and then in all Norway in 2007. The demand for this approach was extended to several other trades in addition to construction. The employers protested when it came to the shipyards, but this decision was finally confirmed, in the Supreme Court in 2013.[15]

Yet, doubts lingered about *the erga omnes* practice. Some feared this might develop into a minimum wage, unilaterally fixed by the state. If so, the case against social dumping might weaken. And some claim that a focus on the general application of wages may take attention away from the decisive core issues, such as fighting for permanent employment, securing skill, recruiting apprentices, et cetera.[16]

Some measures might make the general application law more efficient. One suggestion is for employers to drop the demand for documentation of low wages as a necessary premise for activating *erga omnes*. In return, the unions should accept that only minimum conditions are to be generally applied (Skjærvø 2011: 8).

LESSON THREE: THE MINIMUM WAGE?

The pros and cons were the same in another issue tightly linked to the *erga omnes* question—*the minimum wage*. Norway does not have a statutory, legally based minimum wage. However, the collective agreements often have clauses to this respect. Therefore, the definition of minimum wage, and hence the wage level, was most important. Should it be based on the average wage in the branch? An idea from the 1990s, and since abandoned. Should it be linked to the lowest level in the collective agreement in the sector in question? Should covering costs for lodging and food be included when it came to posted workers? [17]

The minimum wage could be important in other ways. In the shipyards, low-cost labour from countries, such as Romania, was seen as necessary to secure the competitive edge of the firms. Romanian workers were in 2007 hired at a yard on the premise that minimum wages should be paid. This did not happen; the wages were manifestly lower. The local Norwegian shop stewards wanted this deal. They claimed that lower wages, 40 No. crowns, as opposed to thrice the sum for Norwegian skilled workers, would secure the competitive edge of the company. Otherwise, the firms wanted to move production abroad. By paying foreigners lower wages, skilled Norwegian specialists could keep their relatively high wages. So, some trade unionists in *Fellesforbundet* came to see temporarily hired workers as a possible permanent element in the workforce. As a kind of compensation, a so-called social fund should be established in Romania. [18] The construction workers condemned this deal as social dumping (Erne 2008: 76).

However, the dominant attitude in *Fellesforbundet* favoured small wage differentials between Norwegians and foreigners. The Construction Workers' Union demanded that foreign workers, in particular posted workers, should be paid wages, more or less, equivalent to Norwegian wages. In 2010, the unions went on strike for this principle (Rodal 2013: 61).

Here, a self-critical question needs to be asked: Was this an act of solidarity or was it a way of depriving the foreigners of the one competitive advantage they have: a willingness to accept lower wages (Nielsen 2013)? The problem was demonstrated in the 1993 law on general application. The dual purpose of the law is (1) 'to secure foreign workers wages and work conditions that are *likeverdig* (equal or equivalent) to those of Norwegian workers' and (2) 'to counter distortion of competition that is to the disadvantage of the Norwegian labour market'. [19] The original 1993 argument, proequal conditions, was not a concern regarding foreign workers, but a concern that Norwegian workers, who were better paid, might lose out in the competition (Skjærvø 2011: 14). The Oslo Construction Workers' Union was accused by the employers' organization of being protectionist, nationalist, or even racist. [20] The unionists claimed that this was not the case; the intention was not to bar foreigners. But could this, nevertheless, be the objective effect, more or less, consciously influencing their stance?

There was no 'identity of group interests in the short term' (van der Linden 2008). In the short run, there was nothing to be won directly by supporting labour migrants. Yet there was what van der Linden calls an 'identity of group interests in the longer term' or even 'indirect identity of group interests' (van der Linden 2008: 260). The stance on migrants may be interpreted as *'enlightened self-interest'*. Looking somewhat to the future, the unions realized that an unregulated situation would also backfire on Norwegian workers. The unionists argued that a lack of resistance to low pay for labour migrants might lead to a development towards low wages in general. This would also be detrimental to those migrant workers who stayed on in the country, having to cope with Norwegian price levels on a par with other residents. The unionists also pointed to the fact that, for instance, Polish workers did not lose their ability to compete and get jobs—even after having their wages increased three- or fourfold due to the move from the black-grey market rate to a regulated minimum wage. In 2011, the *erga omnes* principle had been practiced for six years— without any concrete cases of generally applied minimum wages causing anyone to lose out in the labor market (Skjærvø 2011: 28). Having the choice between earning 60 or 160 Norwegian crowns, the minimum wage, Poles and Balts chose the latter.

A document from *Fellesforbundet* in 2006 identifies the dilemmas and choices that had to be made:

> We have to heed several important concerns. And these do not always pull in the same direction. Is what we do appropriate to limit wage competition? Does it limit work immigration? What consequences will it have for the agreements? And what consequences will it have for our relations with workers from the new EEA countries, and in particular, the Baltic countries and Poland. Working to minimize wage competition is a core task for trade unions. But a strategy against social dumping cannot have as its purpose the limitation of labour migration. (Quoted in Skjærvø 2011: 32)

The document concluded: 'To limit labour immigration is beyond the purpose of unions. We do not run trade unions for Norwegian workers. We run unions for workers in Norway, regardless of nationality' (Quoted in Skjærvø 2011: 32).

EXPERIENCES OF CONSTRUCTION WORKERS

So far, we have tried to reconstruct the debates and reasoning among the union activists and *how* their stance developed. As stated above, a strategy oriented more towards national closure might have been chosen. So *why* did they reach this conclusion? Were there historical experiences and structural traits that may explain their choice?

An answer should include the situation for both the construction workers and for the union, not being identical entities. A union has to aggregate various demands and points of view from members. As an organization, it also has to heed other relations, to the union movement at large or to the national industrial relations system.

First, the construction workers. They were used to mobility. Many had themselves travelled to building sites inland and abroad. One may surmise that these experiences created empathy—'yesterday it was me, today it is you, tomorrow—who knows, it may be me (again)?' The building workers also remembered that migrant workers had been in Norway before. From the mid-1990s, lots of Nordic construction workers were in Oslo and other towns, in particular Swedes. So the unions were used to foreigners; they knew this generally worked well.

There was also another structural factor that may have caused Norwegian workers and unionists to avoid panicked reactions to greater numbers of migrants coming in 2004. For starters, the times were quite good, there was no serious unemployment, neither in the branch, nor, more generally, in the Norwegian economy. Unemployment as percentage of the labour force fell from 4.5 per cent in 2004 to 2.5 per cent in 2007 (Statistics Norway 2011). The lesson learned was that foreigners per se did not produce economic problems. This differed to, say, the German *IG Bau*, which had to formulate their policy in times of economic decline. So, during the initial formative years of the unions' strategic choice of policy, the attitude was relaxed towards newcomers. The start of the learning process, *the formative moment* for interpreting the foreigner issue, proved crucial. In the following period, the momentum and routines led the union to hold onto this 'open' policy. The importance of the formative years is probably shown in the fact that, according to the interviewees, few union members were openly disgruntled with the inclusive stance of the unions, even when the European financial crisis hit in 2008/2009 and unemployment rose.

LESSONS THE UNION TAUGHT ITSELF

If we move to the organized union, we may observe traits that might explain their choices.

First, a favourable structural fact: The Construction Workers' Union had a good financial situation, and it had resources for organizing. This was the product of a merger of most of the *trade* organizations—masons, tillers, steel fixers, painters, and stone and cement workers. The latter groups were important. Rodal (2013: 22, 25) points out that traditionally this organization was a *class* union rather than a *trade* union, an attitude, we may surmise, that was projected onto the newcomers.

However, this only explains that a possibility was opened, not that this possibility was capitalized upon. An active, interpreting, and organizing subject was necessary. This 'we' was a milieu of active trade unionists, a subculture, radical, but undogmatic and orientated towards exchange of experiences and discussions. Attitudes and policies towards labour migrants were in particular discussed at a formative joint seminar between the Carpenters' Union and Oslo Stone, Soil and Cement Workers' Union in the winter of 2003/2004. Here an agreement on the general line was reached, and the learning process led most of the active participants to the same conclusion.

Of importance here is that the Norwegian trade union movement has not been split organizationally along religious, linguistic, or political cleavages. And its relatively decentralized structure made it possible for a local union to articulate and implement policies not sanctioned by the social democratic union central (Bergh 2009: 87ff, 104ff, 206ff, 333ff, 402). The initiating role of the Construction Workers' Union is noted by sociologist Anne Birgitte Rodal (2013: 51). The importance of internal structure of the unions confirms findings by Stefania Marino (2012) who compared the Dutch and Italian trade unions' practice versus immigrants. This relative autonomy of the lower organizational level, and the middle strata among the cadres, had opened up options for people with political persuasions other than social democracy. Many militants had risen through the ranks from the 1970s and onwards.

'The banner proletariat'—a self-ironical term meaning those who take the union branch banner from the office to a demonstration—has traditionally been leftist in the building trades. They have come from various strands of socialists and communists, and they had the power of definition. But social democrats were not excluded. The common attachment to the union was stronger than various party allegiances.[21] One younger activist, a social democrat and union official, says, 'there was a holy mixture of workers' radicalism, social democracy and leftist groups, yet undogmatic, not sectarian. The milieu has always had a strong attitude advocating pro-internationalism and solidarity'.[22]

So, the building workers union's encounters with immigrants were interpreted through the ideological lens of their leaders, a point also made by Marino (2012). In the learning process, these local cadres offered a diagnosis and a program. The importance of such leadership may be intuitively understood. It has also been shown in an analysis by Tamara Kay (2011)—testing variables that seek to explain which American unions participated actively in the fight against the North American Free Trade Agreement—that their transnationalist stance does not spring directly from the objective situation created by free trade and economic globalization. An interpreting leadership was necessary:

> Unions with a progressive leader—many of whom came to age during the civil rights and anti-Vietnam war movements—altered the calculus of support for transnationalism by seeking out and nurturing relationships and educating, including the rank and file. [North American Free Trade Agreement's] catalytic effect therefore generated labor transna-

tionalism for unions that had certain predisposing characteristics. (Kay 2014)

Such predisposing characteristics were also present among the activists in Oslo. Within this broader milieu, or network, some individuals seem to have played a central role, in particular in the formative phase. In the words of the younger trade union official, 'It is difficult to overrate the role of Kjell Skjærvø and Roy Pedersen in these matters'.[23]

The Italian Marxist Antonio Gramsci saw trade unions as sectional and rather narrow organizations. Opposed to them, he conceived the communist party as a leading force and a 'collective intellectual'. Through the party's 'organic intellectuals', spokespersons who originated in a popular class and brought forth the interest, values, and thoughts of this class, could join forces in an aggregative fashion (Jakopovich 2008).

The real existing parties seldom actually fill this role. In the case of the building workers, the union functioned as a collective intellectual and was the creative vanguard in the field of policies towards labour migrants. A possible counterargument is that the leaders had a left political party background. However, the interpretative answers in 2003/2004 were not given from their previous affiliations. The answers were freshly developed in a phase when the parties did not play any decisive role in this field. And activists with the same party affiliation came up with differing answers in trade union issues.

So far, the story has dealt with the Oslo network. Oslo was the only city with a permanent supply of labour power from outside, giving the Oslo unions a solid experience with newcomers. Also being the capital, the biggest city, and harboring many huge building sites, Oslo also became the centre in these matters.[24] Their experience and political conclusions were disseminated nationally via courses, conferences, seminars, et cetera. From the 1970s, there had been nationwide conferences within the various trades, dealing 'a little with trade and a lot with politics'.[25] These were independent milieus, organized from below, not under the auspices of the central leadership in *Fellesforbundet*. These conferences paved the way for the Oslo fjord conferences, rallying unionists from all trades in construction and all counties around the fjord. They were originally organized as a grassroot opposition and functioned as fora for debates and a channel for dissemination of ideas from the Oslo core.[26] Among ideas hatched at an Oslo fjord conference in 2006/2007 was the demand for *solidaransvar*, joint and several responsibility for employers in a sub-contractors' chain.

EXPERIENCE, INTERPRETATION, AND LEARNING—AND AN AFTERTHOUGHT

How and why did the Construction Workers' Union reach the conclusion about being a union for all workers in Norway?

Let me repeat: The choice was not given or self-evident. A learning process took place, leading away from a demand for transitory arrangements to the active inclusion of migrant workers. To explain the process, one should include enabling structural dimensions—previous experience with own or others' labour migration, a favourable employment situation at the formative moment, and sound financial status for the union in question. These factors removed some hindrances to an open door policy, such as fear among the workers of losing their work. When the situation arose, the active core of the unionists had a leeway for interpretations, for choices. There was no decisive, one-directional pressure from the structural situation. The particular milieu in the union—discussion orientated, inclusive, open to a manifold from the centre to the left, somewhat oppositional and not subservient to trade union leadership—made it possible to articulate a stance which differed from the national union. The union functioned as a Gramscian 'collective intellectual'. Once the policy had been articulated, the centrality of Oslo made the spread of these thoughts fairly easy. And within this milieu, some individuals were the most articulated proponents.

Thus, we advocate an approach emphasizing learning processes and interpretations, the significance of an active leadership core and their agency. This is not to deny the importance of understanding the environment. There had to be a structurally given 'situation' to be learned from, interpreted, and acted upon. Here, the new reality consisted of a large labour migration to Oslo and Norway from 2004. Yet the situation did not immediately and unequivocally produce *one* interpretation and action program. The role of the union as a historical subject was decisive.

Then an afterthought: Strategic guidelines are not definitively chosen. Keeping to them implies both routines, carrying on in the same track—and conscious efforts. So far, the union has kept to the open union principle, also through the years of financial crisis. Yet, in other unions, which in 2005/2006 worked along the same lines as the Oslo construction workers, the active support for this policy has crumbled. They may agree verbally, but do not do very much to greet newcomers.[27] And important defining factors in the formative phase—such as previous personal experience with moving to find work, full employment, an active and radical caucus of elected representatives, and, from 2005, a relatively supportive Red-Green government—are not there anymore.

By 2014, there are circumstances that might lead to a change: A continuous cross turnover of members, and a continuous demand for assistance in individual cases, is 'devouring' organization workers' resources and this has led to some fatigue. There is a discussion on the right balance between 'core' and 'periphery' activity, among the latter is recruitment of temporary workers (see Kjeldstadli forthcoming). Furthermore, the more ideologically committed 'founding fathers' are into their sixties; a demographic shift may, despite the strength of the tradition, lead to other attitudes and different points of view. Also, external factors are a problem. Norway now has a conservative/right populist government, at least until 2017. There is considerable anxiety with regard to criminal activity among employers. Should this spread to several subbranches in the construction sector, cooperation with the police may lead unions to reconsider their position about not being a 'reserve police'. This might estrange the migrant workers. Unemployment and more intensive competition in the labour market may rise. Although the prospects for the national labour market are not bleak, at the time of writing (2014), the Norwegian economy is extrovert, and a sharp fall in demand and a concurrent prolonged crisis might change the picture. *Chi vivrà vedrà.*

NOTES

1. The first public statement seems to be made by union organiser Kjell Skjærvø in an interview in *Klassekampen*, 20 November 2003.

2. http://taspo.de/aktuell/alle-news/detail/beitrag/10500-verband-der-wanderarbeiter-ents

3. Penninx and Roosblad's (2001) third dilemma is whether to organize migrants in the union or separately, as done by German *IG Bau*. The Oslo workers opted for the first of these alternatives, see Kjeldstadli (forthcoming).

4. See Odin.dep Arbeidsdepartementet: Regjeringens handlingsplan mot sosial dumping (2006), Handlingsplan 2 mot sosial dumping (2008), Handlingsplan 3 for et anstendig og seriøst arbeidsliv og mot sosial dumping (2013). Among the measures were authorization of work agencies, joint and several liability for subcontractors' obligations towards their workers (*solidaransvar*), general application of collective agreements, a duty for entrepreneurs to see that the *erga omnes* principle actually was applied, right of inspection (*innsynsrett*) for trade union officials, the right for a union to press charges, identity cards, regional occupational safety officers, strengthened mandate and resources for the Labour Inspection Authority, and demand for Norwegian wages and work conditions to be included in municipal procurement in accordance with International Labour Organization convention 94. Critical voices exist; the resources to control the implementation of these measures are too meagre. If one crooke company is stopped, ten more appear, according to unionist Arne Hagen.

5. A more or less educated guess said that 120,000 to 130,000 Polish citizens were in Norway in 2007 (IMDi-rapport 9-2007).

6. This faction comprised of people, such as Boye Ullmann, trade union secretary in the organization 'No to EU' and Eldar Myhre, union representative in the Aker Kværner corporate group.

7. Frode Rønning, in *Klassekampen*, 11 April 2003.

8. In addition, there was clause saying that the government might regulate the influx of workers, if disturbances emerge in the Norwegian labour market that might constitute a serious risk for the standard of living and employment in a certain region or occupation. Such measure could be adopted for two plus three plus two years; Norway chose to keep to these transitory arrangements from May 2004 and two years onwards, in line with most European Union countries, Sweden, Ireland, and Great

Britain excepted. After twelve months of residence, the transitory rules did not apply, and the person obtained a five years' permit along with other EEA citizens.

9. Among them were Kjell Skjærvø, working at *Fellesforbundet* at the time, organization worker with the Plumbers' Union Tor Moestue and Roy Pedersen, leader of Oslo Stone, Soil and Cement Workers' Union.

10. Interview with Roy Pedersen, leader of Oslo branch, *Landsorganisasjonen i Norge* (Trades Union Congress).

11. This had been the dominant understanding in the 1990s, Boye Ullmann: Arbeidslov og sosial dumping, *Klassekampen*, 10 September 2009.

12. Interview with Roy Pedersen. While Norway has no legally decided minimum wage, collective agreements usually have such a clause.

13. Interview with Boye Ullmann, organizer for the Plumbers' Union.

14. Interview with Kjell Skjærvø, organizer with the Construction Workers' Union, and Petter Vellesen, leader of the Construction Workers' Union.

15. Fafo Østforum: Temaside Allmenngjøring. http://www.fafo.no/Oestforum/Kunnskapsbase/Temasider/allmenngj.htm.

16. Interview with Arne Hagen, branch leader of Construction Workers' Union.

17. The duty for employers of posted workers to pay for food and lodging was settled by a governmental regulation in 2013 (see http://lovdata.no/document/SF/forskrift/2013-04-24-426).

18. This led the prime organizer in this field, Kjell Skjærvø, to resign from his job; later on he was hired by the Oslo Construction Workers' Union.

19. http://lovdata.no/dokument/NL/lov/1993-06-04-58.

20. Interview with Odd Magnar Solbakken, organizer for Construction Workers' Union.

21. Interview with Kjell Skjærvø, organizer for Construction Workers' Union.

22. Interview with Jonas Bals, official in *Fellesforbundet*.

23. Interview with Jonas Bals, official in *Fellesforbundet*.

24. Interview with Arne Hagen, branch leader of Construction Workers' Union.

25. Interview with Arne Hagen, branch leader of Construction Workers' Union.

26. Interview with Steinar Krogstad, official in *Fellesforbundet*.

27. Interview with Kjell Skjærvø, organizer for Construction Workers' Union.

SEVEN

A Pyrrhic Victory?

A Case of National Unions and Immigrant Workers Returned

Tiago Matos[1]

INTRODUCTION

This chapter is a case study that deals with social dumping and the dynamics around an international workforce in construction in Norway. In 2013, an ongoing struggle at the COOP warehouse building site, involving posted workers employed through various subcontractors, became the focus of the mainstream media. By the time the struggle hit the news, the Spanish posted workers had formed solidarity bonds with onsite Norwegian workers and had become organized in the Plumbers' Union (Fellesforbundet). The struggle revolved around wage questions and on-site work conditions, which grossly violated the Norwegian Working Environment Act. The negotiations that ensued led COOP to assume joint liability with its contractor GSE, and subcontractor Eco Iberica, paying the posted plumbers the differential of their wage (circa 50 NOK per hour) and the Norwegian standard wage (163–174 NOK per hour).

This study primarily tries to identify the possibilities and constraints on the Plumbers' Union's actions: How did the regulatory framework influence the struggle; what allowed the union to empower the posted workers; and finally, how did media coverage influence the struggle? I try to answer these questions from a low- and mid-level union representative's point of view. The source material is based on a broad review of mainstream and union media outlets, and on interviews with union officials, including representatives at the regional level for the sectorial federations.

'A Pyrrhic Victory' refers to two things. First of all, in a very direct and case-specific way: The struggle was indeed a victory, but struggles against social dumping are highly taxing on union resources and in the end, the workers were sent home and did not keep their jobs.

Secondly, in a more general fashion, it deals with the victory in a broader sense. As was said by my informants, although this was indeed a victory, it is nearly impossible to be happy and see it as such; yes, the workers got paid, but this case is one out of a hundred cases. The general sentiment was that this struggle was won, but unions are losing the fight against social dumping; which still occurs because nothing structural really changes as a result of the struggles—or, if structural changes do occur, they have been shown to worsen the problem of social dumping and eat away at unions' institutional power (Alsos and Eldring 2008; Woolfson 2007; Woolfson and Sommers 2006).

THEORETICAL APPROACH

The particular positions of workers in production systems make it reasonable to use this as a point of departure for our theoretical framework. This notion has been accompanied by the development of concepts with reference to power resources, some of which I now will briefly turn my attention to.

Silver (2003), on the basis of Wright (2000), identified two main sources of workers power: *Structural power* depends on the position and status of particular groups of workers within the economic system; *associational power*, on the other hand, is based on the capacity to form unions (in a broad sense) among workers in order to contest the control over the means of production (see also Dörre, Holst, and Nachtwey 2009: 35–36; Hardy et al. 2014: 4). The concept of *coalitional power* is similar, but frames this somewhat differently by including 'the capacity of workers to expand the scope of conflict by involving non-labour actors' (Brooks 2013; cited in Hardy et al. 2014), and even the capacity of forming relationships with other unions and drawing on their resources (Hardy et al. 2014). Dörre, Holst, and Nachtwey (2009) suggest the existence of a third source of power, namely *institutional power*. This form of power—as the denomination implies—comes from institutionalized societal power relations, which are based on historical victories, losses, and compromises. Finally, Webster suggests in his contribution to this publication, that *logistical* and *societal power* should be added to the list. Lévesque and Murray's reading of the literature on power leads them to specify that workers and unions' capacity to exert power is a 'power to'—because unions are primarily engaged in empowering workers—and not strictly a 'power over' (2010a: 335).

Most power source theorists point out, in order to fully understand power, one needs to look closely at context. William Sewell's take on agency may also be added; for Sewell, 'agents are empowered . . . by structures . . . [a]gency is implied by the existence of structures' (Sewell 1992: 20). These structures also lay the grounds for differences in power and create possibilities for individual, as well as, collective agency. Imig and Tarrow define political opportunity as,

> consistent—but not necessarily formal or permanent—dimensions of the political environment that provide incentives for collective action by affecting peoples' expectations for success or failure. These political opportunities are *external* to the resources held by the group, and they must be perceived by insurgents, for structural changes that are not experienced can hardly be expected to affect people's behaviour, except indirectly. (2000: 81)

Lastly, we need to address action that then bridges the understanding of 'power to' and the external possibilities. I do so by invoking the Tillyian concept of repertoire meaning 'the "inventory of available means" of collective action . . . [Tilly's] understanding of repertoires merges institutionally created possibilities for power with the popular strategies that actually emerge' (Piven and Cloward 2000: 414).

THE COOP CASE

Posted Workers and Regulatory Framework in Norway

Many have pointed out that subcontracted capitalism is becoming the new state of business (see Wills 2009). The changes this may cause in the working class and in production and social relations may result in new agencies, new sites of conflict, and new forms of struggle and action (Silver 2003: 19). More specifically, there are two impacts of particular importance in this case: First, it reduces or splits the core workforce thereby reducing workers' ability to organize, bargain, and strike; and secondly, it hides the 'real employer' (Manky 2014), allowing them to 'cut costs, shed responsibility, increase flexibility and disempower the workforce' (Wills 2009: 444). Posted workers are by definition a product of subcontracting and emblematic of changes in the world of work.

The precarious position of the posted worker exemplifies a perversion of the *commodification* of labour: A state where not only labour is detached from workers, but even individual and collective rights are left behind in the posting country, while the subject is physically exerting his or her labour in another country. Although some core rights regarding labour conditions, such as minimum wage regulations, apply in the receiving country (Alsos and Eldring 2008), rules governing unfair dismissals, for example, rarely do. This creates a particular set of constraints on national trade union agency.[2] In this sense, the COOP case is not only about a struggle against social dumping; it is a microcosm of unions' struggle for effective strategies in a transnational arena.

Furthermore, the transient nature of employment with a subcontractor—workers move from workplace to workplace, sometimes, with a new employer and new colleagues—makes it hard to create or particularly maintain a collective culture in the often small groups of workers (Wills 2009). This is especially the case among posted workers.

The case should not be viewed as an isolated case; instead, it is seen in the broader context. Social dumping is far from a question that only touches on wages and cutting costs for safety; it's also a question of recruitment and trade sustainability. The informants expressed real fear that the trades were 'rotting from within' because many companies do not see any monetary gains in having apprentices; in order to have apprentices, you need full-time workers.

In Norway, there have been efforts to tackle the case of 'hidden employers', poor working conditions, and substandard wages, although they do not seem to curtail illegal and informal activities (Ødegård, Øyvind, and Alsos 2012: 463). The Red-Green government (2005–2013)—the product of a long-standing grassroots alliance and a testimony to the union's coalitional capability (Helle and Matos forthcoming)—sought to establish a framework in order to deal with the deficit of possible measures to combat social dumping. The so-called toolbox (or even 'institutionally created possibilities') became the mainstream repertoire of the unions. These efforts have been made as a continuation of already established regulations, some of which I want to point out before moving on to case details.

The *legal extension of collective agreements* was introduced as a tool for unions and employers to tackle the foreseen problem of social dumping in the wake of the introduction of the posted workers directive in 1996. However, no extensions were introduced before 2004—in the wake of the European Union enlargement—but have since become a key instrument for unions in tackling social dumping (Eldring, Fitzgerald, and Arnholtz 2012: 26). As a result of the so-called financial crisis and the subsequent influx of migrant and posted workers from Southern Europe, this tool has reassumed its original intention. Applying for legal extensions is primarily left to the union or employer federations. These extensions have been a source of contention and tested several times in the European Free Trade Association Surveillance Authority with varying outcomes.

Furthermore, the Red-Green government introduced a *Joint and Several Liability Act* with the intention of securing workers' payments, even when subcontractors fail to pay wages in accordance with general application laws (Ødegård, Øyvind, and Alsos 2012: 467). Still, many of my informants expressed frustration regarding the distance between work-ers, their experiences, and the policies: 'Let them come here and see for themselves. We have lines of immigrant workers that come with ques-tions regarding wages. They also talk about harassment, threats and so on'. One major problem was that there were no resources, or political will to back the 'tools'. As they see it, in this case and with posted and migrant workers in general, actions are very much confined by the unions' judi-cial resources, possibilities, and capabilities. In a study by Ødegård, Øyvind, and Alsos (2012), their informants point out, similarly, that the unions do not need more regulations, but rather a stricter implementa-tion of the existing rules. The unions experienced a *depoliticization* of problems concerning social dumping rather than a *repoliticization*.

According to my informants, the current bar for the introduction of legal extensions of collective agreements is considered too high. As of now, the documentation requirements for cases of social dumping are strict and solely left to the party that applies for a legal extension. The Norwegian Labour Inspection Authority (LIA) does not have enough resources, and the only consequence of breaching regulation is making sure back payments are paid. For example, when the LIA was featured in the media, they said they had received reports about social dumping, breach of labour safety routines, and substandard accommodation at the site, previous to the news story breaking. Indeed, they not only had been at the site for an unannounced visit the prior evening to the story going public, but according to COOP they had been there seventeen(!) times. According to LIA themselves, they had been there seven times without uncovering anything. Commenting on the current situation, one of my informants equated it to stealing at the supermarket: If you get caught, you pay for what you should have paid for to begin with, if you do not get caught you get free groceries—nowhere else in society would this be accepted.

The lack of preemptive measures, low political will, a high bar for legal extensions, and the inexistence of hard-hitting consequences has made the struggle against social dumping a tough one for the unions, and very taxing on their resources. This struggle became even more diffi-cult in light of various controversial verdicts in the European Court of Justice (Alsos and Eldring 2008; Woolfson 2007; Woolfson and Sommers 2006).

Besides tackling the 'hidden employer' challenge through regulatory means, there has been, on the part of the unions, an attempt at curtailing the splitting effects that subcontracting has on the workforce. This has been covered by Kjeldstadli's contribution to this book and so I will just briefly say this: Trade unions in Norway have adopted what might be called an open strategy towards immigrants. The Construction Workers' Union in particular stand out with their affirmation of 'organising work-

ers in Norway, not only Norwegian workers' (see also Penninx and Roosblad 2000; Hardy, Eldring, and Schulten 2012).

Developing Struggle: Empowering Posted Workers

On 4 July 2011, COOP Norge Handel AS announced that everything
was in place for the building of Europe's most modern warehouse close
to Gardermoen outside of Oslo.[3] The contract went to GSE Norway on
the grounds of 'competitive price' and because the company had completed similar projects in Norway and abroad. The COOP press release
went on to describe GSE as a fairly new contractor in Norway, with its
roots in France and a global actor with operations in thirty-five countries.
According to my informants, the contract was won by underbidding
Norwegian contractors with a substantial differential. GSE Norway subsequently put subcontracts on the European common market, and the
project employed more than five hundred workers from various European countries through a myriad of subcontractors.

During the early winter months of 2013, there were rumours of
'strange things' going on at the building site. A plumber's union member
at Imtek Norge contacted the Plumbers Union at Fellesforbundet. The
Norwegian plumber, of Chilean decent and a native Spanish speaker,
had come in contact with workers posted from Spain, employed by Eco
Iberica to install the sprinkler system.

Boye Ullmann, a union official, was sent up from Oslo to inspect the
claims. At the site, he was assisted by the Spanish-speaking Norwegian
plumber in communicating with the Spanish posted workers. The workers seemed scared to speak with him, but he managed to get them to take
some informational pamphlets.

After the initial visit to the site, there was further contact between
Ullmann and some of the posted workers. A meeting was set up in the
beginning of April 2013 at a desolate forest parking lot at 10 PM. The
workers were scared and wanted to avoid alarming the rest of the workers for fear of being exposed to the company management.[4] As an excuse,
they told their colleagues that they were going for a late night jog in order
not to raise suspicion. They provided evidence to the union in the form of
a video, documenting the unsafe work conditions (in breach of the labour
safety regulations) and payslips proving substandard wages.

GSE had installed the warehouse shelves before the sprinklers. Consequently, there was no room for a lift. Commenting on this, the GSE site
manager reportedly told Ullmann that the cost of one such lift would
amount to that of twenty-five Spanish workers' wages, and that such an
expense would be out of the question. The case was made that safety was
considered each individual worker's responsibility. However, tight
schedules and pressure to meet deadlines meant the workers had to

choose between meeting deadlines or using a safety harness. Not meeting deadlines could cost them their job.

After a lengthy discussion in the forest parking lot, one of the Spanish plumbers, the main whistle blower, joined the union and the rest followed suit. By the end of the meeting, they were all members of the Plumbers Union. Henceforth, the strategy followed along two lines: Through the traditional corporatist system and through the media.

The pragmatic approach of the union differed from 'business as usual'; the union made the membership retroactive in order to include the full employment (posted) period. In a more technical sense, this meant that the union was taking up a struggle of nonmembers. This practice was not completely foreign to the union. The union had previously used such a strategy for a transitional period in order to deal with the influx of Polish workers after the 2004 European Union expansion (Eldring, Fitzgerald, and Arnholtz 2012). However, the decision to act on behalf of these new members was taken locally, contrary to usual procedures, thereby shortening the path to action.

The open organizing strategy, combined with the pragmatic innovative retroactive membership, opened up the possibilities for the union. Indeed, not only did it allow the union to make claims on the workers' behalf as members dating back to the moment they started working in Norway, but also it gave the workers full access to the broad range of sources of power available to the union. Following Sidney Tarrow (1998: 71), it seems intuitive that the chance for contention increases when people gain the external resources and figure out how to use them.

E. P. Thompson (1991) points to the careful approach that is needed when studying such entities as 'crowds', 'cultures', 'workers', and so on, noting that this may cover up the diversity within such entities. Silver (2003) makes a similar point in treating conflict not only as something that occurs between classes, but also within classes: In any case, it is important to remember that collective actors are comprised of various groups and individuals, that various attributes of the collective actor may vary within the group, and the need to study the relation between the various levels.

With this in mind, a note should be made in reference to power sources. The seemingly homogenous groups, such as the working class or labour movement, are indeed not homogeneous and contain within them both resource-strong actors and those with nothing to lose. The union, and these posted workers, have a reciprocal relation between them. In this case, as is the case for most posted workers, the Spanish workers enjoyed a practically nonexistent degree of structural power, but as substantiated and formulated by Dörre, Holst, and Nachtwey, '[t]he organisational power of trade unions can substitute and *extend* the structural power of particular groups of wage earners, but it cannot fully replace it' (2009: 36, author's emphasis). The organizational or associational power exerted in particular struggles then relies on the degree of power retained by the union, as a whole. For obvious reasons, this is of particular importance: by organizing, the posted workers gained access, through the union, to existing sources of organizational power, associational capabilities, and to institutional power while also extending their own, and the union's, structural power within the national labour system (and the European labour market).

According to Tarrow's reading of resource mobilization theory, agents with the least to lose are most likely to act (1998). Tarrow, however, claims that if one examines those that try to seize external opportunities, it is 'those with the most to lose who are most likely to engage in contention, since they face the greatest threat from inaction' (Tarrow 1998: 86). A particularly important distinction needs to be made as a result. By looking at the two, the union and the Spanish workers, as two different groups, one can see that both of these notions are true for the respective groups; the posted workers wanted fair pay and a safe working environment—so did the union. By the time the Spanish workers decided to organize, they considered that they had little to lose, really. The unions, most definitely, had the most to lose from inaction—it would undermine the whole labour system in Norway.

Moreover, if we continue to look at these groups as separate with a differentiated view on gains and losses, there appears to be an energizing dialectic between the groups that is released when the struggle is taken from complaint to action (see Tarrow 1998: 86). The union becomes the vehicle, or the framework, where the development of dissent, claim-making, and action can happen, within a specific set of political possibilities. Tarrow points out that this should not be confused with resource mobilization because political opportunities might serve as a better explanation due to its connection with the externalities of actors (1998); the unions' capacity to act on behalf of the posted workers is dependent on the regulatory framework of labour and on political opportunities. However, action cannot be solely connected to externalities; the dynamic within groups and institutions also have a decisive impact on contentious action.

Regulated Action: Negotiation

Following the news story, which broke in mid-April, COOP assumed joint and several liability. COOP would guarantee that the workers be paid Norwegian salaries and stay employed until the project was finished. In accordance with the Norwegian tripartite system, COOP called for an immediate meeting, first contacting Roar Flåten, the head of Landsorganisasjonen i Norge (the national union federation), then Labour Minister Anniken Huitfeldt, and finally, the Plumbers Union. At the meeting, there were representatives from GSE and COOP, with their respective legal teams, and the COOP union representative and the Plumbers Union representatives. The Plumbers Union's claim came to NOK 1.7 million, based on wages in accordance with the general application of collective wage agreements for skilled workers, and a 40 per cent overtime addition.

Accepting joint liability meant that GSE also acknowledged responsibility for the contracts with their subcontractors. COOP and GSE announced a joint investigation of their own to look into all of the companies at the site, stating that they would cooperate with the Labour Inspection Authorities on this. The result was a revision board set up to collect and investigate the accusations made by the various workers (not just the Spanish). The revision board would also conduct any further negotiations.

Longtime lawyer for the employers, Jan Fougner, headed the revision board, assisted by three other lawyers. They were charged with conducting interviews of workers and engaging in negotiations with the unions. Although it was deemed investigative, the board was also, and perhaps chiefly, a group set up to figure out what the legal landscape was: Where they had to pay and where they did not. Some parallels might be drawn to what Piven and Cloward (2000: 421) have called a re-emergence of 'union busting firms', noting that these groups are no longer comprised of 'detectives and goons' but rather 'staffed by lawyers and publicity experts'; their major forte being the ability to make legal processes 'torturously slow'.

In the negotiations with Boye Ullmann and the Plumbers Union, the revision board made claims that the hours that were counted by the punch-in system would be the grounds for the reimbursement. However, several of the workers had not received identification cards and had used the many gaps in the fencing to get onto the site, resulting in gross discrepancies between the unions' numbers and the punch-in system registered hours. The Red-Green government, in an attempt to 'combat undeclared work in the industry, as well as more effective control of health and safety' (Ødegård, Øyvind, and Alsos 2012: 464), had previously obligated contractors to issue identification cards, which made it the responsibility of GSE Norway.

Furthermore, Fougner and the revision board claimed that retrieving the information about the hours was a delicate personnel protection issue and would have to go through the Norwegian Data Protection Authority. According to union officials, this was a slow up strategy—it stopped the process for four weeks. Boye Ullmann then called the Data Protection Authority who informed him that they had been contacted by Fougner and his group, but had not put limitations on the use of the data for the purpose of uncovering social dumping. The statistics, which were later retrieved from the punch card system, showed that the workers in question were working ten-hour days, six hours on Saturdays, and had Sundays off, making for a total of fifty-six-hour weeks and thus illegal.

An offer of NOK 600,000 came at the end of May. It did not include overtime and was based on the hourly wage rate of an unskilled and inexperienced worker. It also did not take into account any hours not proven by the punch-in gate system. The hours were, according to Fougner, not up for negotiation—if the union thought so, it had misunderstood. At this point the Plumbers Union, who had conducted the negotiations mainly on their own, asked Fellesforbundet to involve the Landsorganisasjonen i Norge law department, which subsequently led to an offer of 1.2 million.

Framing and Shaming

In order to communicate grievances to the broader public, an actor must have the internal resources to perform contentious actions, or the actor must try to use the media as a platform to accentuate dissent (Tarrow 1998: 114). It might then be suggested that the active use of media strategies point to attempts at compensating for power deficits, whether they are structural, associational, or institutional.

Wills (2009) and others have argued that some corporations have become 'hollow organisations'. Such corporations manage a brand and a public image rather than workers and production. COOP is not such a corporation in full, but it shares some traits with these 'hollow corporations'. One such trait is of course the already mentioned subcontracting of major functions and services. The result is that the public image, important to any company, can be an effective target in order to make sure one is striking the 'real employer'.

COOP in Norway is a very public company, in both reputation and in ownership. This has caused the company to receive a 'red' image of sorts—an image they wish to retain. Making the case public gave the unions the upper hand; further media exposure could be used as a bargaining strategy in the negotiations.

The media was instrumental in the COOP case, and it is broadly accepted that it is good to shed light on social dumping and expose such practices to the general public. Only few cases, however, make it to mainstream media, but if they do, they usually get solved positively. Nevertheless, consequentially such exposure might also produce a false image of a winning battle against social dumping.

On the other hand, these public symbols of victory are important. COOP had weaknesses that became evident as soon as wrongdoings were uncovered and the claims were made public. This is something that can be formulated and integrated into a prescriptive strategy. However, it is practically impossible to predict with certainty. Notwithstanding this, action or past experiences of action are important as 'collective action exposes opponents' points of weakness that may not be evident until they are challenged' (Tarrow 1998: 87).

Due to the fact of the symbolic power the case came to achieve, the results might be more fundamentally important in unveiling opportunities than initially perceived by activists as well as opponents. Through connecting their individual, and collective, grievances to the larger and already established frame of social dumping, they were able to 'underscore and embellish the seriousness and injustice of a social condition or redefine as unjust and immoral what was previously seen as unfortunate but perhaps tolerable' (Snow and Benford 1992, quoted in Tarrow 1998: 110).

At an early stage, the Plumbers Union official proposed to involve the media. Initially, the new members met this with some scepticism and fear, but Boye Ullmann made the case that involving the media would function more as insurance against further exploitation, rather than more exposure to it. Aminzade and McAdam suggest that without a mobilization of heightened or strong emotions, collective action will not occur. On the individual level, students of social movements have ignored the power of emotions in assessing gains and costs in a non-instrumental way. After all, it is easy to agree that '[i]ntense fear can motivate action, even in the face of extreme risks and seemingly no hope for payoff' (Aminzade and McAdam 2001: 17). Also, structural relations of power/powerlessness and status can be experienced as inclination to act; the resulting disposition can produce anger, fear, and despair (see Aminzade and McAdam 2001: 20).

It was decided to employ the element of surprise, walking with cameras up to the workers' barracks during lunch in the middle of the site, where the Spanish workers were housed. The housing conditions were far below the standards stipulated in collective agreements: twelve shift workers in bunk beds sharing one bathroom and one shower. The workers talked about the low wages and described feeling exploited and a fear of being let go if they spoke up about the conditions. The reporters also referred to conversations with workers from Latvia, Ireland, and Poland who were experiencing working under similar circumstances, but were not willing to go on camera or on record for fear of losing their job.

The workers described a situation that is mainly foreign to the broad general Norwegian public. Feelings of indignity and powerlessness could therefore be publicly transferred from the workers onto the employer through shaming, in a way that resonated with the Norwegian public. The demands were not only perceived as highly legitimate and fair; they were, in Norwegian terms, also fairly modest. The workers expressed that they had no choice but to accept the situation. The conditions in Spain were even worse and there were no jobs. It was the application of a classic injustice frame.

Attempting to talk to onsite management, the news crew was told to cease filming to leave the site. The COOP management released a statement saying that the company considered the situation unacceptable and that they had a zero tolerance policy for social dumping. The company stated that they had no prior knowledge of the conditions. COOP, together with GSE, would take full responsibility for the plumbers' back payments in accordance with the joint venture liability act, and none of the workers would lose their jobs.

BNL, the construction sector employer's organization, also said that this was unacceptable. The LIA said that they would put three investigators on the case. At one point Anniken Huitfeldt, the minister of labour, also went on television urging COOP to compensate the workers as promised. Making the struggle public created opportunities for other actors to move. The COOP case did not only produce incentives for other unions and parties, it also brought the problems of social dumping to the forefront and successfully framed it as a grave injustice to the subcontracted workers.

Back to Spain

Around the same time as the last offer was made, EcoIberica terminated the workers' contracts, and they were to be sent home. Boye Ullmann called the COOP management personally and asked the head of COOP, Mr. Fanebust, to intervene directly to avoid the situation. COOP had, as mentioned earlier, promised that they would be employed until the end of the project, and this was a breach of that promise. Previously, this had happened once before: Two plumbers had been thrown out of the barracks and sent to the airport. Direct intervention by the COOP management ensured their return to the site. Situations like this show the precarious situation posted workers find themselves in, as housing and work conditions are intrinsically related. If contracts are terminated, it often includes a loss of housing and a practical impossibility to initiate or continue a struggle.

Since the parties had come to an agreement on the wage claim, a final visit was made to the building site. After the union representative left, the workers were threatened that anyone who had talked to him would be sent back to Spain on the first flight available. The posted workers were not sent home in May; they returned to Spain in June, but were paid until July when the project was planned to be finished.

TV2 and the union decided to do a follow-up story and went to Zaragoza, where they met the Spanish workers. After the workers had arrived in Spain, eight of the plumbers were immediately let go. In accordance with Spanish law, they were compensated with severance payments. But the main or initial whistle blower was fired and did not receive such a payment. Five of the workers returned in July/August—because the project was not completed—and received Norwegian salaries and continued as members of the union.

CONCLUSION

As we have seen, the various sources of power are unevenly distributed among groups of workers. Having open strategies towards immigration and being innovation-minded, with regards to organizational practises (for example, membership), can produce stronger workers' organizations, as workers' status can change due to harsher labour systems. Changes in possibility structures may then promote or undermine categories of workers or workers' organizations. Furthermore, unions may appear strong or weak, depending on context. For example, institutional power can be concentrated in some institutions rather than others, and the balance of power within each institution is different.

The specific regulatory context seems to be favourable from the standpoint of unionists. Still, the problem lies with the lack of political will to enforce regulations and transfer the necessary resources to deal with the problems of social dumping. There is a need to create less taxing ways for unions to use the tools at hand, so that existing regulations become more effective. In any case, there lies much power in existing regulations; the mainstream repertoire of the Norwegian unions is judicial and connected to its institutional power. That means that when laws, judicial precedent, and institutions, such as LIA, change or do not have resources, the institutional power can shift quickly. Strategies that are solely based on existing institutional channels seem rather perilous.

The question of leadership should not be underestimated, and it is fairly obvious that Boye Ullmann played a major individual role in the struggle. In addition to handling the negotiations mainly alone for a long time, while mobilizing emotions and instilling the posted workers with the 'idea of power', he was also the main architect behind the media strategy. Depending on how they are framed, highly publicized cases can, to a certain degree, function as or even replace preemptive 'clauses'. The COOP case became a reference point, framed as 'this is the tip of the iceberg', a cautionary symbol that could be used in arguments after the case was over. The very public and shared frame that was developed through the media became an easily accessible frame to apply in the struggle against social dumping and in the pursuit of the general application law. Because the plumbers had won their struggle, they opened up or made visible a path that could light the way for other groups and later struggles.

NOTES

1. A special thanks to Andreas Bieler, Roland Erne, Darragh Golden, Idar Helle, Knut Kjeldstadli and Sabina Stan for their guidance, support, and valuable comments. Some of the theoretical remarks were developed, in part, as work connected with the PhD program at the European University Institute.

2. For example, the Fellesforbundet sectorial federation had a policy of refraining from action that might cause migrant workers to be expelled from Norway in order to build trust with Central and Eastern Europe workers (see Eldring, Fitzgerald, and Arnholtz 2012).

3. COOP Handel AS is a subsidiary company of COOP Norge SA. COOP is a Norwegian chain of grocery shops collectively owned and run by cooperative societies locally across Norway. According to the press release the warehouse had a capital-spending budget of NOK 1.5 billion. Once operational, the building would be in use for twenty to thirty years, offering employment to four hundred workers.

4. The initial group were five out of the seventeen posted plumbers (three from Bulgaria, four from Latin America, two from Senegal, and the rest from Spain) employed by the Spanish company EcoIberica.

Part III

Power and Strategy

Introduction

Tiago Matos

Common to the chapters in the following section are the themes of power and strategy, but perhaps also, underlying in all the chapters, is the question of action ability or union capabilities. As globalization's many effects continue to rearrange previous power configurations, unions are left having to reassess how to retain, regain, or reestablish structural and associational power. The bargaining power of unions has slowly been eroded for decades, and this erosion has been intensified over the last decade. Nevertheless, globalization has also led to shifts in production systems and power, which may also create new opportunities and innovations in action repertoires. In her much-cited book, Beverly Silver suggests that, since production systems are in perpetual development, the working class will have to be viewed in constant transformation as well, ultimately defining the nature of the conflict between labour and capital. The result, Silver says, is new agencies, in new places, and new forms of struggle (Silver 2003: 19). Moreover, structural change, resulting from globalization, undoubtedly creates constraints on agency as well as possibilities, new participating actors, new alignments, and changes in the relations of power not only pertaining to unions. With the experience from modular forms of contention, whether they take the form of disruptive industrial action or of campaigns directed at companies, national or transnational institutions, innovative strategies emerge, where inherited forms meet new conditions (Tarrow 1998: 71–105).

Edward Webster offers an outline of the various sources of power, distinguishing between 'old' and 'new' sources. Drawing on the notion of labour as an active agent in hashing out innovative ways of dealing with globalization and providing examples of struggles from three different sectors, Webster sets out to develop a conceptual framework for understanding changes in power sources. He suggests that *logistical power* and *societal power* be considered new sources of power, while institutional power is a neglected dimension with regards to incorporating 'new' sources of power, and innovations in forms of action and power exertion that emerge at the periphery of the traditional labour movement.

Marissa Brookes tackles the problem of applying various types of power effectively by reviewing various Transnational Labour Alliances and their outcomes. *Context-appropriate power exertion* is dependant, says Brookes, on targeting employer's core interests, related to the fulfilment of the company's material interests. These interests exist within sectors, where labour can exert its structural, institutional, and coalitional power. Only by acknowledging that power is relational, and that interests ultimately are informed by these relationships, can strategies be context appropriate and thus effective.

Although codes of conduct and global framework agreements have been around for some time, Jamie McCallum tries to make sense of their increased use for empowering workers by theorizing the contention for governance, an innovation McCallum coins *governance struggles*. McCallum argues that this strategic shift towards governance struggles seeks to change the 'rules of engagement', which may reestablish actionable power, albeit in different arenas. In order to empower workers, governance struggles do not emphasize the traditional push for new rights, but rather the creation of new rules—new spaces for associational power to develop—where none have existed or existing ones are unfavourable.

The final chapter of this section discusses how trade union education can be used as a resource in building union capacities. Through her research on a European Works Council training event at the European Trade Union Institute, Bianca Föhrer argues that educational activities create a set of spaces in which labour representatives' transnational personal, collective, and social identities can develop. By actively creating *space for cross-border encounters, exchange and action,* and *reflection and insight,* the ensuing personal development, as well as development in collective identities can ultimately further transnational solidarity and promote cross-border solidarity action.

EIGHT

Labour after Globalization

Old and New Sources of Power

Edward Webster[1]

The nature of globalization's impact on workers is contested, both in the workplace and on the streets. Paul Bowles (2010) identifies two dominant paradigms. The first, the neoclassical liberal paradigm, views a liberal trading order as the main manifestation of globalization and beneficial to the majority of workers. It accepts that there will be job losses and growing wage inequality, and believes that the best way for workers in industrial countries to respond is by increasing their human capital through job retraining. The solution to the globalization problematic, neoliberals believe, 'is for the adjustment costs to be minimized perhaps by protection from import surges, but more importantly by longer term retraining programs which shift workers in industrial countries out of those industries in which developing countries have a comparative advantage' (Bowles 2010: 16).

The second paradigm, which Bowles terms antineoliberal globalism, starts from the proposition that globalization is a political project to increase the power of capital over the nation state and labour. Workers' responses vary from global social democracy to support for 'delinking' from the global capitalist system. The policy instruments for labour include corporate codes of conduct, including the demand for a social clause in trade agreements, international framework agreements, global unionism, international minimum wage campaigns, international labour standards, regulation of global capital, and re-establishing the political autonomy of the state (Bowles 2010: 17–20).

There is, however, a third paradigm emerging which challenges the conventional 'end of labour' thesis expressed by leading social scientists such as Manuel Castells (1996) and Guy Standing (2010). Instead of dismissing labour as a product of the past, this approach sees labour as an active agent responding to globalization in innovative ways. It takes as its point of departure the assumption that the labour movement was built around its capacity to disrupt the economy (its structural power within the workplace) and its ability to organize collectively into trade unions and political parties (associational power) (Piven 2000; Silver 2003; Wright 2002). While structural power has been weakened by neoliberal globalization, and associational power is under attack by the ideologues of the 'free market', new sources of power are emerging. One of these is *logistical power*, a form of structural power where disruptive politics are drawn from the workplace into the public arena (Webster, Lambert, and Bezuidenhout 2008: 13). Another is *societal power*, which depends on unions' ability to frame their struggle in ways that aim at organizing a counterhegemonic force, based on *cooperative power* through coalition-building with social movements or *discourse power* through influencing public discourses around issues of justice. Jennifer Chun (2009) has called these symbolic or moral powers. Using these forms of power, union organizers have successfully drawn on the public arena with the aim of restoring the dignity of, and justice for, socially devalued and economically marginalized workers. She demonstrates the use of symbolic power through an analysis of public demonstrations by caddies in Korea and janitors and home care workers in California (Chun 2009).

In this chapter, I focus on building a conceptual framework for understanding the changing dynamics of labour and workers' sources of power. I begin by identifying worker action that draws on traditional sources of structural and associational power. I then show how the emergence of new forms of labour action is drawing on both old and new sources of power. New global forms of worker power are examined, and I conclude by suggesting that the missing dimension in the three sources of power identified—structural, associational, and societal—is institutional power. If these new initiatives are to be sustainable, they will need to include one of labour's traditional sources of power, institutional power. These four-fold sources of power provide the basis for a strategy of union renewal in the age of globalization.

SOURCES OF WORKERS' POWER

Contrary to the 'end of labour' prognosis, strikes and uprisings have become commonplace worldwide. South Africa is no exception. Since 2006, strike activity has increased in duration, number of workdays lost, and levels of violence (Webster 2013: 349). Indeed, Alexander (2012) has argued that South Africa is 'the protest capital of the world', describing these protests as a 'rebellion of the poor', and linking them to labour-related demands for increases in wages, demands for jobs, and improved service delivery. These protests are symptomatic of larger issues: 'At the most fundamental level, community protests are a natural and probable consequence of systematic institutional problems that exist in the provision of basic services to the most poverty-stricken members of South African society' (Jain 2010: 10).

A turning point for South Africa was the Marikana Massacre in August 2012, in which striking workers and policemen clashed, resulting in thirty-four deaths, the largest number of civilians killed by security forces since the end of apartheid (Alexander 2012). In the incidents leading up to the massacre, workers, policemen, and security guards were killed. While the employer, Lonmin, refused to talk to its striking workers, the dispute was complicated by the emergence of a breakaway union—the Association of Mineworkers and Construction Union—from the previously hegemonic National Union of Mineworkers.

From the outset, workers rejected representation by National Union of Mineworkers, the recognized union, and the formal collective bargaining system. The massacre at Marikana brought sharply to the fore the changing nature of the employment relationship in the age of globalization, and the emergence of new actors in the workplace. As Cooke and Wood (2011: 3) argue,

> the growing inadequacy of the traditional institutional actors (e.g. the state and national unions) in defending workers' rights has created both the space and the need for 'new' actors to fill the gap. Examples of these actors include: [nongovernmental organizations], employment agencies, [human resources] consultancy firms, counsellors, chaplains, health advisors/trainers, citizens' advice bureaus, global union federations, employment arbitrators, grassroots activists and social movements, and so forth.

All of these new actors, and more, were present in Marikana. Most significant were the large number of temporary employment agencies, side-by-side with grassroots activists, traditional healers, chaplains and nongovernmental organizations.

But popular protest is not peculiar to South Africa; it is a global phenomenon in which the financialization of capitalism has substantially altered the grammar of social conflict. From the Arab Spring to the 'movement of the squares' in Southern Europe, streets have become the site of massive demonstrations, strikes, occupations, riots, rebellions, and revolutions. These popular uprisings include Tunisia, Egypt, Greece, Spain, Italy, Portugal, Brazil, and Turkey. Institutionalized industrial conflict is being eroded and the labour market is fragmenting society along new fault lines. Alongside the decline of traditional unions, new movements are emerging. As Klaus Dörre (2010: 66) writes:

> What is crucial is that even in developed countries, collective (labour) interests are often articulated outside the scope of normalised conflict. In abandoned neighbourhoods and regions, 'bargaining by riots' is quite common, a practise which despite the undeniable relevance of ethnic or gender-specific constructions, originates to a great extent in spontaneous or unconventionally organized class action.

These protests are class-specific, bread-and-butter conflicts in which protesters feel powerless in the face of the international financial institutions and vent their anger in the destruction of property and in militant forms of action.

It is important to note that these new initiatives, organizational forms, and sources of power are emerging at the periphery of traditional labour, leading to the flowering of new global labour studies. Importantly, the strikes at Marikana were not led by a union, but were a product of the self-activity of workers, as Sinwell and Mbatha (2013: 32) argue:

> The agency of workers, and more specifically the independent worker's committee, is arguably the key feature surrounding the event of the Marikana Massacre. . . . The committee at Marikana is important in understanding the strike wave along the Rustenburg Platinum Belt where these independent organisations emerged. Industrial sociology more generally has been dominated by investigations into formalised unions.

Underlying this analysis are historical critiques of formal industrial relations structures from a broadly syndicalist perspective.

Another example is that of informal workers in India. Rina Agarwala (2013: 98) challenges the conventional view that informalization is the 'final nail in the labour movement's coffin'. Informal workers, she demonstrates, are creating new institutions and forging a new social contract between the state and labour. Agarwala shows how informal worker movements are most successful when operating within electoral contexts where parties must compete for mass votes from the poor. She calls this competitive populism. These informal worker organizations are not attached to a particular party, nor do they espouse a specific political or economic ideology. In this way, they have successfully organized informal workers. As one organizer observed: 'The informal sector is entering into the previously formal sector, and the formal sector is being cut in size. . . . We cannot differentiate between formal and informal workers, because politicians only care about getting most votes' (cited in Agarwala 2013: 98).

I am not suggesting that organizing informal workers is an easy task. From research among vulnerable immigrant clothing workers in the inner city of Johannesburg, we found that these workers often operate in family-type microenterprises that blur the boundaries between employer and employee (Joynt and Webster 2013). Instead of joining unions, they prefer faith-based organizations, such as the growing number of Pentecostal churches, which often perform economic as well as spiritual functions. They assist in job searches, find accommodation for newcomers to the city, and even act as 'bankers' by carrying money to home villages.

But the important point is that there are also newer forms of power emerging. I illustrate the changing sources of workers' power in the matrix shown in Table 8.1. As the table illustrates, it is possible to identify both new and traditional sources of power in contemporary protests. I now turn to the ways in which workers are taking advantage of points of vulnerability within the present global order. There are a growing number of examples where globalization has opened up new sources of power. For example, workers on the large grape farms in Northeastern Brazil have been able to maintain high wages and permanent employment by taking advantage of the pressures on suppliers to deliver high-quality grapes on time for the European market (Selwyn 2012). The exporters, large commercial farmers, are subject to quality pressures from retailers in Europe and need a permanent workforce that possesses the required skills.

This has given the workers structural power—workplace bargaining power in the heart of the production process, not unlike the pressures of Fordist production—as well as marketplace bargaining power (their skills are needed by employers). But it is a new form of power in that workers are able to take advantage of capital's vulnerability in the global production network. These previously low-wage farm workers can disrupt production if they are not satisfied with their working conditions,

Table 8.1. Old and New Sources of Workers' Power

'Traditional' forms of workers' power	Structural power: Marketplace bargaining power Workplace bargaining power Example: The ability to disrupt production through strikes	Associational power: Example: The ability to form unions and influence government policy through political processes
'New' forms of workers' power	Logistical power: Example: Blocking roads and burning tires in the rural uprising in the Western Cape	Societal power: Example: Johannesburg municipal workers' demonstrations and anticorruption campaign

Source: adapted from Lambert, Webster & Bezuidenhout, A. (2012): 294.

and employers cannot afford to allow this to happen given the strict delivery requirements from the retailers.

Below I look at three examples of this newfound workers' power: The struggles of municipal workers in Johannesburg, the farm workers' uprisings in 2012/2013 in the Western Cape, and the global campaign against Group 4 Securicor (G4S) led by the global union, Union Network International.

NEW FORMS OF GLOBAL POWER

Municipal Workers in Johannesburg

Among the struggles of municipal workers in Johannesburg, we can identify three cycles of contestation framed around the repertoires of inclusion and exclusion (Ludwig and Webster 2014). The first cycle, 1980 to 1995, was framed against racial discrimination and the demand for inclusive, democratic citizenship. It culminated in 1995 in a brief honeymoon period and the promise of a participatory labour regime. The second cycle, 1996 to 2001, covers the shift to privatization, when intense ideological contention focused around the opposition to privatization, with workers demanding access to public goods. In the third cycle, 2001 to 2011, the union—the South African Municipal Workers Union—confronted the consequences of flexibilization and the return of contract labour. The union responded to capital's strategy by embarking on a campaign against corruption and demanding job security. This culminated in the 2011 strike against the quasiprivate Pikitup (a waste collection company) that brought together casual and permanent workers in a successful demand for permanent jobs and an investigation into corruption.

We suggest that there is a shift from traditional sources of worker power to 'new' forms of logistical and symbolic power. In the second and third cycles, framed in terms of anticorruption and broader coalitions, the South African Municipal Workers Union went beyond pressurizing their Alliance[2] partner, the African National Congress. They were able to gain public recognition through discourse power. Framing, therefore, relates to the generalization of a grievance, shaping grievances into broader and more resonant claims (Tarrow 2011: 31). For example, precarious workers can compensate for their lack of associational power 'by drawing upon the contested arena of culture and public debates about values' (Chun 2009: 7), and by winning public recognition and legitimacy for workers' struggles.

In entities like Pikitup, where the public is intensely affected by a strike, influencing public opinion plays an important role. Shop stewards believed that communities were sympathetic and in support of the strike because the union was blowing the whistle on corruption in Pikitup.

However, these new sources of power remain embryonic and sporadic. The South African Municipal Workers Union was not able to uphold its strategy of inclusive solidarity and social movement unionism because the union was torn between loyalty to its Alliance partner and support for social movements, fundamentally contesting neoliberal politics.

At the same time, power resources also depend on agency, on the unions' mobilizing capacity, and on their strategic choices (Brinkmann et al. 2008; McGuire 2012). As studies on social movements show, 'material conditions do not necessarily and automatically generate mobilizing grievances' (Levésque and Murray 2013: 779). It is therefore necessary for actors to assign meaning to these conditions in order to transform grievances into mobilization. The 'repertoire of contention', defined as 'the ways people act together in pursuit of shared interests' (Tilly 1995a: 41), can take three distinct forms of collective action—disruption, violence, and contained behaviour—thereby combining to different degrees the properties of challenge, uncertainty and solidarity (Tarrow 2011: 99).

Rural Uprising at De Doorns

The De Doorns Uprisings in 2012/2013 were confrontational in nature. They included direct action through marching, blocking roads, collective refusal to go to work, and the destruction of property. This challenged the dominant discourse of farm workers, namely, that the impediments to collective farm worker resistance results in workers relying on 'weapons of the weak' such as individual appeals and avoidance of open conflict within a paternalistic, moral universe. Andries du Toit argues that 'paternalism smothers any possibility of resistance' (cited in Wilderman 2014: 23). Paternalism, he argues, is reinforced by fear and isolation; farms are spread over long distances, and the strict enforcement of private property rights 'means that the ability to gather any sort of strength or safety in numbers is very challenging' (Du Toit, cited in Wilderman 2014: 23).

Wilderman's case study of the rural uprisings of 2012/2013 demonstrates this challenge to the conventional view by showing how the agricultural sector 'is facing increasing global competition, decreased protection and subsidies from government, and the increasing power of consolidated buyers imposing greater demands in terms of lower costs and higher quality' (Wilderman 2014: 14). Farmers have responded, he suggests, by shifting away from live-on-farm labourers to the use of workers who live off-farm and are seasonal, casual, or contract (migrant) labour. But this shift in the composition of the workforce is not only the result of 'push factors'; there is also the 'pull factor' of a Reconstruction and Development Programme house[3] in the informal settlements, 'creating the possibility of a more independent life for farm workers' (Wilderman 2014: 14).

The implications of this erosion, of the workers' paternalistic dependence on the farm owner, through the sociospatial shift to seasonal labourers living in informal settlements is, Wilderman argues, a contradictory one. On the one hand, seasonal employment, in the context of a large reserve of labour, adds to the vulnerability of workers; on the other hand, gathering together large numbers of workers with shared grievances in one place facilitates collective mass action, not just of farm workers. As a farm worker from De Doorns observed, it also included 'taxi drivers, construction workers, security guards, teachers, nurses—the whole town shut down and every time we would march it would get bigger' (Wilderman 2014: 26).

Importantly, Wilderman explores how the strikes spread from the local level to the region. The accessibility of television and other media coverage of De Doorns, and two months earlier of Marikana, provided both a mechanism for disseminating the strike as well as a source of inspiration. But what turned this energy into collective action were the Coordinating Units, 'locally based organisations or vanguard groups of pre-existing community based leadership' (Wilderman 2014: 45). A good example is the small socialist trade union, the Commercial, Stevedoring, Agricultural and Allied Workers Union based in Borrowdale, that had the capacity to turn energy and anger at the local level into a broad social base, and link it to the larger movement. In addition, the tactics chosen— blocking roads, burning tires, marches, refusing to work, and stopping others from working—were easily replicable without large resources. Materials such as petrol, tires, stones, and hand-written placards were relatively easy for farm workers to acquire and did not require much coordination. The existence of information technology and social media ensured the rapid spread of the strike, and the coercive action of the police turned the strike into a human rights–based discourse. It was, Wilderman concludes, the unplanned way in which the strike spread that made it 'spontaneous' (Wilderman 2014: 30).

Wilderman concludes his study by raising the question of whether the uprising has translated into the growth of existing or new organizations. At the level of formal trade union membership, there was an initial modest increase but it was short-lived. In part, this was because there has been an intense employer backlash against farm workers, resulting in dismissals, evictions, and refusal to rehire activists, as well as 'stealing any sense of victory from the increased minimum wage by imposing greater deductions from pay checks . . . and a more rigid performance based piece rate system' (Wilderman 2014: 86). Furthermore, Wilderman argues, this was partially brought on by an ineffective approach to interaction and organisation during the protest, which built a sense of disillusionment and cynicism. In other words, the unions had attempted to mediate rather than to engage, empower, and support farm workers.

Wilderman's study shows how the macro changes in agriculture have created a new kind of worker, no longer tied to the farm owner but easily mobilized in the densely populated informal settlements. However, although they are readily mobilized, this militant collective action has not translated into sustainable organization.

The Global Campaign against Group 4 Securicor

A final example of the new forms of power emerging in the age of globalization takes the actor-driven approach a step further by arguing that labour is an agent of global governance (McCallum 2013). Workers, McCallum suggests, are not simply victims of the global juggernaut; they can change the rules of global engagement. Global framework agreements, he suggests, are part of this strategy to expand the bargaining power of national unions over entire industries by forcing major companies to play by union rules. McCallum illustrates this theoretical argument through an analysis of a global campaign led by the global union, Union Network International, against the multinational G4S, the largest employer in Africa and, surprisingly, also listed on the London Stock Exchange.

The campaign began in the United States with the Service Employee International Union, an affiliate of Union Network International, and its successful Justice for Janitors Campaign. McCallum (2013) shows how the organizational model they developed was globalized and transferred to the United Kingdom, Australia, New Zealand, and then to Europe, and the Netherlands and Germany in particular.

In a nutshell, the model involved the relocation of resources towards new organizing and an increased reliance on strategic research to drive the industrial strategy. The empirical core of McCallum's book examines the extension of the campaign in 2008 to South Africa and India. McCallum argues that the campaign was successful because it neutralized the management of these enterprises while simultaneously creating the conditions for workers to organize, build new structures, renew old traditions, and experiment with new strategies.

The centre of McCallum's argument is that the campaign did not win new rights, but instead used global power to make new rules of engagement for local unions. He calls this new approach 'governance struggles'. Governance struggles refer, he says, 'broadly to the exercise of power in the absence of an overarching political authority, usually by a constellation of institutions that make decisions and enforce compliance with norms and rules at the supranational level' (McCallum 2013: 12). This allows him to theorize global unions themselves as potential agents of governance. In South Africa, this meant, for example, that for every thousand union members, the union was entitled to one full-time shop steward. It now has four nationwide.

McCallum has identified a new source of power: global power. This is an important insight, as it allows us to go beyond the widespread view that globalization disables labour—the pessimistic school—and to begin to explore the new sources of vulnerability and the strategic possibilities that globalization has created for labour. This case study raises four issues: what is new in the new labour internationalism, old and new sources of worker power, union democracy and the bureaucratization of shop stewards, and the limits of transferring union models to other countries.

First, there is an ambiguity in the question of how 'new' the new governance struggles are. As McCallum (2013) acknowledges, Charles Levinson from International Chemical, Energy and Mining, a global trade union secretariat, argued for what he called company councils in the early 1970s—that is, worker committees extending across countries in multinational companies. In South Africa, the emerging black unions targeted transnational corporations and entered into what were called 'recognition agreements' at plant level. These established new rules on the shop floor enabling unions to gain access to the workplace. These are examples of governance struggles where unions were agents filling the 'governance gap' in a context where the rights of black workers were not recognized. These agreements relied on navigating between the local and the global—that is, between local workplace resistance and the global sanctions campaign of the anti-apartheid movement. But this combination of the local and the global was driven overwhelmingly by the power of local union organisation, as Seidman (2009) has pointed out in her comparative study of codes of conduct.

Secondly, is it possible to sustain engagement in these 'new rules' through associational power alone? Put differently, is associational power sustainable without institutional power? To be sustainable, these new rules need to be consolidated. Can they be consolidated without institutions to enforce them? For example, McCallum (2013: 29) writes: 'In South Africa, guards used the agreement to demand access rights. Once organizers were able to talk to workers without fear of management reprisal, organizing exploded'. I would argue that rules on their own are not lasting unless they are supported by institutional power. It is institutions that create new 'rules of the game'. Without the sanctions that go with new rules, local management has not really changed in G4S in South Africa. Indeed, it required the state-funded Commission for Conciliation, Mediation and Arbitration to facilitate the establishment of an industry-wide National Bargaining Forum in 2009 to ensure a successful three-year wage agreement (Sefalafala and Webster 2013).

Thirdly, the outcome of the governance struggles, the creation of four full-time shop stewards in G4S, is what Sakhela Buhlungu (2010) has called the 'paradox of victory'. On the one hand, having elected shop stewards paid by management and able to work full time on union business is a major gain for workers. On the other hand, these shop stewards have increasingly come under attack within the labour movement for being too close to management. As full-time shop stewards, they are entitled to a range of privileges that has often distanced them from the shop floor. By focusing on one multinational in a context where only 16 per cent of the industry is organized, has the campaign not entrenched union leaders at G4S as a union bureaucracy amid a majority of low-wage, precarious workers (Sefalafala and Webster 2013)?

Fourthly, McCallum (2013) argues convincingly that the US organizing model is growing in influence globally. As he notes, this is ironic given the experience of many European, African, and Asian trade unions of the legacy of US trade union imperialism. The sentiment is captured in this comment by a European trade unionist: 'If the [International Monetary Fund] had a trade union wing, it would do what the [Service Employee International Union] does. It's weird, but in a way those people [Service Employee International Union leaders] are our role models, but they are also a huge pain in the ass' (cited in McCallum 2013: 150).

The globalization of the US model is ironic for another reason. I have argued earlier that innovative union organizing linking the workplace to the community in the 1980s, in countries of the South was circulating in the opposite direction from South to North (Lipsig-Mumme and Webster 2012). More recently, Ercu Celik (2014) has shown how the concept of social movement unionism, used in South Africa, Brazil, and the Philippines in the 1980s, travelled North to the United States mediated through Northern scholars, a case, he suggests, of learning from the periphery. Importantly, both authors stress the differences of social context between the Global South and Global North, reminding scholars of the dangers of transferring union models.

CONCLUSION

Our identification of sources of power is incomplete without an account of institutional power and strategic capabilities.[4] Institutional power embeds past social compromises by the incorporation of associational and structural power into institutions (Dörre, Holst, and Nachtwey 2009). As McGuire argues, this source of power continues to be applied during ongoing economic cycles, even where power relations within society may have changed. It may take the form of labour law, wage setting, and bargaining arrangements, as well as institutionalized forms of social dialogue such as the National Economic Development and Labour Council, South Africa's premier peak level social dialogue institution (McGuire 2012: 43). The important point about institutional power is that it grants rights but also limits the space for action (Dörre, Holst, and Nachtwey 2009). The Jena power resources approach argues that institutions shape the relationship between structural and associational/organizational power, but that power resources are not sufficient; they need strategic capabilities—that is, the capability to detect power resources in order to make use of them as well as the organizational flexibility to optimize associational power (Dörre, Holst, and Nachtwey 2009).

In this chapter, I have identified the new sources of power that are emerging in the age of globalization. If it is premature to call these forms of action a countermovement, they have nevertheless shaken up our research agenda and challenged us to rethink the relationship between global capital, global labour, and the new forms of action and social movements that are emerging at the periphery of the traditional labour movement. This emerging research agenda will require a multilevel analysis if it is to contribute to renewing the labour movement.

The fourfold sources of power—structural, associational, societal, and institutional—provide the basis for a strategy of union renewal. It is worth noting the pessimism that faced the labour movement in the 1930s in the United States. As labour historian David Brody has argued:

> Perhaps one of the more famous stories illustrating the labor movement's unpredictable course is the one historians often tell of multitude and solemn pronouncements made by august labor scholars in 1932 heralding the certain death of the American labor movement. These dire predictions, of course, were issued literally on the eve of the dramatic and widespread upsurge of labor organizing that began in 1932. (Brody 1980, cited in Cobble 1992: 82)

The development of capitalism is a contradictory process; in each phase of its development, it faces obstacles to the accumulation process and, in overcoming these obstacles, generates new opportunities for collective worker action and organisation. The rise of factory-based production overcame the limits of home-based production, but in the process created the conditions for the emergence of trade unions. The rise of Fordism led to a shift from craft unionism—where the power of the workers lay in their skill (market-based power) to industrial unionism, where worker power lay in a new political subject—the semiskilled worker, whose new source of power was workplace bargaining (Webster 1985).

Neoliberal globalization and the information technology that accompanied it have increased productivity to unprecedented levels worldwide, overcoming the impediments to capital that arose from militant industrial unions. However, globalization has opened up new sources of power and opportunities for transnational action and organisation on a global scale (Evans 2010).

NOTES

1. Edward Webster is Professor Emeritus at the Society, Work and Development Institute at the University of the Witwatersrand, and Director of the Chris Hani Institute, both in Johannesburg, South Africa.

2. The Tripartite Alliance has deep roots in the struggle for liberation in South Africa. In its current form, it consists of the African National Congress, the South African Communist Party, and the Congress of South African Trade Unions. However, sections of the Congress of South African Trade Unions have been very critical of the leadership of the Tripartite Alliance for following what they see as orthodox neoliberal economic and social policy.

3. The Reconstruction and Development Programme was introduced shortly after the democratic transition. Among other benefits, it promised free or affordable housing for those previously denied it by the apartheid regime.

4. Donna McGuire (2012) develops the notion that institutional power is a neglected dimension of power in her doctoral thesis at the University of Kassel.

NINE

Power, Labour, and Globalization

How Context-Appropriate Strategies Help Transnational Labour Alliances Succeed

Marissa Brookes

INTRODUCTION

Recent years have seen a rise in workers' cooperation across national borders. These transnational labour alliances (TLAs)—defined as active collaborations among organized groups of workers based in two or more different countries—have used targeted campaigns to pressure multinational corporations into improving or maintaining wage levels, working conditions, union recognition, job security, and collective bargaining rights. TLAs enable workers from different countries to collaborate in launching waves of international protest, disrupting supply chains, sparking shareholder revolts, promoting global boycotts, and stalling production processes. Walmart, Tesco, IKEA, Carrefour, Siemens, Bosch, Gap, Nike, H&M, Accor, Hyatt, Volkswagen, Ford, DaimlerChrysler, Chiquita, Citra Mina, Coca-Cola, Unilever, Turkish Airlines, Securitas, Group 4 Securicor, United Parcel Service (UPS), DHL, Rio Tinto, and Vale are among the numerous companies that have been targeted by TLAs in just the past twenty years. Though only some TLAs succeed, their ongoing activities nevertheless suggest that organized labour has agency as an actor in the global economy.

While scholars of labour transnationalism generally agree that workers have some power to influence corporate behaviour, they disagree over how to categorize and analyse the different types of power workers exercise in transnational campaigns. Moreover, the connection between the type of power workers exercise and the success or failure of TLAs has yet to be fully explored. This chapter thus combines and critiques existing theories of power, globalization, and labour transnationalism in an effort to explain what makes the exercise of some types of power effective in some cases but not others.

Building on previous work (Brookes 2013), I argue that TLAs draw on three types of power to influence the behaviour of multinational employers: *structural power, institutional power,* and *coalitional power.* Structural power is the capacity of workers to physically disrupt an employer's operations. Institutional power is the capacity to hold an employer accountable by invoking the formal or informal rules that structure the employment relationship. Coalitional power is the capacity to mobilize and leverage the influence of nonlabour stakeholders to whom the employer must respond. I explain these three power types, along with the importance of associational power for their exercise, in greater detail below. I then argue that each power type is only effective in certain contexts. When workers exercise a type of power that does not threaten the target employer's core material interests, it will not be effective in compelling the employer to change its behaviour. Only a context-appropriate power strategy—meaning the use of a power type that directly impacts an employer's core interests—is likely to have some effect.

This chapter proceeds first by defining power in general. I then explain the concepts of structural, institutional, and coalitional power. Third, I discuss the concept of associational power in the context of the other three power types. Next, I highlight the conditions under which workers' different power types are effective in transnational campaigns. Finally, I illustrate what is meant by the context-appropriate exercise of power through examples of TLAs in practice.

DEFINING POWER

Following Knight (1992: 41), I define power generally as the ability of an actor A to make another actor B do something B otherwise would not do. This definition has three important advantages over competing definitions. First, power is conceptualized not as that which produces an outcome but, rather, as a capacity that can remain latent indefinitely. This corrects for what is by now a well-known flaw in the classic pluralist view (Dahl 1961), which sees power as something evidenced only by who prevails in decision making. As Lukes (2005: 69) argues, 'power is a potentiality, not an actuality—indeed a potentiality that may never be actualized.' Viewing power as a capacity prevents the researcher from ascribing power post hoc to those who gained from the outcome of a campaign. This is not to say that outcomes cannot tell us anything about the capacities of the actors involved. Rather, the essential point is that power can exist as a capacity at any point in time, even if it is not being exercised and even if actors' capacities fluctuate throughout the time period under analysis.

Secondly, Knight, like Piven (2008) and Lukes (2005), conceives of power as relational: 'to have power is to have power *over* another or others' (Lukes 2005: 73, emphasis in original). In contrast, Wright's definition of power as 'the capacity of individuals and organizations to realize class interests' (Wright 2000: 962) is somewhat problematic. Leaving aside the limited utility of focusing solely on class interests, Wright's general definition of power is only relational to the extent that realizing one's class interests requires directly affecting the behaviour of those opposed to and capable of thwarting those interests. Yet if, as Wright implies, there are other ways of exercising power that do not involve influencing the behaviour of other actors, it is not clear what such a solitary exercise of power would entail. Presumably, power in that sense is visible only through its supposed effects, leading again to the problem of identifying power only as something revealed by an outcome.

A third analytic advantage of Knight's definition, which distinguishes it from both Lukes' and Wright's, is that Knight allows the researcher to focus on actors' behaviours rather than their interests. This is in contrast to Lukes, who defines power by saying that '*A* exercises power over *B* when *A* affects *B* in a manner contrary to *B's* interests' (Lukes 2005: 37). It is true that actors exercise power in attempt to serve their own interests. It is also true that the exercise of power implies an asymmetry in the capacities of the actors involved. Nonetheless, the difference between A compelling B to do something B otherwise would not do (Knight's definition) and A compelling B to go against B's own interests (Lukes' definition) is that the former scenario allows for exercises of power that result in mutual benefit. It is therefore possible to have a relational view of power that takes into account the potential mutual benefit to both actors involved in a conflict. For example, a TLA (A) could launch a campaign to improve occupational safety measures across a particular employer's (B) operations, and the result of the successful campaign could ultimately improve the firm's productivity and therefore increase profits for B, an outcome very much in B's long-term interests. Knight's definition allows for the possibility that sometimes B acts a certain way, not because such actions are necessarily in B's objective interests, but because B is short-sighted, lacks information, or is subject to other factors related to the complex process of organizational decision making.

While power can take several different forms in the context of employment relations, of greatest relevance to TLAs are the types of power that workers exercise in situations of overt conflict with multinational corporations or other employers. These three types of power—structural power, institutional power, and coalitional power—are discussed below.

I also discuss a fourth type of power, associational power, which is the capacity of workers to act collectively in the first place and a necessary condition for exercising the other three power types.

VARIETIES OF POWER

Structural power is the ability of workers to influence employers because of their location in the economic system (Silver 2003: 13; Wright 2000: 962). It involves physical action (or sometimes inaction), such as preventing the delivery of parts to an assembly line that relies on just-in-time production or shutting down an entire transport system by striking at key transit stations. Structural power is especially effective when workers are selective and tactical so that actions at one worksite impact an employer's operations in other locations (Juravich 2007: 21; Selwyn 2007: 549). Not only might a relatively small number of strategic strikes 'disrupt the output of an entire plant', it could also 'bring all downstream plants, and even an entire corporation, to a standstill' (Silver 2003: 15). In extreme cases, the impact could ripple through an entire industry.

There is something new and distinctly transnational about workers' use of structural power in recent years. According to Piven (2008), economic globalization has created new interdependencies that can be exploited by unions and other organized groups of workers. Numerous employers depend on extensive chains of offshoring, whose individual links are vulnerable to strike action. The use of just-in-time production further 'removes the protective cushion of accumulated inventories' (Piven and Cloward 2000: 423). These structural vulnerabilities enable labour to create the 'bullwhip effect' in global value chains so that 'a small disruption at one point in a supply chain becomes increasingly magnified further up or down the chain' (Selwyn 2007: 549). Courier services, transportation networks, manufacturing, and agricultural export are all inherently vulnerable to TLAs' use of structural power.

A second type of power is *institutional power*. Unlike structural power, which workers derive from their embeddedness in the economic system, institutional power comes from workers' embeddedness in institutions, defined as laws, regulations, practices, procedures, and other formal and informal rules that persist over time, structuring actors' incentives, channelling their interests, and creating rational expectations of each other's behaviour. Institutions are of special significance to understanding power dynamics because they are themselves the product of past and ongoing power struggles (Hall 1986; Mahoney and Thelen 2010; Streeck and Thelen 2005; Thelen 1999). Collective bargaining procedures, corporate governance systems, and other institutions at the subnational, national, and international levels significantly shape workers' employment conditions, political resources, and relationships with employers. Institutions are therefore a source of workers' power.

I thus define institutional power as the capacity of workers to influence the behaviour of an employer by invoking the formal or informal rules that structure their relationship and interactions. Institutional power could be as straightforward as taking an employer to court for the alleged violation of labour laws, or it could be as complicated as the (actual or implied) threat of a breakdown in the stable, cooperative relationship between a union and management on which the company relies for its productivity and overall competitiveness. Even when companies adopt codes of conduct that are legally nonbinding, this signals a public commitment on the part of that company to meet certain expectations. If these expectations are not met, then there are grounds for pressuring the company into compliance.

The third type of power workers exercise in the global economy comes neither from their embeddedness in the economic system nor from the institutional contexts in which they are embedded. Rather, *coalitional power*—defined as the capacity of workers to leverage the influence of nonlabour stakeholders to alter an employer's behaviour—derives from workers' embeddedness in social and professional networks. Examples of nonlabour stakeholders include community leaders, religious associations, environmental activists, human rights organisations, students, shareholders, international nongovernmental organizations (INGOs), and political parties. In contrast to institutional power, which involves rules that directly affect the employment relationship, coalitional power mobilizes actors who affect other aspects of a company's operations, such as its profits or public reputation. Moreover, unlike community unionism, which is a long-term strategy for better integrating unions into their local communities (Tattersall 2010; Yates 2003: 232), coalitional power describes the capacity of workers to leverage their relationships with other stakeholders in general, including but not limited to those deriving from their local ties.

Transnational labour alliances have the potential to magnify the impact of structural, institutional, and coalitional power to the extent that TLA members are embedded in multiple different nodes of global production networks (the basis of structural power), multiple different institutional frameworks (the basis of institutional power), and multiple different networks of nonlabour stakeholders (the basis of coalitional power). Using these multiple and overlapping positions, TLAs can attempt to strategically relocate conflicts with employers to other countries or other geographic scales[1] on which workers have some advantage. Moreover, power can be multiscalar in its exercise (Ellem 2006), so that 'jumping scales'—the process whereby an actor strategically shifts the locus of its engagement with other actors—entails not a wholesale relocation of conflict to a different 'level' or 'stage' but rather a remapping of conflict to play out on multiple scales simultaneously (Cox 1998: 2; Herod 2001: 43; Lier 2007: 824). TLAs thus allow workers to exercise power to an extent that is impossible for a single union to do on its own.

A NOTE ON ASSOCIATIONAL POWER

The three power types discussed above—structural, institutional, and coalitional power—all describe a capacity workers have to compel an employer to do something it otherwise would not do. Labour studies scholars have tended to divide workers' power into only two types: structural power and associational power, relying on Wright's (2000) definition of the former as the power workers derive from their location in the economic system and the latter as the power workers have by virtue of being organized into a collective entity such as a trade union or political party. Conceiving of structural power as a capacity is not difficult: its substance lies in the capacity of workers to physically disrupt the production or distribution of goods and services. Likewise, the substance of institutional power is in workers' capacity to invoke rules that structure employment relations, while the substance of coalitional power is in their capacity to mobilize influential nonlabour stakeholders.

Conceiving of associational power as a capacity is problematic, however, because it is not clear what the substance of associational power actually is or what exactly associational power enables workers to do or to whom. Although associational power derives from the organization of workers into collective entities such as unions, such organizations are not themselves the substance of associational power. Unions, parties, and works councils are not capacities; they are actors or perhaps vehicles for action. What, then, is the substance of associational power?

Part of the problem with conceptualizing associational power is that nearly every reference to the concept involves a confusing semantic overlay in which the reader is told only where associational power comes from but never what it actually *is*. Wright's own definition—'the various forms of power *that result from* the formation of collective organisations of workers' (Wright 2000: 962, emphasis added)—explains nothing about what associational power actually enables workers to do. The same is true for Selwyn's definition, '*a product of* workers' collective organisation' (Selwyn 2011b: 16, emphasis added), and Chun's definition, '*the process whereby* a group of workers actively transform themselves from a state of invisibility and marginality to one of explicit recognition as a collective social group' (Chun 2005: 490, emphasis added). Wright and Selwyn identify the source, not the substance, of associational power, while Chun explains not what associational power is, only the process of attaining it.

The problem with associational power is not merely semantic. Scholars, union officials, and labour activists frequently emphasize that simply belonging to a union or other organization does not necessarily empower workers (Hyman 2010), who might discover that the potential for collective action is precluded by a divided, apathetic, or unwilling membership or stifled under the weight of a leaden bureaucracy. A union can exist on paper without ever engaging workers in collective action. The same problems prevail on the international level with organizations such as the International Trade Union Confederation and the global union federations, whose memberships face a host of coordination issues and collective action problems.

The failure of scholars to conceptualize associational power as a capacity is thus a failure to analytically differentiate between an organization that simply exists and a true actor capable of influencing the behaviour of others. Associational power must therefore be identified not simply as the product of collective organization but through the specific qualities that make it possible for a collective actor to have agency. For example, a union must have both a coordinated leadership and high membership participation to have associational power (Hyman 2010: 23).

More specifically, to have associational power, unions need not only resources—which Lévesque and Murray define as 'fixed or path-dependent assets that an actor can normally access and mobilize' (2010b: 335)—but also capabilities—which enable 'union leaders and activists to develop, use and transform those resources as required by the circumstances they face' (2010b: 341). Resources include tangible assets such as money and office space as well as less tangible assets such as a common identity, unity of purpose, and linkages to other actors. Capabilities include the ability of union members and leaders to autonomously and proactively create an agenda for action, form a consensus for action, learn from past experiences, and otherwise consciously direct the union's actions across space and time (Lévesque and Murray 2010b: 341–44).

With the above formulation in mind, I thus propose a conceptual clarification that is meant not as a challenge to Wright (2000) and others but, rather, an attempt to dispel the ambiguities inherent in present uses of the term associational power. To that end, I define associational power as the capacity of workers to mobilize themselves and to act collectively. That capacity, in turn, comes from the resources and capabilities internal to a labour organisation (Lévesque and Murray 2010b). The *substance* of associational power is thus neither the organization itself nor the laws and regulations that make it possible for workers to organize in the first place. The substance of associational power is the capacity of workers to act through their organization. It follows that the 'power' in associational power is not exercised by workers on outside actors but rather by workers on other workers. That is, associational power is the ability of A (e.g., union officials, rank-and-file activists, or labour party leaders) to get B (the other workers comprising the union or other organization) to do something B otherwise would not do (such as speak with one voice in contract negotiations, go on strike, etc.), perhaps by making use of resources (common identity, internal democracy, union dues, and so on) and capabilities (mediating contending interests, learning, and so on) in a way that solves collective action problems.

This adjustment to the standard definition of associational power clarifies, for example, the difference between the capacity of workers to disrupt the production process by withdrawing their labour (structural power) and the capacity of workers to come together and consciously decide to take such action (associational power). It also implies that associational power is a precondition for exercising any of the three other types of power described above.

Associational power facilitates the exercise of structural, institutional, and coalitional power not only by individual unions but also by TLAs. Nevertheless, exercising power and succeeding in a transnational campaign are not the same thing. For a TLA, success—defined as an outcome of a transnational campaign that results in a material or strategic gain for members of the labour alliance—requires a power strategy that actually compels an employer to alter its behaviour.

HOW CORE INTERESTS CONDITION POWER'S EFFECTIVENESS

Structural, institutional, and coalitional power only result in material or strategic gains for workers when their exercise directly impacts (or threatens to impact) something on which the employer in question depends for fulfilling its present or future material interests. Put simply, the power type exercised must be *context-appropriate* in order to contribute to success. Defining 'context' requires a recognition that power is relational; hence, the circumstances under which structural, institutional, and coalitional power are each effective depend not only on workers' embeddedness in global production networks, institutions, and social networks, but also, crucially, the target employer's core interests and needs.

Structural power is therefore effective because employers have a core interest in the smooth and profitable functioning of business and depend fundamentally on workers performing their assigned tasks. When workers withdraw their labour this directly disrupts business operations and threatens the basic functioning of business on which the employer depends. Nevertheless, structural power will be less effective on an employer that can endure a brief or even extended disruption to its operations, easily replace its existing workforce, or isolate instances of industrial action to avoid ripple effects throughout its production network. Moreover, highly mobile industries, such as customer service and clothing manufacturing, enable employers to react to labour unrest by relocating call centres and garment factories to other countries with relative ease. This spatial fix also enables employers to quell potential industrial action through the threat of job losses (Silver 2003: 41). Even some site-specific industries pose problems for structural power. A strike at a mine owned by a major multinational energy company would not have the same effect as a work stoppage would in the transport sector or in manufacturing processes that rely on the single sourcing of parts.

Institutional power is effective because employers have a core interest in the perpetuation of certain institutional arrangements for securing profit and ensuring the long-term functioning of the firm. Hence, invoking the authority of laws, regulations, standard practices, and other institutions works best with an employer that has premised its viability on its own and others' compliance with the law, or some other set of formal or informal rules. A firm whose production strategy depends on institutions that enable management to receive input from a stable, skilled workforce with accumulated shop floor knowledge, for example, is more likely to negotiate with workers in ways that maintain those institutional structures than an employer for whom those institutions are not as important. Nevertheless, institutional power is less effective when employers face no threat of third-party sanctions for failing to comply with institutionalized practices, when workers lack the resources to endure drawn-out court cases, and when employers are willing to change the rules of the game rather than maintain long-standing institutions.

Finally, coalitional power is effective because employers have a core interest in maintaining a good image with key stakeholders, such as investors who provide capital, consumers who purchase the firm's goods or services, or politicians who pass business-friendly legislation. When workers draw on their social networks to leverage the capacity of these nonlabour stakeholders to boycott, disinvest, exert political pressure, or otherwise disrupt the processes on which a company depends for its functioning and profitability, they threaten the viability of the target employer. Nonetheless, not all employers are equally vulnerable to coalitional power. A company that does not depend for its business on maintaining a positive public image will be less vulnerable to consumer-based campaigns than one for whom public image is essential, such as a hotel, restaurant, or retail chain. Likewise, calling attention to a corporation's poor environmental record is only likely to rally shareholders towards a protest vote when the company in question bases its business model on widespread recognition of that firm's promotion of environmental sustainability or other 'green' credentials.

CONTEXT-APPROPRIATE POWER IN PRACTICE

The past two decades offer numerous examples of TLAs exercising structural, institutional, and coalitional power. Successful labour alliances not only used context-appropriate power strategies but also took advantage of the transnational nature of the target employer by relocating the conflict to countries or geographic scales different from that in which the conflict originated. TLAs thus appear to be most successful when their members not only take advantage of the employer's interdependent relationships with workers or nonlabour stakeholders, but also make a deliberate effort to reshape the dynamics of these relationships at multiple scales.

The successful campaign aimed at UPS in 1997 is an early example of the exercise of structural power by a TLA. Through the International Transport Federation World Council of UPS, the Teamsters union in the United States reached out to other UPS employees around the world to take actions that would complement their national strike. UPS workers in Belgium commenced a wildcat strike, German and Dutch employees of Mercedes Benz and Philips convinced their respective employers to stop using UPS services, a motorcade of local workers in the Philippines shut down UPS operations in Manila, and the French union CGT threatened to prevent UPS deliveries going through Paris Orly Airport (Banks and Russo 1998; Urata 2010: 61). As a result of these transnational acts of structural power, UPS agreed to longer rest periods, improved occupational health and safety measures, renewed health insurance plans, and a new collective agreement with the Teamsters (Urata 2010: 64). The UPS campaign entailed the use of multiple scales, in that it involved a national strike by the Teamsters, which was complemented by international industrial actions and other forms of protest, which in turn could be understood as local actions spatially linked by the economic network of a global company.

Another example of a TLA successfully exercising structural power is the Flags of Convenience campaign, coordinated by the International Transport Workers' Federation and its affiliate unions. The time-sensitive nature of international shipping, and shipping's indispensable role in countless global production networks, renders the industry particularly vulnerable to physical disruption, and hence structural power. Thus, in addition to other negotiating tactics, the Flags of Convenience campaign used industrial action by seafarers and dockers to win a standard collective agreement, which ensures minimum wages for all seafarers working on approximately one-quarter of all Flags of Convenience[2] vessels, regardless of nationality (Lillie 2006).

TLAs have also exercised structural power in the nonmobile service industries, including the property maintenance and security services industries. In doing so, TLAs have taken advantage of the geography of capitalism, particularly the rise of global cities, epicentres of trade and finance 'where corporations are concentrating, not dispersing' and which 'cannot operate without the global workers, who literally feed, protect, and serve the richest and most powerful corporations and people in the world' (Lerner 2007: 21). The site-specific nature of these service jobs not only makes structural power viable (since companies cannot threaten to offshore the jobs of janitors and security guards) but also contributes to TLAs' internal cohesion since workers in different countries are not competing with each other for these jobs (Anderson, Hamilton, and Wills 2010: 387; Piven and Cloward 2000: 424).

TLAs have also taken strategic advantage of the geography of capitalism to exercise institutional power. A well-known campaign in the hotel industry illustrates this point. In the late 1990s, the North American union HERE, having faced years of difficulty attempting to unionize workers at the Novotel hotel in New York City, finally won a union election — only to have Novotel's managers dispute the results through continual court appeals (Wills 2002: 692). Through the International Union of Food, Agricultural, Hotel, Restaurant, Catering, Tobacco, and Allied Workers' Associations (IUF), HERE learned that Novotel's parent company, the Paris-based corporation Accor, maintains a positive and cooperative relationship not only with unions in France but also with the Accor European Works Council, which allows Accor employees throughout Europe to influence corporate decision-making. HERE officials then flew to Geneva to attend a meeting of the European Works Council, during which they expressed their concern about Novotel managers' union avoidance tactics to their European colleagues, who in turn pressed Accor's corporate leaders to address the situation. Accor heads quickly appointed three new managers to lead their North American operations. The new managers agreed to recognize and negotiate with HERE, not only at Novotel but also in the soon-to-be built Sofitel luxury hotel in New York City (Wills 2002: 695–96). HERE thus successfully jumped scales, leveraging its European allies' institutional power to convince Accor's head management to support the union in New York.

Another example of a TLA leveraging supranational institutions is the Causal-T campaign coordinated by the IUF in 2009. Workers at a Lipton tea processing facility in Khanewal, Pakistan, fought against their precarious labour conditions by connecting to the IUF, which filed an official complaint under the Organisation for Economic Co-operation and Development (OECD) Guidelines for Multinational Enterprises on behalf of the workers in Pakistan against their employer, Unilever, an Anglo-Dutch MNC. Pressure from the OECD, combined with other campaign tactics, ultimately compelled Unilever to raise salaries and increase the number of full-time and permanent jobs at the Khanewal plant. The TLA thus used an agreement on the international level to successfully exercise institutional power (IUF 2009).

Finally, TLAs have exercised coalitional power in numerous ways. Antisweatshop campaigns illustrate the multiscalar dimensions of expanding the scope of conflict to mobilize nonlabour stakeholders (see McCallum, this volume). Because industrial action in garment factories (mainly in developing countries) fuels whipsawing and capital flight (Silver 2003), workers have initiated campaigns that instead encourage consumers (mainly in developed countries) to put pressure on retailers to source their garments from factories with ethical labour practices (Johns and Vural 2000: 1202). Campaigns against sweatshop conditions in garment factories have shifted the *scale* of conflict from the local factory floor (the 'sphere of production') to various overseas clothing retail stores and other 'spaces of consumption' (Johns and Vural 2000: 1196; Sadler 2004: 38), thereby simultaneously expanding the *scope* of conflict by enlisting the support of countless potential purchasers of these stores' products (Merk 2009: 606). Because they have the capacity to threaten companies' profits and public images, consumers are better positioned than factory workers to alter the behaviour of retailers and the garment manufacturers that supply them.

For instance, a group of garment workers in Bangladesh fighting to improve labour conditions in a factory that is a major supplier for a US-based retail corporation might form an alliance with a union in the United States, who then uses its ties to consumer organizations to generate public pressure against the retail company to better monitor its suppliers. Such a TLA-consumer coalition could involve general support from a relatively undefined mass of consumers, or it could consist of a well-defined network of prominent NGOs and unions. An example of the latter is the union-NGO coalition that created the Accord on Fire and Building Safety in Bangladesh following the collapse of the Rana Plaza factory complex that killed 1,130 garment workers in 2013. This coalition included several Bangladeshi unions, two global union federations (IndustriALL and UNI), and four NGOs (Clean Clothes Campaign, Worker Rights Consortium, International Labor Rights Forum, and Maquila Solidarity Network). The Accord, which is legally binding, has been signed by over 150 apparel corporations from twenty countries across Europe, North America, Asia, and Australia (Knudsen 2014: 20).

CONCLUSION

Whether the exercise of structural power, institutional power, or coalitional power is context-appropriate—and therefore likely to be effective in compelling an employer to do something it otherwise would not do—depends crucially on that particular employer's core material interests. Core interests, in turn, are informed by the interdependent relationships between that employer and other actors in the global economy, including the members of the TLA with which the employer is in conflict. Relocating conflict across countries or onto other geographic scales further enhances workers' power, especially since conflict can play out in multiple different countries and on several different scales simultaneously. 'Power is not mobilized at one scale or another but at many—and in diverse ways' (Ellem 2006: 374). Transnational labour alliances are in a unique position to counter the power of transnational capital, and evidence suggests that they have begun to do so in increasingly sophisticated ways.

NOTES

1. 'Scale' refers to geographic and socially constructed notions of the local, national, regional, international, and global spaces of human interaction (Lier 2007: 823). Analytically, one can conceive of scale as the 'geographical mechanism whereby spaces exhibiting similarity of conditions are delineated from those experiencing different conditions' (Herod, Rainnie, and McGrath-Champ 2007: 257).

2. In commercial shipping, a 'flag of convenience' vessel is a ship that is registered in a country other than its country of ownership in order to take advantage of the former country's regulatory framework and thus legally justify lower wages and more lax working conditions. See http://www.itfglobal.org/flags-convenience/index.cfm.

TEN

Governance Struggles and Worker Power

The New Spirit of Labour Transnationalism

Jamie K. McCallum[1]

INTRODUCTION

Recent shifts in power among states, corporations, and labour groups have encouraged unions to seek gains through governance struggles, a strategy that enhances the potential for unions to empower workers without winning new rights, and often avoiding the existing regime of rights workers do enjoy. Governance struggles exert a degree of discipline and control over the business practices of corporations, trade agreements, and multilateral governance institutions. In so doing, they alter the otherwise unilinear channels of decision-making that impact workers' ability to organize. Although 'governance' usually implies a generalized political authority vested in nonstate actors and institutions, I use it here specifically to connote worker struggles that seek to enforce new 'rules of engagement' with large corporations. Whereas traditional union strategies seek to exert pressure on management or the state to increase wages or benefits, or to respect a panoply of rights, governance struggles target the corporation at a level removed from the workplace in the hope of establishing rules that will enable workers to exercise power. These rules include neutrality agreements but also, social clauses, codes of conduct, jobbers agreements, and global framework agreements (GFAs), all explained in some detail below. Governance struggles represent a new 'spirit' in labour organizing and activism, an evolving idea about how best to approach the labour question in the twenty-first century.

I begin by examining the idea of 'governance' as it pertains to labour struggles and then outline a genealogy of how governance struggles emerged as an important form of labour activism. Next, this chapter's two case studies draw on lessons from the last two decades of labour transnationalism, or sustained cross-national activism by workers and their allies. The first deals with an interrelated series of campaigns in the private security industry by unions and nongovernmental organizations, and is based on original fieldwork from 2008 to 2012 in North America, Europe, South Africa, and India. The second, based largely on an evaluation of recent scholarship, entails attempts to increase labour standards in the garment industry.

THE IDEA OF GOVERNANCE STRUGGLES—FIGHTING FOR RULES, NOT RIGHTS

Having emerged alongside processes normally associated with globalization, governance is a contested term that broadly refers to the exercise of power in the absence of an overarching political authority. This is usually a constellation of institutions that make decisions and enforce compliance with norms and rules at the supranational level. Political scientists emphasize the significance of the Bretton Woods institutions—the World Trade Organization, the International Monetary Fund, and the World Bank—as governance bodies, especially since the end of the Cold War. International political economy, in contrast, stresses the 'worldwide tilt from states to markets' and the emergence of an arena of 'governance without government'. Still others focus on 'soft law'. Following Foucault, sociologists often use the concept to signify an artful and subtle power formed through networks of knowledge, communication, and control, often resting in social institutions (hospitals, schools, churches, and so on). If the Westphalian system and the New Deal represented the apogee of a state-based system of government, the neoliberalism of the early part of the twenty-first century marks a transition to an era of global governance.

Frances Fox Piven (2008) suggests that ordinary people can exercise power when they break the rules that structure a given social context. In other words, power entails disrupting the interdependent relationships in society that are normally bound by the legal and social rules that comprise the social fabric. More than championing acts of principled civil disobedience, Piven's theory offers an explanation for why acts of disruption, even violent outbursts, are rational responses to exploitation. In contrast, I put Piven's concept in the service of *rulemaking*. More precisely, this means new terms of engagement between labour and capital that allow associational power to become actionable. Modifying the normative framework of employment regulation and the cultural logic that proscribed workers as submissive—in effect, new rules governing the industrial context—is the central way otherwise powerless workers are able to fight back. Although this tendency is true almost everywhere, it is especially evident at the global level where formal rights are virtually nonexistent.

Regulating labour rights across borders would seem to be an ideal test case for the governance paradigm. The dismantling of state protections for workers has increasingly subjected labour conditions to the vicissitudes of the market. International labour law is nonexistent, and unions everywhere are becoming an endangered species. In this instance, the governance paradigm usually proposes a 'participatory' quasidemocratic process involving a variety of generic stakeholders—nongovernmental organizations, unions, business and political leaders—and, occasionally, some kind of human rights campaigner. This logic assumes a nonexistent equivalency between the parties, as though there is some sort of 'democracy' created by allowing business and labour to hash it out in a utopian pluralist society. The end result is, typically, domination by the leading power, yet without any accountability mechanism, leading to what Rodriguez-Garavito (2005) calls 'governance failure'.

Yet several important studies have suggested that the governance institutions not only exert a pull effect on labour strategies (Anner 2011), but they also offer workers political opportunities through which to raise standards, settle grievances, and win rights (Kay 2005, 2011). My analysis extends beyond such 'opportunities' to argue that governance struggles have been most successful when they have been able to rewrite or alter the rules of engagement with capital, whether or not they have won a spectrum of rights.

To highlight the distinction between rules and rights, imagine that workers at a given company's supply chain are granted the right to organize without a change in management's antiunion behaviour. Compare this to a global agreement, jointly signed and won after a campaign that creates a rule stating management must apply universal standards to its full-time and subcontracted employees. Labour, a central factor in much debate about private regulation, has rarely been considered an agent of global governance. Nor is it common to hear of a 'governance gap' with regard to labour conditions, yet such a gap is exactly what GFAs are seeking to fill. This approach therefore joins a handful of others seeking to 'bring labour in' to debates on governance, asserting their fundamental significance in shaping the world economy (Fichter and Helfen 2011, 2012; Kay 2011; Papadakis 2008; Stevis and Boswell 2007).

Governance struggles constitute the primary *modus operandi* of transnational labour activism since the late 1960s. The global union federations (GUFs) are the latest actors to modify this general repertoire through the implementation of GFAs. GFAs are policy instruments signed by trans-national corporations and GUFs that seek to create an arena for global labour relations (Fichter and Helfen 2011). GFAs also link unions around the world in an effort to impact the behaviour of companies throughout their supply chains. GFAs have been studied from myriad directions, but my analysis suggests their greatest utility is as part of a larger strategy to expand the bargaining power of national unions over entire industries by forcing major companies to play by union rules.

Governance struggles have come to play such a large role in global labour activism as a direct outcome of three interrelated phenomena. First, the post–Cold War analysis that placed transnational corporations as the main actors of the world economy, and largely outside the purview of national states, has convinced many parts of the labour movement that it cannot rely on government protections. This is a reasonable theory, for as Peter Evans (2010) demonstrates, the view that states were once friends of labour, and now no longer are, is nostalgic for something that was never truly there. Although it is intended to support the normative globalization thesis, Tilly's (1995b: 21) maxim nonetheless captures a fundamental historic development: 'As states decline, so do workers' rights'. This is exactly why labour turned towards governance struggles—to fight about rules, not rights. Some of the largest and most successful recent victories for unions have been won not through the power vested in them by the National Labor Relations Act, for example, but by circumventing it. The relatively recent failure of unions to successfully win the Employee Free Choice Act, despite massive resources spent trying, is even more of an indication that labour will be unable to depend on national legislation. Instead, the erosion of the right to organize, bargain, and win a contract has pushed some unions towards a strategy of creating new rules. This is even more crucial at the global level, where international labour rights barely exist or are unenforceable. Second, rapidly changing investment patterns and employment regimes, especially in the growing services sector, have emphasized the perceived need for labour to insert itself more firmly into the operating protocols of global business. For many unions, even those without the capacity, resources, or know-how to change, it is now clear that waging battles in one country (against a corporation in many countries) is a recipe for failure. Finally, the increasing consolidation of corporate ownership into fewer hands presents an opportunity for unions to reach more workers and apply more leverage to a sector as a whole with a single campaign.

It is easy to challenge the efficacy of a union movement that is dependent on working collaboratively with corporate management to secure its gains and future power. Likewise, any union that ties its fate to the prosperity of its employer is doomed to be no more than a business agent for the company. But as much as governance processes tie workers' hands, so do state-sanctioned rights regimes. Union elections, run through the

National Labor Relations Act's board, are notoriously bogged down by delays and antiunion appointments to the committee. Unions often find themselves in interminable litigation proceedings, defending their rights through courts and other fora, often with unfavourable outcomes. Unlike the more successful use of individual rights won by people of colour and women during and after the Civil Rights and feminist movements, collective workplace rights have been infamous dead ends. Central to Nelson Lichtenstein's *State of the Union* (2002), the magisterial history of the twentieth-century labour US movement, is the contention that the rights consciousness of the 1960s and 1970s served to undermine the solidarity principle of American unions by deflecting worker struggles from the workplace to the courts. Since that time, he argues, 'If a new set of work rights was to be won, the decisive battle would take place, not in the union hall or across the bargaining table, but in the courts and the legislative chambers' (Lichtenstein 2012: 192).

Some argue that rights, broadly conceived, are fundamentally stronger ways to mobilize workers and communities. In other words, rights are principled statements of entitlement and social access that allow people to make viable and legitimate claims on governments, companies, and other entities. As one labour lawyer put it, 'rights are enabling' (private correspondence with Cesar Rodriguez 2014). Rules, by contrast, are said to come 'from outside' and usually seek to limit rather than expand collective action.

But forms of governance can also be seen as empowering, however, because workers can be said to have a genuine impact within their own workplaces. The governance model implies that workers become comanagers of corporations. The most dramatic example of this is the German model of codetermination, where unions, at least in theory, help set production schedules and output quotas, and other rules governing the labour process and employment relationship—wages, hours, benefits, vacation, pension investments, and so on. At the global industrial relations level, another example is the GFA signed between UNI Global Union and ISS, a large property-services company in 2003 (renegotiated in 2008). The agreement extends beyond the required four core International Labour Organization conventions to include 'a commitment to pay the legally required minimum wages and to respect limitations on the hours of work and overtime obligations' (ISS and UNI 2008). Moreover, searching for a platform from which to launch a global organizing campaign, one that also helped to stabilize labour relations within the company's corporate periphery, it convinced management to seed an 'organizing fund'. Such a pool could be tapped when union and corporate priorities concurred that a campaign would positively impact the company's portfolio and worker standards. Obviously, winning this involved working with a supportive management. While this model is more cooperative, the risk that the labour organization becomes just another planning apparatus, rather than a political and social force, is worth considering.

A competing governance model, the one embodied in the GFA signed by UNI and Group 4 Securicor (G4S), is more adversarial. This less collaborative model can be seen as an archetypical example of what Müller-Jentsch (2004) call a 'conflict partnership'. The union has inserted itself into the boardroom by force and has demanded the company accept a series of its demands. While this has granted them less 'voice' in the quotidian workplace, the risks associated with bureaucratization are decreased.

General tendencies towards informalization and precarity almost everywhere, including the Rhineland social democracies, suggest that the cooperative governance model is unlikely to flourish within large corporations. This fact is one of the driving forces for governance struggles: Those with anticipated outcomes that are inherently adversarial, even if they appear on the surface to be collaborative. This is what was meant when a unionist I interviewed described her union as 'frenemies' with the company after a corporate campaign. Campaigns to win a semblance of governance will expand in the future, and they will conclude less as genuine partners and more as reluctant cosigners of a tenuous accord.

GOVERNANCE STRUGGLES: A BRIEF HISTORY

There are three avenues through which unions have tried to exercise governance in the public and private sphere: social clauses, codes of conduct, and GFAs. Can a governance regime oversee the observance/implementation of basic rules and regulations pertaining to labour standards? One method allows the World Trade Organization or North American Free Trade Agreement, to take two examples, the power to sanction those member-states that are out of compliance with agreed-upon norms. This strategy is called a 'social clause'. Space constraints require that we save the examination of the social clause for a later time, and instead I will devote the remainder of this chapter to addressing two other pathways: codes of conduct and GFAs.

Codes of Conduct

A panoply of organizations has proposed corporate regulation schemes since the 1960s. The Sullivan Principles, which in 1977 enforced a code of conduct on transnational corporations operating in apartheid South Africa, and the MacBride Principles, which set standards for US companies operating in Northern Ireland, are two classic examples. Beginning in the 1970s, corporate social responsibility groups diluted actual governance efforts with public relations ploys, as corporations began adopting certain core values, standards, or practices in some formal fashion en masse. As a result, codes of conduct suffered, or went into abeyance, under the new idea that business could govern itself.

About a decade later, however, a variety of labour-initiated worker struggles erupted that took the form of governance struggles, reinvigorating the codes of conduct strategy (see Anner and Evans 2004; Armbruster-Sandoval 2005; Compa 2004; Esbenshade 2004; Seidman 2008). Such struggles sought to 'shape corporate conduct' and restrain corporate power through 'binding rules' (Murray 1998).

Most of these codes began as principled statements on corporate behaviour, but quickly evolved into dense juridical documents. Most attempted to apply a set of standards to be followed, a local implementation procedure, and a monitoring provision. The code strategy provided an obvious inroad towards transnational advocacy networks (Keck and Sikkink 1998) that helped establish a broad base of support and a greater degree of legitimacy and international media attention to the struggle. Almost all the successful codes were won and defended by such networks of linked activists.

By now, most codes of conduct are understood as abject failures. They have proliferated—hundreds, if not thousands, of corporate codes of conduct have been signed—as labour conditions within the sweatshop economy have worsened. In most cases, companies submitted so willingly because the regulatory sanctions were so minimal and the monitoring process voluntary (Pearson and Seyfang 2001).

Global Framework Agreements

GFAs are contracts signed between GUFs and transnational corporations that attempt to secure labour standards throughout a company's operations. GFAs also link unions around the world in an effort to impact the behaviour of companies throughout their supply chains. Twenty years ago, there was only one GFA; today, there are over one hundred. By creating new employment rules, workers get a voice in how their work lives are structured.

The overwhelming majority of GFAs are not enforceable in court and can therefore be considered nonbinding. (Their status as voluntary agreements, however, does not make them nonbinding, as many voluntary agreements in the United States have such standing.) While this has been seen as a primary weakness, scholars and labour activists routinely argue that hard law regulations simply do not work—the prevalence of wage theft and other 'unfair labour practices' in the United States is ample testament to this. In other words, the problem is not one of soft versus hard law, but hard versus soft power.

GFAs are significant for many reasons. Here, I am most interested in their power as a tool for labour governance. Global agreements are potentially part of a long-term industrial strategy to build power within a sector or region's largest players. In other words, as global employers within a particular industry agree to union neutrality (through a GFA), they provide employees with potential strength beyond the workplace, as these companies can become part of an effort to pressure other industrial leaders to sign GFAs as well. Moreover, because union organizing in the services sector is usually driven by regional market imperatives, not specific corporate targets, a GFA's impact should be measured by the extent to which it expands the union's influence over the industrial landscape. In this way, GFAs offer a route to challenge company power in the absence of worker rights by establishing new rules. Global agreements can be considered the result of a historical struggle to govern global capitalism and build worker power in an arena in which a more traditional approach based on worker rights in insufficient. Such a perspective contributes an understanding of GFAs as not mere policy instruments, but useful platforms for worker organising.

Interviews with the staff of several GUFs reveal a mix of cynicism and optimism about the prospects for GFAs to become effective union tools anytime soon. The perception of GFAs as weak, even by those whose mission it is to secure them, does not inspire confidence in the strategy. Nonetheless, this chapter explains a few ways in which they are used rather well.

CASE STUDIES

Conduct Codes and Jobbers Agreements

The garment sector was the dominant industry of the nineteenth century across the world (Silver 2003). Consequently, garment sector worker activity has a long history of transnationalism, or sustained collaboration across national borders. In many ways, garment workers have always been responding to globalization. However, in the final decades of the twentieth century, trade agreements and other political-economic developments increased the connections between producers and consumers in Latin America. Unions made a point, therefore, to encourage collaboration of worker movements across the North-South divide.

In 1997, US college students formed United Students against Sweatshops (USAS), and by the early 2000s, it boasted over two hundred chapters in the United States (Featherstone 2002). USAS sought explicitly to change the conversation about why labour standards are so low in the global garment industry. The problem was not, in the main, corrupt governments or low-road factory managers, but rather the leading firms of the global apparel industry. They therefore set themselves to the task of disciplining those firms. In particular, activists developed a strategy that involved forcing garment companies to sign 'codes of conduct' that would govern their behaviour within a growing sector composed of maquiladoras and free trade zones (see Anner 2011).

Students and their universities played a decisive role, given their position in the global supply chain of college apparel. Although universities comprise a meagre 2 per cent of US apparel sales (Traub-Werner 2002: 194), USAS used its leverage to insert itself into an inchoate movement. Seeking to increase the monitoring and implementation of codes of conduct, USAS and its allies founded the Worker Rights Consortium (WRC) and funded by-products from apparel sales in over one hundred US universities and colleges. The WRC played a critical role in many campaigns for garment sector labour rights by trying to hold corporations more accountable to a new set of industrial rules and more transparent business practices.

Compa (2004) suggests that such codes stake out a 'third way' to enforce labour rights and standards, and substitute a government's apparent inability to monitor the growing number of factories within its borders, and to compensate for the declining success of trade unionism. Given the private nature of the codes, the content varied considerably, but most attempted to apply a set of standards to be followed, a local implementation procedure, and a monitoring provision. The code strategy provided an obvious inroad towards transnational advocacy networks (Keck and Sikkink 1998) that helped establish a broad base of support, and a greater degree of legitimacy and international media attention to the struggle.

Almost all the successful codes were won and defended by such networks of linked activists. The Kukdong factory in Mexico, the Korean-owned Kimi plant in Honduras, the Phillips-Van Heusen plant in Guatemala, and the Mandarin plant in El Salvador all won better standards through codes of conduct, not traditional union organizing (Anner and Evans 2004). But even these cases proved ephemeral as management often relocated after workers won wage increases (Anner 2011).

In 2005, USAS developed the Designated Suppliers Program (DSP) to help solidify gains won through campaigning. Universities that were pressured to adopt the DSP would have to source their materials from garment factories with a set of rules governing the industrial context, usually regarding fair wages, conditions, and union access. This usually meant that brands would be required to subsidize minimum wages and other benefits even at factories they did not own. The heads of leading apparel brands embarked on a tour of college campuses to dissuade major universities from signing the DSP. Even against this pressure, almost fifty universities in the United States signed on. However, the DSP fell victim to dubious potential antitrust violations and has not been fully implemented. Likewise, gains won through campaigns at individual factories slowly disappeared as factories migrated to Asia after the conclusion of the Multifibre Agreement in 2005.

The recent campaign to organize the apparel manufacturer Russell Athletics, in Honduras, offers a new dimension of transnational garment worker activity, and one that offers promise where others have failed, as they were able to constrain management's ability to simply relocate. In 2007, Honduran workers began a campaign alongside the General Confederation of Workers that targeted the Russell Athletics apparel manufacturer, a corporate stepchild of Fruit of the Loom. According to local organizers, the union began with a tepid and 'conciliatory' approach, seeking to avoid conflict, which they quickly learned would not be insufficient. Early in the process, 145 workers were fired illegally for union activity, and the General Confederation of Workers was unable to fight successfully for their jobs back. Russell had remained a union-free company for one hundred years in the United States, and it was not about to change its position in Honduras.[2]

Nearly defeated, a union activist later stumbled upon an old business card of the WRC in her office. She telephoned its Washington office, thereby starting the union's first transnational labour campaign. In the mid- to late 1990s, the emergence of new organizations such as USAS and the WRC, both outgrowths of student-worker international solidarity campaigns, was a critical phase in the movement to target global sweatshops, especially in Latin America. Through these institutions, campus groups came together in a buyer-driven campaign for labour rights at the companies that produced their college's apparel. They forced their college administrators to only source garments from companies that had signed a code of conduct.

After hearing from the union in Honduras, the WRC produced a report that denounced Russell for firing the workers for what they determined was legal union activity. The report, widely distributed throughout North American activist networks, caught the attention of USAS, which quickly joined the campaign against Russell. USAS organized speaking tours of the fired Honduran workers and pressured campus administrations to choose union-friendly sources for its apparel. Eventually, this work led to the largest boycott in its history, with over one hundred universities terminating their apparel contracts with Russell based on its track record in Honduras. Everywhere the demand was the same—let Russell workers organize without fear of management retaliation.

Within months, the company entered into good-faith negotiations with the local union and the WRC. In 2009, it announced plans to open a new factory, rehire all the fired workers, begin contract negotiations with its workers at one plant, and remain neutral at its other seven plants when workers tried to organize. The *New York Times* called it the 'biggest victory by far' for organizers of apparel sweatshops (Greenhouse 2009), and it is perhaps the clearest example of the boomerang campaign strategy involving labour organizations.

Organizers are hoping that the revival of an older strategy—so-called jobbers agreements—will offer garment sector workers a better future. A recent flurry of academic work has mirrored a renewed interest in labour activists in this idea (see Anner, Bair, and Blasi 2012; Kumar and Mahoney 2013; Robbins 2013). Jobbers agreements are agreements between unions and brands that govern working conditions in the factories of suppliers. A jobber is a brand—today the familiar names such as Nike, Adidas, Reebok, and Russell—that subcontracts the production of garments, which they then sell to major retailers. Jobbers agreements are different from collective bargaining agreements because they extend control beyond the purview of the factories owned by the brands to their suppliers, regardless of there being a union there or not. The original jobbers agreements, in the garment industries of the 1920s, were certainly not responses to 'globalization' in the way we typically think of today. But the revival of the strategy has been because the major brands produce garments in other countries, often beyond the level of regulation and union activity. These more recent jobbers agreements sometimes establish rules similar to those found in strong GFAs. For example, a recent agreement signed by the Liz Claiborne company and the garment workers' union includes provisions whereby the company will pay for an industry-wide independent monitoring process to help regulate working conditions.[3]

Jobbers agreements, similar to the codes described above, are textbook governance struggles, as they seek to discipline a company's business strategy through pressure applied from outside the workplace, and sometimes on an entity that does not even directly employee the workers in question.

Almost two decades after the birth of the modern antisweatshop movement, almost all the evidence points to a dramatic failure to improve working and living conditions for workers in the global garment industry, the main target of myriad campaigns. This has prompted the search for a new approach. Time will tell whether the Russell victory lasts longer than others in the area. Ultimately, however, codes of conduct and regional pressure campaigns have obvious limitations. With concentrations of cheap labour in so many places around the globe, capital flight still provides a way around submitting to a code. Given these conditions, unions have increasingly sought global corporate governance. The GFAs' strategy therefore demands examination.

The Global Campaign against Group 4 Securicor

From 2003 until 2008, private security guards and their unions around the world waged a global campaign against G4S, the third largest employer in the world behind Walmart and Foxconn. G4S security guards

stand watch over everything from strip malls to nuclear weapons labora-
tories, from the tennis courts at Wimbledon to the battlefields of Iraq.
Through a series of coordinated actions—some involving everyday
workers, some almost exclusively through the top staff of various unions—G4S was forced to submit to a GFA in December of 2008, a contract
of sorts that commits the corporate leadership to respect four basic International Labour Organization conventions against forced labour, child
labour, nondiscrimination, and, most contentiously, the freedom to form
a union without management interference. This latter commitment, often
known as a 'neutrality agreement', was a significant step forward for
UNI Global Union and Service Employees International Union (SEIU),
the two unions primarily involved in the campaign. Workers won wage
increases, access for union organizers, union recognition, benefits increases, and political gains as well. This chapter explores this campaign,
one of the most successful and aggressive, ever waged at the global level.
While there are many important lessons to be drawn from its broad scope
and transnational character, I find what is most compelling is the way it
illuminates a recent tendency within the labour movement to engage in
what I call 'governance struggles'.

Against the failed attempts to unionize the company's US-based subsidiary, Wackenhut, the achievements of the global effort are all the more
perplexing. During the years-long campaign to win the GFA, UNI built a
network of other unions and nongovernmental organizations that pressured the company from above and below. The result was perhaps the
most aggressive and comprehensive campaign for worker power ever
undertaken by the global labour movement. Below, I consider the campaign as a paradigmatic governance struggle, both in its dimension as a
corporate campaign and in the way it used a GFA.

In 2003, some of the same union organizers who had worked on the
Justice for Janitors campaign began organizing low-wage workers in the
security industry. They made significant headway. Whereas the janitors'
struggles had been accomplished by low-income Latino/a migrants, security guard organizing became the largest labour campaign for African
American workers since A. Philip Randolph organized the Pullman Car
Porters in the 1920s. But almost immediately, it became clear that G4S's
antiunion stance was sufficiently determined to negate the possibility of a
successful domestic campaign. It was the company's intransigence that
eventually propelled the SEIU to abandon a purely national strategy,
setting the stage for a dramatic global confrontation.

SEIU looked outside the United States for allies—first in Europe, then
in the Global South. As workers occupied corporate headquarters in Indonesia, struck in South Africa and Malawi, and crashed shareholder
meetings in London, the SEIU and UNI worked to tarnish the company's
public profile and weaken its status with potential clients through a corporate campaign. Eventually, and after more than a little prodding, the

Organisation for Economic Co-operation and Development determined that the company had violated fundamental worker rights in four countries, and a major investor in G4S withdrew its financial support out of moral outrage. In 2008, after five years of battle, the company finally capitulated and submitted to a GFA.

When management's retaliatory threats were neutralized via the global agreement, security guards went on the offensive, winning concrete economic gains in India, South Africa, Malawi, Mozambique, Indonesia, and Poland. New security guard unions emerged in Nepal, Congo, and Ghana. Security guards in the United States, who began the campaign years earlier, won a clear path to union recognition in nine major cities.

South African guards ousted racist managers who had regularly referred to workers as *kefirs* and built stronger workplace unions. The social movement character of trade unionism that all but disappeared in the postapartheid era seemed reinvigorated through this campaign—a massive strike, workplace militancy, transnational collaboration, and community involvement. In contrast, the Indian situation did not recall an old tradition; it reflected a new one: The growing tendency in India's labour movement towards independent unionism outside of political party control.

In both places, the commitment to a global strategy paid off locally, as workers won wage gains and increased their membership. Keck and Sikkink (1998) demonstrate that social movements in poor countries can make use of a 'boomerang strategy' by enlisting the support of rich country allies. That process is indeed present here, but we also see how unions in the North were strengthened by recruiting solidarity from unions in the Global South, a 'boomerang in reverse'. The campaign against G4S is probably the most extensive and aggressive campaign ever waged by unions in so many places at once.

Corporate campaigns are first and foremost top-down endeavours, as their critics are quick to point out. But they are not only that. The GFA was in this case enforceable in South Africa and helped inspire unintended positive outcomes among Indian guards as well. In South Africa, guards used the agreement to demand access rules. Once organizers were able to talk to workers without fear of management reprisal, organizing exploded. The local union brought thousands of guards into the union, increasing its membership among guards by 40 per cent. By contrast, in India, the company's largest market, workers were unable to hold management accountable to respect the GFA. Instead, the social dialogue process that ensued did win some legislative gains for average security guards—wage increases, pension benefits, time off, and identification cards. In this sense, gains at the 'top' of the campaign had direct impacts on workers' ability to organize at the bottom.

This brief sketch suggests just one instance where a corporate campaign restricted management's freedom to completely govern the employment relationship. Instead, without winning any rights, they were nonetheless able to discipline the company sufficiently to organize. While the expectation is that rules are upheld, the largely voluntary nature of the agreements means that they are technically more easily broken too. However, my research suggests that they are also, in practice, sometimes stronger modes of enforcing norms and regulations. As one union organizer said, 'We've had a better track record of holding them [companies] to things we set together than laws and formal regulations. . . . When things go wrong, we just point—"hey you signed this, now do it."'

CONCLUSION

This chapter explores the emergence of a new form of transnational labour organizing. These new strategies, that I call governance struggles, are directed at modifying the normative framework of employment regulation and the cultural logic that proscribes workers as submissive. It is an attempt to theorize the strategic transition towards a kind of activism that seeks to make new rules rather than win new rights. One of the reasons governance struggles evolved was because they mirror broader transformations of political economy generally. It is in many ways the most logical form of labour regulation in the neoliberal era, even if not the most effective.

However, the G4S campaign was successful because it neutralized the company while simultaneously creating the conditions for workers to organize, build new organizations, renew old traditions, and experiment with new strategies. That happened because unions and workers found a way to unleash their power—not because of capitalist globalization, but despite it, and not because they won new rights, but because they made new rules. Now that the three largest global providers (G4S, Securitas, and International Services) have agreed to respect the union's access to worksites, there is greater capacity to organize guards and pressure other companies to work with the union. From this perspective, the G4S campaign was the most important component of a long-term industrial strategy to exert governance over the private security industry that could, in turn, lead to mass organizing on a scale that was previously impossible.

The kinds of new rules that are developed by GFAs and codes of conduct are almost uniformly described as rights by those who win or seek them. That they are conceived as rights is important and logical. Rights have long been considered *the* goal of social movement organizing, and the main perceived path to power for those who lack basic privileges. But this doesn't make them rights. Codes of conduct and GFAs provide a rules-based logic that can often be seen as an addendum to the normal operating protocols of big business. As such, they may have a limited impact in the long run. This chapter, however, was inspired by some cautious optimism. Governance struggles try to carve out a space, within the private sphere of global capital, often outside or underneath the purview of the state, where workers can organize and, once in a while, win.

NOTES

1. This chapter builds on the book *Global Unions, Local Power* (McCallum 2013).

2. Information on the Honduras campaign was gleaned from a public presentation by some of its primary participants during Autumn 2013 via Skype at Middlebury College.

3. See "Article 11" in the jobbers agreement by and between Liz Claiborne Inc. and UNITE.

ELEVEN

What Role Can Trade Union Education Play in Enhancing Transnational Labour Solidarity?

Bianca Föhrer

INTRODUCTION

Trade union education is considered 'a key resource for the construction of trade unionism' (Bridgford and Stirling 2000: 5), or 'the key to trade union capacity building' (International Labour Organization 2007). As to Ulisses Garrido, current education director of the European Trade Union Institute (ETUI), labour education is 'education in the service of trade union action, socio-political in nature. It helps to build an identity' (ETUI 2013: iii).

Shelley (2007) and Spencer (2007) argue that trade union education can support union activism. Indeed, there is much empirical evidence where education played a vital role in forging successful cross-border solidarity action (e.g., Croucher 2004; Erne 2008; Novelli 2011).

A policy officer at the European Public Services Union pushes the purpose of labour education even further. For him, it is not only about activating trade union members and shaping their view towards certain values. It is also about activating society and shaping the view of citizens towards certain values (interview, 29 January 2014).

Despite the obvious importance of specialized education for workers' representatives, research on trade union education has remained sparse (Ball 2003; Miller and Stirling 1998; Stirling 2007), not only in Europe, but also worldwide (Croucher and Cotton 2009).

The purpose of this chapter is to address this gap. It proposes that educational activities can enhance transnational labour solidarity by creating five spaces: (1) space of encounter, (2) space of exchange, (3) space of insight, and (4) space of action. Together, they can form a further (5) space of development as a person as well as a group.

Arguably, educational activities may especially develop labour representatives' transnational personal, collective, and social identity. Identity is crucial for sustaining solidarity action. Yet, the concept of identity has remained rather marginalized in the industrial relations discipline (Bridgman and McLaughlin 2013), in particular with a view to how actors actively construct identities (Greer and Hauptmeier 2012).

METHODOLOGY

All empirical material was compiled during a research period at the ETUI between September 2013 and February 2014.[1] In an effort to triangulate, data was collected from different perspectives both qualitatively and quantitatively.

Besides literature review, empirical material stems from a selected European Works Council (EWC) training event. It is a critical case, because the ETUI is unquestionably the continent's exemplary service provider in the area of cross-border labour education. In addition to nonparticipant observations during the educational activity, empirical evidence originates from interviews, surveys, and documents.

Informal face-to-face conversations were held with the EWC coordinator and three EWC members during the training days. Follow-up emails were sent to both the EWC coordinator and chair. Other relevant interviews were conducted with the ETUI education director, as well as two education officers who are responsible for EWC training. All conversations were face to face. Some were formal and semistructured; others less structured and more informal.

Data was retrieved through two nonrepresentative online surveys. The first questionnaire addressed the Beckers EWC members. Six of eight participants from France (three), the United Kingdom (one), Sweden (one), and Germany (one) replied. The five men and one woman were all unionized. The second was composed for the ETUI Education Day/Conference 2013 and was sent to seventy-six event participants. Of the forty-two respondents, all but one are representatives from thirty-one European Trade Union Confederation–affiliated national trade union confederations, in twenty-one European countries. Nearly two-thirds of them belong to union management, mostly in the role of head of education department. The survey results are hence likely biased in favour of a top-down view. A third of all respondents are active trainers. The sample comprised 40 per cent females and 60 per cent males.

Documents were gathered from the ETUI internal database for getting information on the process of organizing the EWC training.

THEORETICAL APPROACH

Labour representatives may have the knowledge to collaborate with comrades beyond national borders. They may not also have the skills to engage in transnational solidarity actions. Yet, in order to put theory into practice and act transnationally with powerful impact, workers, and their representatives, have to consider cross-border actions as a meaningful priority. Hence, the appropriate attitude is at the heart of effective crossnational labour collaboration. Workers' representatives need to identify transnationally, both as a person and a representative body. Therefore, three kinds of identity shall build the theoretical frame for this chapter, namely personal, collective, and social identity.

Personal Identity

Scholars appear divided about the definition of personal identity. According to Bratton et al. (2010: 116), it is 'the ongoing process of self-development through which we construct a unique sense of ourselves'. Polletta and Jasper (2001: 298) point similarly to 'the bundle of traits that we believe make us unique'. These traits are what Bratton et al. (2010) would however distinguish as 'personality'. All of them seem agreed with Pries (2013: 25) that personal identity is 'a complex interplay of perceiving, interpreting, negotiating and defining'. These deliberations aim to answer a question, which is not only fairly philosophical, but also very intimate and challenging for every human being: Who am I?

In short, personal identity is the definition of and connection to self. It creates meaning for our actions and beliefs (Melucci 1996). And yet, this concept has remained 'an underanalysed level of the self' (Hitlin 2003: 118).

Defining ourselves involves the mind, heart, and soul, respectively, 'rational calculation', 'affective bonds', and 'intuitive capacity' (Melucci 1996: 66). Hitlin (2003) advocates correspondingly that commitments to certain values are core to personal identity formation. Thus, personal identity seems to originate from certain knowledge, attitudes, and roles which either nature has predetermined or we have chosen individually and collectively within our man-made economic-financial, political-institutional, and sociocultural structures: Identities are 'outcomes of external opportunity structures [and] internal self-awareness' (Pries 2013: 25).

One form of personal identity that appears particularly promising for fostering cross-border collaboration is *transnational personal identity*. According to Chaney (1979: 209, cited in Park 2007: 202), this means to have one's 'feet in two societies'. This definition appears quite limited, though. Today, having a transnational personal identity arguably means to have one's feet in *at least* two societies.

The logic behind transnational personal identity is therefore not 'either or' but 'as well as'. It means adding to the national identity an equally appreciated transnational dimension that can comprise again, one or more other national identities. It means to be culturally hybrid: a person who chooses to live 'with and within cultural difference' (Pries 2013: 334), who embraces the 'strength of combination' (Beck 2008: 226), who acknowledges what is general and specific, common and special, or what Pries (2013: 26) calls a combination of 'universalism and particularism'. In so being, workers' representatives would overcome boundaries that are both external and internal to self, and make mental, emotional and spiritual, as well as physical, connections to people and places around the world.

Collective Identity

Like personal identity, collective identity describes an ongoing human process to create meaning for ourselves and our actions (Holland, Fox, and Daro 2008; Knudsen, Whittall, and Huijgen 2007; Melucci 1996). Whereas for personal identity, meaning derives from characteristics and roles that make sense to us individually, meaning nurturing collective identity arises through feeling membership to a particular group. This group can either be real or imagined (Knudsen, Whittall, and Huijgen 2007; Polletta and Jasper 2001).

The group or 'we-feeling' (Gamson 1991; Kotthoff 2007) is the result of mutually reinforcing interplay of the group members' individual cognition, emotion, and active relationships (Melucci 1995). Of these three components, emotions and their role in shaping collective identity have hitherto remained underresearched (Polletta and Jasper 2001). Emotions are obviously underrepresented in collective action too: 'there is a lot of talking, but an inability to produce emotional connection, to *sense* the feeling of the other' (McDonald 2002: 121, emphasis in original).

Central to collective identity formation are the perceptions of unity, mutual recognition, and equilibrium (Melucci 1995) as well as sameness and congruence (Knudsen, Whittall, and Huijgen 2007). Group unity cannot, however, be extrinsically imposed, but must be intrinsically created (Hyman 1994). It must also be constantly maintained (Melucci 1995, 1996).

Corresponding to personal transnational identity, *transnational collective identity* appears inevitable if cross-national labour action is to arise (Knudsen, Whittall, and Huijgen 2007; Kohler 2006). But, collective identity can conflict with personal identity (Gamson 1991). To align both, collective action may help if it has a wider purpose than constructing collective identity, namely finding one's place in the world, as individual as much as part of a group (McDonald 2002).

McDonald therefore suggests moving from the conception of 'collective identity' to 'public experience of self'. This would require a paradigm shift from analyzing social movements and conflicts fairly instrumentally through a view on mobilizing mechanisms, to a more organic perspective on the group members' 'shared struggle for personal experience' (McDonald 2002: 125).

Social Identity

Social identity is 'the perception of a "sameness" or "belongingness" to a human collective with common values, goals or experiences' (Bratton et al. 2010: 116). Put otherwise, social identity is the perceived connection of self to a certain group of people who we believe to have something in common with, without being a group member. We arrive at this kind of 'collective self' through comparisons and self-categorisation (Hogg and Ridgeway 2003). Social identity seems thus a particular area of personal identity, which hints at who we are as an individual at a given point in time, and might want to be as part of a group.

We can, and certainly usually have more than one group affiliation, that is called plural or 'multiple identities' (Bratton et al. 2010: 116; Deaux and Martin 2003: 105; Timming and Veersma 2007: 41). Consequently, social identity can be sourced from one or more collective identities, without being part of every respective group. For example, we may identify with a certain soccer team, trade union, or multinational company brand without playing, affiliating, or working for any of them.

Given this, collective identities may be found at multiple levels, such as local, national, supranational, and international. The reach of our sense of belonging can therefore fall rather short or long. Representatives whose social identity is not influenced by collective identities beyond national borders would arguably hamper transnational solidarity, because their perception of sameness does not reach far enough.

Perceiving an international community of labour is admittedly quite challenging, because only a small portion of this perception can stem from personal contacts or 'real attachment'. The vast remainder of it would have to originate from 'imagined attachment'. As Deaux and Martin (2003: 114) note, 'social identity can include great numbers of people whom one has never met or will never meet'. Thus, global, as much as European labour, must predominantly be a 'community of the mind' (Chayko 2002, quoted in Park 2007) or an 'imagined community' (Anderson 2006; Polletta and Jasper 2001) instead of what might be introduced conversely as 'community of the body' or 'corporeal community'.

Special to communities of the mind is that they are enabled 'not by way of their travels and social activities, but through identity practices'

(Park 2007: 207). These identity practices would aim at creating a '*socio-mental* space' (Chayko 2002, cited in Park 2007: 207, emphasis in original). Arguably, this space would invite thoughts and memories into our minds, emotions into our hearts, and images in front of our inner eye. From this state of being, we can create what Park (2007) calls 'cognitive' or 'interpersonal social bonds'.

Ultimately, social identity—whether real or imagined—is the basis for solidarity (Knudsen, Whittall, and Huijgen 2007).

EUROPEAN WORKS COUNCIL TRAINING AT THE EUROPEAN TRADE UNION INSTITUTE: THE BECKERS BASE

The following section investigates, through the example of an ETUI EWC training, the extent that trade union education, at the European level, facilitates representatives' transnational personal, collective, and social identity.

The Beckers EWC training took place from 9 to 11 December 2013 in a hotel very close to the ETUI in Brussels.[2] The EWC had met seven months earlier in London for the very first time. The delegates were a selection of the total of fourteen EWC members from eight countries. The group of eight came from France (four), the United Kingdom (one), Sweden (one), Germany (one), and Poland (one). They met in order to:

- become familiar with the new legal standards for EWCs and compare them to the practice and the EWC agreement of Beckers;
- improve communication and cohesion among the members and deputies of the EWC;
- familiarize the participants with the differences and similarities between the systems of workers representation in the European Union in general and the Beckers subsidiaries in particular;
- be able to anticipate changes in the company, and to represent the workforces' interests; and
- develop a common view and understanding about the role and responsibilities of the EWC representatives.

Six translators (two German, two Polish, and two French) facilitated cross-border communication. The transnational trainer switched between German, French, English, and he spoke Swedish, like a native. Also the executive manager involved in the planning participated constructively from the first evening until the following afternoon in fluent English. Not all EWC members appreciated his participation, though some felt inhibited to talk freely. Eventually, the educational activity was a learning opportunity in many ways.

Space of Encounter (Ort der Begegnung)

As a residential activity, the Beckers training was firstly an opportunity for the EWC members to meet each other as well as other people in person. As the Swedish delegate described 'I had possibility to . . . meet the old and new nice people of course' (email, 12 December 2013). Since the EWC had met once before, the training provided space to meet some national colleagues, the EWC coordinator, as well as the management representative again. New people were obviously the trainer, the translators, the information technology technician, and the author.

New for the participants was also the venue in Brussels. Thus, educational activities are also opportunities to meet people (again) in a different environment. Usually, this environment holds two different settings where one is more formal than the other. The training room is more formal, because here the participants are asked to perform tasks. Coffee/lunch breaks, dinner, and any other rather informal situations inside and outside the training room invite people to speak about more than work-related issues. In this way, EWC members may encounter known and previously unknown people, and gain insight into their behaviour as well as learn of different circumstances from several perspectives.

Space of Exchange (Ort des Austausches)

Thanks to the space of encounter, the EWC training offered opportunities for the Beckers delegates to communicate with each other and other people. The communication flow went in multiple ways. The participants received information rather passively by listening to and observing the trainer's PowerPoint presentations. Sometimes, both trainer and the group posed questions to each other. The trainer also encouraged the group to share information more actively among themselves. This included past theoretical knowledge and practical experiences, but also present opinions and future ideas.

The introductory session, for example, was an opportunity to present oneself and exchange facts regarding everybody's country, national industrial relations system, challenges at work, and personal hobbies. In so doing, the trainer created a basis for further formal, more work-related, and more informal personal communication. It was also an initial opportunity to recognise 'mutuality despite difference' (Hyman 2011) and acknowledge how 'united in diversity' the supranational labour representatives actually are.

Mutuality showed itself not only privately in some hobbies, but also professionally in their experience as local labour representatives. Sharing the challenges, which the EWC members had been facing with their local employers for approximately the last two years, seemed an especially welcomed opportunity to open up and release their emotional pain. With

the exception of the Swedish delegate, the author could see the despera-
tion in their faces and hear the feelings of powerlessness and insecurity
through their speech. Their anger concerned not only management and
their often disrespectful and deceitful behaviour. In particular, the German delegate was also concerned about inefficiencies in the production
process, as well as the damages these can cause to the health of both
employees and nature.

Besides local challenges, local solutions were discussed. The German
and the Swedish colleague, for instance, shared information on the production conditions in their respective subsidiary. Through exchanging
knowledge on Swedish best practices and those German (which should
not be copied), both delegates are now in a position to better evaluate
their own situation. Moreover, the German comrade has now got a powerful argument to create upward change in production which can be seen
a triple win-win, namely for employees, environment, and business expenditure.

Space of Insight (Ort der Erkenntnis)

Exchanging information may result in hearing content we already
know and learn anew. Based on such data, the EWC activity invited
participants to reflect on self, others, and the context.

Reflections had started already during the educational activity. In a
conversation with the author, the German delegate realized at the second
evening that 'in London, I was a stranger. Here [in Brussels] I am already
a bit better' (translation by the author). Initially put up as a reserve member, he came to feel more comfortable among his colleagues, since he was
meeting some of them for the second time. The EWC chair concluded at
the end of the session in plenary that 'training gives you confidence—and
confidence drives things'. A French select committee member suggested
after the final lunch that the EWC had become more of a team.

Reflections continued beyond the training days too. The German delegate believed that 'the more we meet, the better we will get to know each
other' (quoted from the survey, translation by the author). At the same
time, he found the training too short. Another French select committee
member realized that the training had provided her with plenty of information that will enable her to better fulfil her supranational duties. The
Swedish and a third French delegate agreed similarly that they had
gained better knowledge of their task as EWC. Remarkably, while the
former stresses his individual representative role, like the aforementioned French select committee member, the latter refers to 'notre' (our)
EWC as a group.

Thus, thanks to the deliberations which the EWC training encouraged,
assumedly all course participants arrived at new insights. These illumi-

nations can concern the individual representative as much as the collectives they are committed to.

Space of Action (Ort des Handelns)

The increased confidence which the EWC chair noted earlier is very likely interconnected with the fourth function of labour educational activities, namely to provide opportunities to act in a safe environment with immediate feedback from an expert. In order to act, the participants were confronted by the trainer with case studies, which either mirror or are taken from the real world. Their solutions were then discussed in plenary. Such exercises are supposed to prepare the participants for similar upcoming situations so that suitable common approaches, strategies, communication, behaviour, and so on can be identified.

In an effort to make the two days a participatory learning experience, the trainer used group, pair, and individual tasks to activate the participants. In pairs, the participants analysed the Beckers EWC agreement in view of key elements of the recast directive. The aim was to find out strengths and weaknesses of their own EWC agreement in comparison to another anonymous (but real) one. Since the Beckers EWC is a newly established representation body, the trainer asked the participants furthermore to debate, in two groups of four (French speakers/others), what the purpose of their EWC is, and what internal rules the members should give themselves in order to become an effective transnational representation body. Particularly enlightening was an exercise on intercultural communication where also the management representative plus, exceptionally, the author took part in. The results of the three groups showed, on the one hand, that the perception of right and wrong human behaviour may diverge considerably. On the other, individual opinions may deviate from the collectively negotiated outcome.

Space of Development (Ort der Entwicklung)

How participant-centred the learning experience becomes is, however, not only dependent on the trainers' facilitation abilities. It depends also on how the participants engage with the learning opportunities provided. This being said, EWC training can eventually open up a space of further development. Whether the course participants indeed tap into this space and use it to advance their knowledge, attitudes, and skills is left to their discretion.

The participants' statements indicate that they have probably all gained in terms of knowledge and attitude. Besides confidence, the EWC chair developed especially 'knowledge of [European Union] trade union structures' (quoted from the survey). One French select committee member emphasized likewise that her confidence and trust in herself has improved. Another French colleague benefitted from knowledge on different mentalities in other countries and improved his understanding of diverse human reactions to certain problems. He realized, and very much appreciated, that misunderstandings may occur if one does not consider that what is normal in one country, may not be normal in another.

Whether the participants' skills have developed is difficult to evaluate, since we do not know how successfully in the future they will apply what they have learned. Nevertheless, remembering the exchange of local policies and practices, the EWC delegates might have developed their skill in finding cross-border commonalities and differences between their subsidiaries. By contrast, the EWC chair expresses feeling still somewhat lost in defining transnational issues which EWCs can influence. He has, furthermore, remained unsure about the legal power and procedures EWCs could utilize to challenge company decisions through the courts, because the recast directive appears too imprecise to be of any help in these matters (email on 5 February 2014 survey).

Obviously, the chair's newly gained confidence does not go as far as to allow him to create his own definition of transnational issues. In a multinational company, basically every issue is transnational, as the other ETUI EWC trainer argues (interview on 20 February 2014).

Despite one or other personal deficiency left, ultimately, every participant appears to have gained something from the training. Through everyone's individual development, the EWC members have evidently grown as a group too. Besides increased confidence, they have arrived at 'a more integrated approach to common issues' (EWC chair, quoted from the survey). We may also recall the previously mentioned perception that the representative body has become more of a team. Thus, the course participants have apparently developed, in addition to transnational personal identity, some transnational collective identity or feeling of cross-border cohesion.

These newly built personal and collective identities not only seem to feel good/ Also, they seem to have released intrinsic motivation and uplifted spirits: 'I am pretty happy with everything during my stay in Brussels', the Swedish delegate wrote one day after the training (email from 12 December 2013). He also commented on the conversations he had with the author during breaks and appreciated that 'through our discussion, I got some of your energy, enthusiasm and positivism, on that way I will be able to fight on'. Also the German colleague sounds more energetic. He took on board the author's suggestion to go to language classes since he is unable to communicate in the EWC's official language: 'I will improve my English, which will make easier the interaction with each other' (survey, translation by the author).

Quality and Usefulness of European Trade Union Institute European Works Council Training

The obviously overall positive education experience is reflected in the survey respondents' usefulness and quality ratings. Despite having missed some more legal training, the members of the EWC found the occasion very useful. On a scale of 1 (very) to 4 (not at all), all surveyed colleagues gave best usefulness ratings. The German delegate expressed correspondingly that 'the training has given me very much' (quoted from the survey, translation by the author). However, what exactly these personal benefits are, he leaves open to interpretation.

Not as unanimous is the participants' opinion on the quality of their training. Probably because they perceived the two days as being too short, a German and French delegate gave only second best marking on a scale between 1 (absolutely delighted) and 5 (very unsatisfied). A French select committee member considers the quality of her learning experience to have been 'very excellent' (email from 5 February 2014). The British, Swedish, and the other French colleagues obviously agree with their comrade and gave best quality evaluations too.

The picture slightly changes, however, when taking separate emails into account. Three weeks after the survey participation, the British EWC chair and one French member respectively downgraded their best quality ratings by one. They did so for different reasons, though. The British chair explains his choice by referring to his perceived lack of information on legal power resources. The French colleague contends that 'excellent' renders improvement impossible, and there would always be room for improvement. Unfortunately, he offers no suggestions on how to make this improvement (emails from 5 February 2014).

Not only does this issue indicate that different ways of thinking can lead to the same result, it also points to certain limits of survey data to reflect the truth. The difference between survey results and follow-up emails prove moreover that perceptions may change over time. How accurate are then the results of the ETUI evaluation questionnaires which course participants are asked to fill in after every activity?

When comparing the evaluations of the Beckers training event against the general opinions on EWC expressed in the ETUI conference survey, we see that the results are not straightforward. On the same abovementioned scales, a delegate from the Italian General Confederation of Labour in Italy and Comisiones Obreras in Spain found their learning experience very useful. An official from the French Confédération Française des Travailleurs Chrétiens evaluated his EWC training as being useful. The Hungarian colleague from the Democratic Confederation of Free Trade Unions did not comment on the usefulness, yet conveyed his extreme dissatisfaction regarding the course quality. The Comisiones Obreras official sounded also unsatisfied in this respect. Contrarily, both the

Italian and French delegates were obviously fairly happy with the quality of their EWC training and gave the second best rating.

Given the quite common opinion about the usefulness of ETUI EWC training, it appears that the contents are considerably useful. Since the perception of quality is divided, the didactics seem to suit some but may displease others. In other words, what ETUI officers and their affiliated EWC trainers deliver appear comparably more appropriate than how they do it.

CONCLUSION

This chapter proposes that trade union education can play a pivotal role in enhancing transnational labour solidarity by providing five development spaces. In fact, any educational activity—whether inside or outside the labour movement—is arguably an opportunity to meet other people (space of encounter); to exchange experiences and ideas (space of exchange); to reflect on self, others, and context (space of insight); and to act in a safe environment with the immediate feedback of a trainer or otherwise expert (space of action). Together, these four spaces can eventually facilitate further development both individually and collectively (space of development).

The chapter argues furthermore that transnational labour solidarity requires educational activities that develop, besides knowledge and skills, appropriate attitudes. Crucial for creating attitudes is identity, as it provides meaning for actions. Therefore, the concepts of personal, collective, and social identity are highlighted.

The critical case study of ETUI EWC training shows that labour educational activities can develop both personal and collective transnational identity. They do so by opening up four fields of education, namely ideology, cognition, emotion, and function. These fields mirror the four basic human elements, which are soul, mind, heart, and body.

On the functional field, the participants can shape their personal and collective identity by developing most of all their skills in communicating and networking. They may form their identities through individual and collective traveling, team-playing, problem-solving, and identifying transnational issues and win-win solutions.

Improving the skill to respond appropriately and in unison to typical situations such as 'whipsawing' games (Greer and Hauptmeier 2008) closure in combination with relocation and wage freeze, profit-sharing schemes, trade union recognition, the use of experts, and so on addresses participants' collective identity. Likewise for exercises which sketch out a more favourable EWC agreement and create rules for effective transnational collaboration.

Regarding emotions, educational activities can be a place to grow high-energy feelings like encouragement and enthusiasm, intrinsic motivation, respect, and happiness. It can also be a place to release low energies coming from emotional pain such as disrespect, disappointment, dissatisfaction, and discomfort. Both personal and collective identity may be strengthened through increased confidence, coherence, and trust regarding self and the group. Furthermore, the feeling of improved integration of group members and commonness in approaching tasks can be beneficial for collective identity.

In terms of cognition, participants may gain a better understanding of their role as individual transnational labour representative, as well as the role of the (national) representative body and movement they are a member of. Both personal and collective identity are shaped, on the one hand, by the trainer through explaining topics like the European legal framework for employee information and consultation (Directive 2002/14 EC), especially the conditions and competences stipulated. On the other hand, the participants may arrive at a better understanding of their transnational roles by outlining to themselves the conditions and competences regarding information and consultation in their local companies. Eventually, participants can learn how to learn and reflect about self, others, and their environment.

Improvements in ideology can result personally in an uplifted spirit, determination to fight, and increased energy levels. Both personally and collectively, educational activities can create and revitalize purpose and meaning for the representative self and body. Collective identity may moreover be formed through establishing and renewing intragroup norms.

Labour educational activities can develop social identity along the same four educational fields as human elements too. Functionally, the participants' skill to identify cross-border commonalities and differences between their local subsidiaries is sharpened through exercises on cross-cultural communication and social mapping of the company. This involves presenting knowledge on various national legal and cultural policies and practices among Europe concerning employees' representation as well as those affecting the plants at hand. Thus, the participants are encouraged emotionally to cultivate empathy, tolerance, and respect for workers from other countries. They are also inspired ideologically through imagining company colleagues on the European continent. These imaginations can certainly act as a source for purpose, meaning, and other normative orientation.

Social identity building has arguably fallen too short in terms of reach, though. The EWC training touched upon the European Trade Union Confederation member organizations as well as the ETUI, albeit marginally. EWC delegates might however want to additionally connect functionally, emotionally, cognitively, and ideologically with other transnational labour representatives and their workers. These may include other EWCs, World Works Councils, European Company Representative Bodies, Special Negotiation Bodies, Interregional Trade Union Councils, as well as the European Economic and Social Committee, to name but a few.

In facilitating such wider connections within the movement, educational activities would enhance labour solidarity not only beyond national borders within a certain multinational company, but also between labour in other companies and countries. This was essential especially, yet not exclusively, along transnational supply chains. On top of that, social identity development should arguably reach out beyond the labour movement to other movements, social interest groups, companies' consumers, (trans)national citizens, and, ultimately, all living beings of this world.

Whether ETUI training extends the reach of workers' representatives' social identity and deepens their personal and collective identity in other activities and educational stages needs further investigation.

NOTES

1. Special thanks go to Ulisses Garrido and his team for giving me the opportunity to study the world of the ETUI and its education department. Very much appreciated is also the enlightening conversations with ETUI researchers, especially Magdalena Bernaciak, Romuald Jagodziński, Aline Hoffmann, and Andreas Botsch, as well as with my PhD supervisor, Roland Erne. Finally, I would like to acknowledge the Irish Research Council for facilitating my dissertation through a Postgraduate Scholarship 2012–2015.

2. AB Wilh. Becker is the parent company of two international operations, namely Becker Industrial Coatings and ColArt, which are headquartered in Berlin (Germany) and London (United Kingdom), respectively. The two subsidiaries are called the Beckers Group and employ around three thousand employees worldwide in the chemical industry. Their European activity spans across the Benelux, France, Germany, Italy, Poland, Spain, Sweden, and the United Kingdom. AB Wilh. Becker is owned by the Swedish family business Lindéngruppen AB. The Beckers Group EWC agreement came into effect on 1 January 2013. Because of the novelty of both the agreement and the training event, the Beckers case can be considered a critical case.

Part IV

Varieties of Internationalism

An Introduction

Knut Kjeldstadli

The theme of this section may be called varieties of internationalism. This partly points to a manifold of internationalist practices in the real world, partly to varying theoretical premises.

Charles Umney's text is a complex conceptual analysis on the possibility of internationalism. As his point of departure he takes the concept of 'cosmopolitanism', understood as a universal orientation where global concerns have primacy over other more parochial interests. Then he goes on to analyse two types of internationalism within the trade union movement: 'Managerial internationalism' is the ordinary, routine variety, dominant in stable periods—and carried more by union officials than members. This internationalism may be more sustained and independent of particular situations, as it is often geared by the political convictions of the union officials. 'Mobilizing internationalism' has a stronger grassroots orientation and tends to emerge in times of crises as a response to concrete grievances. It means internationally coordinated industrial action or campaigns against policymaking elites.

Discussing under what conditions internationalism may occur and lead to cosmopolitanism, Umney evokes the notion of transnationality, not understood as an ideological notion or mental state, but as an objective situation based in the economy. When workers are drawn into such a transnational situation by the expansion of the global capitalist market and increased competition, they may react in order to protect their immediate local interest; they may also swing towards a more cosmopolitan stance.

In her contribution, Jenny Jungehülsing discusses the political potential of migrants for transnational solidarity. In particular, she draws attention to the phenomenon of 'felt solidarity' or even 'lived solidarity'. If solidarity work across borders shall become more than a high-level and bureaucratic practice, an element of 'felt solidarity' is necessary. Drawing on field work experience in a union of US steel workers, with about 20 per cent of members of Mexican descent, she shows that those with a Mexican background are more likely to participate in keeping up relations with a corresponding Mexican union.

Sabrina Zajak deals with the possibility of influencing the conditions of labour in a country from abroad. She argues for the concept of 'multiple transnational pathways of influence'. Four such paths are identified: (1) the international-organizational pathway (targeting international organizations, such as the International Labour Organization), (2) the bilateral pathway (directed towards other states or regions), (3) the market pathway (targeting transnational companies and private regulations), and (4) the civil society pathway (supporting domestic civil society organisations). More than one path may be travelled at the same time, and it is sometimes possible to shift venue if the first one is blocked.

The strength of the Chinese state tends to counter most efforts. One may ask whether the mostly normative power in the various initiatives yields results. If the state is immune to outside pressure, might economic pressure for instance have more impact? Yet, the International Labour Organization engagement shows that there is an opening, that a state such as China may choose at least to argue within a human rights and trade union rights perspective.

An interesting question arises when looking at Umney and Jungehülsing: Is there a possible tension between the ethnic and national, more links and class solidarity, between the universal and the local? This may be the case, but in the American union, the Mexican-American and Mexican contacts were seen as positive; however, it seems that migrant workers with home land contacts are not very able to transfer this to the majority members in the union. One may wonder, what happens in a union with several nationalities, all wanting to prioritize contacts with the respective home countries?

Sabrina Zajak shows varieties of solidarity work, categorized after the target. Her angle is primarily the practical undertakings involved in the four paths and the possible impact they make on Chinese state policy towards workers and unions. As there is weak independent labour organizing in China, action cannot rest on a mobilization 'from below'. It has to be undertaken 'from outside' and even 'from above'. The best prospect for the development of a more autonomous action may perhaps rest with the independent organizations in path 4.

TWELVE

Pathways of Influence

Transnational Activism and Labour Rights in China

Sabrina Zajak

INTRODUCTION

On 14 April 2014, ten thousand workers at the Yue Yuen Dongguan shoe factory took to the streets protesting the company's failure to pay full social security and housing allowance to its seventy thousand employees (see, for example, Caster 2014). Workers protested the largest sports shoe manufacturer in the world, supplying Adidas, Nike, Puma, and other international brand companies. This is not the only recent strike and large-scale protest event in China. In fact, China counts as one of the most protest-intensive countries in the world. China Labour Bulletin, a labour rights organization based in Hong Kong, which maintains a strike map on workers conflicts in China (China Labour Bulletin n.d.) counts 1,171 strikes and protests from the beginning of June 2011 to the end of December 2013 (China Labour Bulletin 2014).

Some common worker concerns include the nonpayment of the legal minimum wage, quality of the dormitories, high work load including massive overtime work, and the lack of independent worker representation. The suicides, which have been taking place as a severe form of protest against the Taiwanese company Foxconn, the world's largest electronics contractor employing roughly 1.4 million workers, has been debated in news around the world (Chan, Pun, and Selden 2013). Foxconn is the principal manufacturer for Apple, and the case has been taken as an example by labour scholars to highlight the role of worker agency and labour struggles in global supply chains (Chan, Pun, and Selden 2013). These local struggles were accompanied by international campaigns from labour advocates and trade unions urging Apple to intervene with its major supplier (Ngai et al. 2014). And indeed, transnational labour rights activism targeting global buyers has become a major tool of interference and transnational support work (Connor and Phelan 2013; Fransen and Burgoon 2013; Merk 2009; Zajak 2014b). It is assumed that as China is a nondemocratic and strong state, which makes it difficult to intervene via state politics or private politics (Baron 2003). Thus, targeting transnational companies in strategic campaigns is the major, or only, way for the international labour movement and labour rights organizations to support local workers' struggles.

This chapter departs from the assumption that private politics, or as I call it mobilization in the market path, is the only way labour rights organizations from abroad have to impact on working conditions in China. It shows that labour rights organizations use multiple ways and strategies to support international core labour standards in China—with partial success. I argue that it is time to go beyond the individual case studies on single campaigns and instead take a longitudinal perspective on joint strategizing along multiple transnational pathways of influence, in order to discern and identify long-term effects, as well as assessing the often neglected synergies, and the combined outcomes, resulting from different forms of transnational activism.

This chapter presents and exemplifies an analytical framework to analyse and explore multilevel labour rights activism within the current global governance architecture, and its local effects on Chinese supply chains. Empirically, the paper differentiates between four different paths: Activists can try to mobilize from within or target international organizations (the international-organizational pathway), other states or regions (the bilateral pathway), or transnational companies and private regulatory arrangements (the market pathway). In addition, they can also support domestic civil society organizations (civil society pathway).

The chapter will first elaborate the framework of transnational pathways of influence and how to operationalize it. It then gives examples of transnational activism targeting labour rights violations in the People's Republic of China. The conclusion discusses the implication of this framework for understanding transnational labour rights activism within the current system of global economic and labour governance, and the integration of nondemocratic states into the world economy and politics.

CONCEPTUALIZING LABOUR RIGHTS ACTIVISM ALONG MULTIPLE PATHWAYS

There is a burgeoning literature on the emergence of labour transnationalism and, in particular, on the question: Why and how do particular trade unions transnationalize? Erne (2014) stresses the importance of politicization of an issue as a precondition for transnationalization. Kay (2014) adds that ideational and organizational factors, next to economic factors, are important in understanding why trade unions transnationalize. Others have stressed the importance of network building and the rise of global supply chains as a new economic opportunity structure, which not only hampers, but sometimes facilitates transnational collective action (Armbruster-Sandoval 2005; Rodriguez-Garavito 2005).

The perspective taken here departs from this literature in two important ways: First, instead of asking why labour transnationalizes, it asks about the variety of forms such transnationalization can take. Second, it not only considers trade union activities as a key element of labour transnationalization, but also sees other labour advocacy organizations as part of transnational collective action. In the case of China, organizations such as China Labour Bulletin, Asian Monitoring Resource Centre, or Students and Scholars Against Corporate Misbehaviour are important organizations with international ties to trade unions and social movement organizations in other countries. Thus, I see cooperation (and sometimes conflict) between trade unions, social movement organizations, and multilevel strategizing as key features of transnational labour rights activism.

In order to better understand this multilevel strategizing, it is important to take a closer look at the specific international regulatory environment. Today's global labour governance architecture is characterised by multiple coexisting and overlapping bodies of regulation, inter- and intraorganizational networks of autonomous, but interdependent actors with multiple sources of power and enforcement mechanisms (Hassel 2008). These layers of regulation include national and international law, transnational and private rules, and local conventions which take the form of social practices (Bartley 2011). Institutional theories, within international relations and transnational governance, have paid careful attention to how these layers of regulation relate to each other, whether they compete or complement each other (Büthe and Mattli 2011; Locke, Rissing, and Pal 2013; Trubek and Trubek 2006). There is also the rise and diffusion of soft instruments of regulation, such as the monitoring and auditing of factories, which are used to implement labour rights in global supply chains (Barrientos and Smith 2007; Locke 2013).

The concept of transnational pathways of influence aims at integrating the idea of multiplicity and interconnectedness of transnational governance arrangements, with the concept of transnational activism, as it helps us to more completely understand the structuration of the institutional settings and the relationship between different settings as a context for activist mobilization.

Looking at the current global labour governance architecture, one can differentiate between four major pathways of influence: The international-organizational pathway, where activists use their influence or existing complaint procedures; the bi- or multilateral pathway where activists mobilize other states; and the market pathway, where activists target and/or cooperate with transnational companies and private regulatory arrangements. Still, it is not enough to look at the major regulatory layers in order to capture all forms of transnational influence. As the governance concept tends to neglect outside actors without access, there is one form of transnational influence which is overlooked when only the institutional infrastructure is examined: The transnational support of domestic civil society organizations (Caraway 2006). This is an important path of influence for two reasons, as empowering local civil society actors (e.g., workers, trade unions, nongovernment organizations [NGOs], and social movements) could strengthen their capacity to claim and realize their rights on the ground.

Analyzing transnational pathways of influence has two major advantages: It allows one to see each governance arrangement as a particular institutional setting, which means a particular set of rules, procedures, and actors engaged in rule making and rule enforcement, which present a specific environment for activism, with particular opportunities and hindrances. While 'traveling' a certain path (operating within a certain setting or applying certain strategies vis-à-vis the institutional arrangement), activists can shift venues when the road is blocked, they can try to change the setting, or they can collaborate across different paths.

Second, it helps us to better understand the effects and outcomes of transnational labour rights activism. Each of these institutional settings has a specific link to the domestic context (Bernstein and Cashore 2000). This is important for transnational mobilization because—even if activists are relatively successful at the transnational level (the proximate target)—it does not mean that change is actually produced at the local level (ultimate target). In fact, one key claim of this paper is that the nature of the ultimate target (the state and private actors within the state) affects not only local outcomes, but also how transnational activism plays out within the global governance landscape. I highlight the sensitivity of each path to interference from the targeted state. China is an interesting case in this respect, as it is both internally and externally a strong and nondemocratic country. The chapter identifies different 'boomerang defence' mechanisms, which strong states use against transnational activism, for example, by transforming existing transnational opportunities or by undermining local actors who seek to go transnational.

The next section exemplifies activism in different paths and identifies specific opportunities and hindrances in each path and the strategies taken by activists to reach their goal.

STUDYING PATHWAYS OF INFLUENCE—SOME EMPIRICAL EVIDENCE

It is beyond this section to present a full-fledged analysis of labour rights activism in all pathways, and this has been done elsewhere (Zajak 2013a). Instead, I focus on the most important developments between 1989 and 2010. The year 1989 was a decisive one for the beginning of transnational activism targeting labour rights violations in China. The violent repression of the independent labour and democratic movement at Tiananmen Square in Beijing had two major consequences: First, mobilization and independent labour organization had become virtually impossible since the beginning of the 1990s in China, when labour rights activists flew abroad to the (then) independent city of Hong Kong, so as to continue their engagement with mainland China, and in particular Southern China and the Guangdong province (Xu 2013). Hong Kong–based organizations, such as China Labour Bulletin or the Asian Monitoring Resource Centre, are important sources of information and cooperation for international labour rights organizations. Second, this was the starting point for international labour and human rights activists to target China (Fleay 2006). Since then, transnational labour rights activism has continued until today. Yet it has changed its face (specific targets, demands, and strategies) many times since—co-evolving and continuously changing with the global labour governance landscape in multiple episodes of contention. The empirical evidence discussed next is based on seventy interviews with NGOs, trade unions, international organizations, companies, and multistakeholder initiatives I conducted in Europe (Germany, Brussels, Geneva, Amsterdam), the United States (Washington, New York), and China (Hong Kong, Guangdong, Beijing) between 2008 and 2010, participant observations of network meetings, factory visits and analysis of documents, such as International Labour Organization (ILO) complaints, European Union documents, trade union statements, and websites of activist organizations.

The International Organizational Pathway: The Case of the International Labour Organization

One of the first strategies labour rights activists used was the ILO complaint procedure. The ILO is one of the oldest (founded in 1919) and most important international organizations for transnational labour rights activism. The ILO provides a stable institutional framework, as its tripartite governance structure has given labour unions unique opportunities for participation and influence. Three major opportunity dimensions for trade union influence can be differentiated: (1) unions have a say within the ILO's three main bodies: The international labour conference, the governing body and the ILO office. (2) They can use the complaint procedure at the Committee on Freedom of Association. (3) The ILO provides a venue for dialogue and exchange between trade unions across nations. Particularly, points 2 and 3 have become relevant for transnational labour rights activism during the 1990s, which shall be exemplified next.

The complaint mechanism is very insensitive to China's internal or external strength, as it does not require the involvement of domestic actors of the targeted country, and the targeted state cannot block or prevent the filing of complaints. If the Committee on Freedom of Association decides to hear the case, it establishes a dialogue with the government concerned, issues a report, and makes recommendations on how the situation could be remedied (Gravel, Duplessis, and Gernigon 2001). This has made it a viable instrument in the early 1990s, in the aftermath of the Tiananmen massacre in 1989 (Kent 2002).

The International Confederation of Free Trade Unions (ICFTU later the International Trade Union Confederation [ITUC]) submitted six complaints during the time of investigation between 1989 and 2010; the first and last one was handed in 1989 and 2002, respectively. Such complaint procedures usually comprise of several rounds of discussions, with statements from participants, providing in-depth documentation from the union filing the complaint, the Chinese official statement, and the governing bodies' recommendation. Resolving a complaint can take several years.

All complaints dealt with the violations of human and trade union rights, the detention of trade unionists, physical assaults, and imprisonment. What is particularly interesting about these complaints is that the Chinese government soon started to argue within the parameters of international labour law. It concluded in 2000 that the ICFTU's allegation of freedom of association violation 'is completely unjustified' and 'constitutes a distortion of the reality' (Case No. 2031, Report No. 321, paragraph 179), as the 1992 Trade Union Act does not violate principles of freedom of association: 'The Government stresses the importance that it attaches to the protection of the democratic rights of its citizens, including freedom of association, and reaffirms that the civil and political rights of the Chinese people are effectively guaranteed by law' (Case No. 2031, Report No. 321, paragraph 158). In terms of effects, this suggests at least a discursive convergence between international rights and government rhetoric, which over time also found, on occasion, its expression in the (re)formulation of the national labour law (Zajak 2013a: chapter 4).

But why then did the complaints stop in 2002 even though the ITUC continued to report violations vis-à-vis labour rights and trade union rights in its annual survey, and the ITUC World Trade Organization report (see ITUC 2010). Neither learning from defeat nor a Chinese victory in the diagnostic struggle seems to explain the absence of further complaints. Especially if we consider that the ITUC continued to direct criticisms towards others. Thus, explanations have to be found in developments in other pathways, and the development of a new strategy of the ITUC dealing with the All China Confederation of Trade Unions (ACFTU) and China. An interviewee of ITUC explains the hesitation to continue the use of the complaint mechanism: 'The judges always uphold our complaint, but it doesn't really add anything, doesn't change things much. So I think it is not really worth diverting so much time to formulate complaints. And we have always tried to do other things as much as possible. And now we are also trying to have this kind of dialogue with the ACFTU. We don't have an open conflict so much' (interview ITUC, Brussels, 10 April 2010). This quote suggests that considerations, other than the availability of transnational opportunities and the existence of labour rights violations, play a role in strategizing along this path. The ITUC has to take into account the rising significance of the ACFTU in other global governance issues, as the following quote from an ITUC document suggests: 'Nevertheless, there are circumstances that require ICFTU contact with the ACFTU. Most importantly, dialogue is necessary, in the context of the Worker's group of the ILO. There are also contacts and dialogue in relation to regional and inter-regional forums, for example, [Asia-Pacific Economic Cooperation] and [Asia-Europe Meetings]. In the context of those relationships, the ICFTU expects a minimum of cooperation from the ACFTU' (ITUC China policy 2002: para. 10).

This brief analysis shows that new opportunities and constraints for the ITUC opened up other paths, and strategizing in other paths also feeds back into the strategy of using the complaint procedure at the ILO. This indicates that the usage of an existing (and in this case even highly stable) transnational opportunity is also linked to the presence and absence of other opportunities within this complex multilevel governance system of labour rights, and the strategy formation of labour advocates within this system. Two other major opportunities arose during the 1990s. Operating in the market path (targeting transnational companies or cooperating with them in multistakeholder initiatives) and using bi- and multilateral relations in trade negotiations with China.

The Bi- and Multilateral Pathway: European Union, China, and the Asia-Europe Meetings

The bilateral pathway states that activists can use other states to exert pressure on the ultimate target (Keck and Sikkink 1999), or they can try to mobilize states to establish labour rights clauses in trade agreements— the mobilization targeting the North American Free Trade Agreement is an example of this (Gereffi, Spener, and Bair 2002; Kay 2005). Here, I propose to extend the concept of a bilateral pathway towards a multilateral pathway, as activists might try and mobilize states via supranational institutions or interregional arrangements. Still, both pathways have similar characteristics: In contrast to the usage of international complaint procedures (as in the case of the ILO), mobilization in the bi- or multilateral is intended to trigger unilateral interventions. The major mechanism of influence is the power of one state to limit another state's access to its internal market (Bernstein and Cashore 2000; Kent 2001). In contrast to the ILO complaint procedure, the political and economic power of the targeted state plays a considerable role, and we might expect, however, it is difficult to simply enforce new rules from the outside on a powerful country such as China (this path is particularly sensitive to the target's external strength). Moreover, there is no exclusive access for a particular kind of organization. Thus, trade unions and other social movement organizations, or advocacy NGOs, can travel along this path, having to decide if they want to work in tandem.

In the European Union, the decision to negotiate a Partnership and Cooperation Agreement with China in 2006 created a new window of opportunity for labour rights activism. These negotiations were embedded in a broader web of European Union–China relations, which are otherwise comprised of agreements, joint statements, memoranda of understanding, summits, ministerial exchange, and sector-specific dialogues. Labour advocates can try to gain access and have a voice within this web of relations. However, opportunities in the European Union are limited given the behind-closed-doors nature of European trade negotiations, the slow progress in negotiations due to political differences, and no direct opportunities to influence. Labour rights activists focused their attention on the broader process of interregional integration between Europe and Asia for their mobilization.

More specifically, the Asia-Europe Meetings (ASEM), which started in 1996, are a rather informal process of dialogue and cooperation between Association of Southeast Asian Nations countries (China being the decisive player in it), and representatives of European Union member-states. It is supposed to foster closer political, economic, and cultural relations and enhance economic cooperation, trade, investment, and business networking (Maull 2010). It emerged as a response to the growing economic, and therefore political, importance of Asia. From the beginning, ASEM was challenged by trade unions, in the form of a trade union summit organized in parallel to the meetings, and the Asia-Europe People's Forum, a transnational counter-forum debating an alternative 'People's Vision' (Asia-Europe People's Forum 1998) to interregional integration. In this structure, labour rights activism has had at least some impact on the European Union–China relations with regards to labour rights issues: a decisive innovation was the establishment of labour and employment ministers' meeting (Helsinki 2006) with consultative capacities for trade unions. The decision for a labour and employment ministers' meeting was prepared by a German-Chinese alliance, as a response (at least in part) to lobbying efforts and mobilisation by trade unions and NGOs (Zajak 2014a). ITUC welcomed this development: 'The reference to the involvement of social partners in further ASEM work, although not defined in specific terms, represents solid ground for the recognition of unions' formal status within the ASEM structure' (ITUC 2008: 8 No. 42).

The increased access for trade unions cannot alone be attributed to transnational labour rights activism. Access also has to be understood in the context of international developments, in particular the increasing acceptance of the ILO's core labour standards and decent work agenda, as well as domestic developments within Asian countries, and particularly China looking for ways to cope with the challenges and negative consequences of globalization. One member of the European Commission summarizes the combination of factors the following way:

> I think the situation is changing in Asia and also in China. External pressure is one element, because obviously these countries have signed up to the ILO conventions and different international conventions, and there is pressure on them to abide by that. But I think what will transform the debate in Asia, is the internal development. When growth and development really take off . . . I think trade unions will become more influential, more powerful. And also social activists become more important. And they make very strong demands for changes in labour conditions; there are strikes and pressure from consumer organisations. So I think a great deal of different factors comes into this debate.[1]

In the conclusion, I refer to the intersection of these different developments as activist interventions, institutional co-evolution, and interaction.

The Market Pathway

There are considerable differences between the international and multilateral pathway, and the market pathway: In contrast to the first two pathways, where the primary target is the nation state, the market pathway penetrates national boundaries and influences the factory level directly. Thus, the regulatory scope and depth of this pathway goes beyond the nation state (Rodriguez-Garavito 2005: 207). By operating in the market path, activists not only try to influence public rule makers, which might contribute to the implementation of domestic and international labour law within China. This leads one to expect a much more successful path in relation to China, compared to the others. However, my empirical findings suggest that the market path is also very sensitive to China's internal strength. In particular, the absence of an independent labour movement, or more prominent domestic labour rights organizations, makes it difficult to effectively intervene. This indicates that global supply chains are not a stable opportunity structure across different countries, but transnational opportunities vary in relation to the domestic context (see Brookes in this volume).

In very general terms, labour rights activists can either campaign against transnational companies to enforce international labour rights within global supply chains or they can cooperate with transnational companies. Research has pointed out that particularly fruitful are combinations of both strategies in transnational organizing campaigns where workers, seeking to organize a union, involve transnational activist networks, which, in turn, make use of company codes of conduct and monitoring systems to support the local unionizing efforts (Armbruster-Sandoval 2005; Lesley 2009; Rodriguez-Garavito 2005). Such transnational organizing campaigns require a strong involvement of local organizations and independent trade unions and, therefore, could not be conducted in China.

Yet, perhaps contrary to what is expected, the other two strategies—campaigns against transnational companies or cooperation in multistakeholder initiatives—are also significantly affected by the political and economic environment in China. The prospects and limits for implementing standards in supply chains by auditing, monitoring, and capacity building has been researched in multiple studies (Barrientos and Smith 2007; Locke 2013), also specifically for China (Bartley and Zhang 2012; Egels-Zandén 2013; Xiaomin 2008). This line of research indicates that the ability of transnational companies to enforce standards in its supply chains, without including workers, local trade unions, or other labour rights organizations, is difficult and produces only selective results in some issue areas.

But even targeting transnational companies and regulatory initiatives becomes difficult when we consider the topic of working conditions in China. One good example is the toy industry, which predominantly sources in China. It is also an interesting case, as the toy industry has an international business association, the International Council of Toy Industries (ICTI), which already engages in the regulation of health and safety standards of toy products. So why not include labour regulation in the already existing regulatory structure and work with trade unions and labour rights organizations on its implementation?

Unions, in particular the ICFTU, were engaged in an international toy campaign throughout the 1990s, together with other NGOs in Europe and the United States. The ICFTU entered negotiations with companies and ICTI. But member companies and ICTI rejected demands for the inclusion of freedom of association provisions (it only refers to national law) and engagement with unions. As a representative of ICTI explained, 'It is a difficult topic for the international association. Which unions should or should not be included. This is why we focus rather on NGOs, with whom we have good relations with. As our major field of activity is

China, we try to be careful. The topic of unions is still a "hot iron"'.[2] In this case, the Chinese political context provided justifications for the rejection of union demands for the respect of freedom of association *and* their participation in transnational governance. It highlights how China's internal strength influences transnational contention over institutional designs of governance arrangements. In particular, the dominance of sourcing from nondemocratic countries with weak or nonexistent labour movements can additionally weaken the international bargaining position of labour organizations vis-à-vis business, but also of labour organizations vis-à-vis NGOs or nongovernmental labour advocacy organizations. This is not only the case for the toy industry, but also other so-called multistakeholder initiatives, where business rather prefers to cooperate and work with NGOs over trade unions (Egels-Zandén 2009).

The example suggest that the Chinese sociopolitical context, and in particular the lack of independent trade unions, negatively affects the opportunities for labour advocates within the transnational governance fields, even if neither the Chinese state nor Chinese organizations have direct access to transnational private governance institutions.

The Civil Society Pathway

While the other three pathways form institutional environments for labour advocates' activities, the civil society path is characterized by building linkages between advocate organizations across countries. These linkages involve a flow of resources with the objective of supporting the organizational emergence and survival of domestic labour organizations. In China, independent labour organizations are still prohibited. And yet, labour support organizations[3] have been noticeably developing since 2000 (Chan 2013; Xu 2013). Since then, the rise and development of domestic labour support organizations in China is supported by international donors, often via their Hong Kong–based allies. But the establishment and acceptance of private regulation and corporate social responsibility (CSR) in China (also as a response to what happened in the market path) created an additional policy space for organisations to emerge as CSR service providers. This creates new possibilities, but also new challenges for international trade unions and labour rights organizations, who wish to strengthen the role of workers in the implementation and formulation of labour rights (Zajak 2013b): On the one hand, new opportunities arise to network with organizations and to get them access to local factories via the 'CSR channel'. On the other hand, new constraints arise due to the business logic of the CSR service provision. A Hong Kong–based organization explains: 'Some companies co-opt these NGOs into their CSR program. There are *many categories of NGOs*. Some are company friendly. They need the funding. So if Nike can pay me [ten thousand dollars] for one talk, I go. I don't care about the reactions. *I do the show*. If I do five shows it's a very good income for me'.[4]

At the other end of the spectrum, there are more independent small-scale organizations and worker support centres, which mainly depend on external funding from external donors. These are individuals, sometimes small groups or very informal organizations, which are often run by former migrant workers (Chan 2013). Another Hong Kong labour rights–based organization working closely with them describes them the following way: '[T]hey have a very grassroots, authentic character, because these people have dealt with these issues personally and they care about these issues because they have suffered from them' (interview, China Labour Bulletin, 23 April 2009). As they operate informally, they have not (yet) been absorbed into the Chinese corporatist structures and operate more at arm's length to (but not against) the state (Friedman 2009: 226). Under these conditions, external support is particularly crucial as they often lack the ability to obtain domestic resources. Thus, transnational connections *compensate for the lack of domestic sources* and ensure that these individuals and groups do not have to move closer to the state. But it is also important in order to prevent these organizations turning to the business side and becoming CSR service providers.

Overall, there is no easy answer to the question whether civil society building contributed to worker empowerment or better working conditions, given the considerable political and business constrains for labour support organizations in China. However, there is also no determinist structural influence, and organizations can carve out room for manoeuvre and find strategies in support of workers. Beyond the domestic context, the development of the labour support organizations in China could also have important implications for the balance between capital and labour on the global scale, and affect transnational labour rights activism in all other parts. Some observers hope to witness the emergence of organizations, through which true transnational collective action might be possible in the future. However, considering the strong state, but also private capacities, which channel societal activities, the emergence of strong domestic organizations seems unlikely in the near future.

ADVANTAGES, CONTRIBUTIONS, AND FUTURE RESEARCH

This chapter has shown the multifaceted nature of transnational labour rights activism targeting labour rights violations in China. The final section summarizes the overall strategies chosen by labour rights activists between 1989 and 2010. It then discusses the overall effects of these continuous forms of activism. Table 12.1 gives an overview of the main pathways, when these paths became relevant in relation to China. It shows that all paths are relevant over time, while the market and civil society

Table 12.1. Activism in Different Pathways of Influence

Paths	Time Since	Actors	Strategies and Used Opportunities	Proximate and Ultimate Target
International organizations (International Labour Organization)	1989	Trade unions	Complaint procedure Exchange with All China Confederation of Trade Unions Country programs	international organization (IO)/ state
Bi- and multilateral (European Union–China; Asia-Europe Meetings)	1996	Trade unions and nongovernmental organizations	Different opportunities for participation and mobilization in European Union–China and Asia-Europe relations	State/state
Market (transnational companies [TNCs] and MSIs)	1997	Nongovernmental organizations and trade unions	Corporate campaigns Participation in multistakeholder initiatives (MSIs)	TNCs/ Factories
Civil society	After 2000	Nongovernmental organizations and trade unions	Resource provision and support	Local organizations/factories

• Combined effects: New laws and regulations, rise in minimum wages, rise of alternative labour support organizations and corporate social responsibility service providers, contained multipartism

Source: Author's compilation.

path emerged and gained relevance at later stages in the development, strongly interacting with each other and other paths.

Thus, the chapter makes two broader claims: First, by focusing on one particular path, and one setting at one particular point in time, we are not fully doing justice to today's transnational activism, which operates in multiple institutional settings, country-specific contexts, and actor constellations. Such an approach might lead to an unrepresentative picture of transnational activism and its outcomes by overestimating the impact of a particular form of activism within a certain pathway. Second, the targeted state can impact transnational activism in various ways, the facets of which have not yet been spelled out completely in the literature. In recursive struggles over labour regulation and its enforcement, the targeted state can channel and redirect activists' influence by exercising a variety of counterstrategies, namely, exhibiting selective responsiveness, undermining the establishment of transnational linkages, or engaging in diagnostic struggles and trying to reframe international core labour standards, in particular the right of freedom of association, as the example of ILO complaints highlighted.

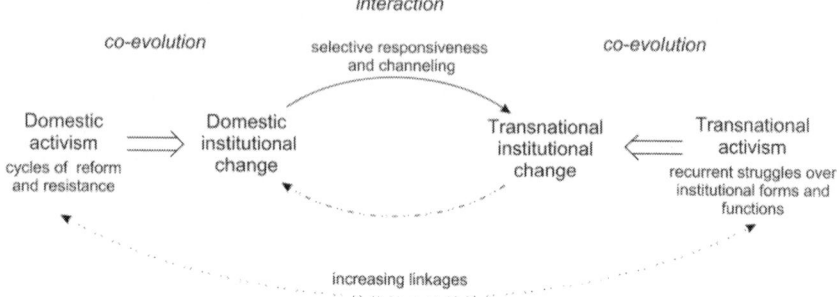

Figure 12.1.   Recurrent activist intervention, institutional co-evolution, and interaction. Source: author compilation.

What do we learn by studying activism along the different pathways? The framework makes it possible to understand combined effects of transnational activism. It helps us get a clearer picture of the outcomes of transnational activism or, more specifically, situate and understand the role and contribution of transnational activism in the context of global and local developments. Figure 12.1 summarizes the dynamic of change across all pathways for the case of China. It shows that change is as much a result of activist interventions as it is of institutional co-evolution and interaction. Each factor alone cannot explain why certain standards become established and put into practice. This does not mean that recurrent cycles of contention automatically contribute to continual improvements. Overall in the case of China, the effects remain fragmented, partially isolated, sometimes unintended, and contribute to a process of selective convergence, where legal changes (e.g., rises in minimum wages and the introduction of collective bargaining rights locally) go hand in hand with new opportunity spaces for emerging local labour support organizations and international opportunities for networking learning and exchange.

Future studies could use and modify this framework in different transnational governance fields and in relation to other countries. Integrating other countries into the framework could also enrich our understanding of the potential of transnational activism.

NOTES

1. Interview, European Commission official, DG Employment, Brussels, 2010.
2. Interview via telephone, director of ICTI CARE, January 2009.
3. I use the term 'labour support organizations' as an umbrella term for all societal organizations engaged in supporting the application of the labour law and workers' claim-making in order to avoid any pre-labelling about the degree of dependency towards business or the state. Labour support organization and worker organizing efforts already existed during the 1980s and 1990s. However, those organizations rather had to operate underground as worker organisers were imprisoned (compare ILO complaints).
4. Interview with Asian Monitoring Resource Centre official, Hong Kong, April 2009.

THIRTEEN

Labour in the Era of Transnational Migration

What Prospects for International Solidarity?

Jenny Jungehülsing

INTRODUCTION

In times of economic globalization, labour unions increasingly view a need for international solidarity. With constantly growing global economic interdependence, and capital operating more and more transnationally, the possibilities to defend workers' rights on a national scale seem increasingly limited. While international solidarity is certainly not the only strategy to be pursued by labour—in fact, many of workers' interests can still be successfully pursued on a national scale (e.g., Castree 2000; Herod 2003)—in the long term, prospects to defend workers' rights exclusively within nation-states, whose government policies are dominated by a global competitiveness rhetoric, are dim (Moody 1997; Zeuner 2004).

Unions' experiences in building international solidarity are a prominent topic in recent labour research. What the mostly empirical, and limited theoretical, research implicitly or explicitly agrees upon is that stable cross-border solidarity between workers involves more than a mere community of interests, but also includes an emotional element, or mutual identification among partners. That emotional element or mutual identification could be called a 'felt solidarity'. Also, this felt solidarity is often hindered by a lack of direct cross-border contact and communication at the grassroots level: a limited understanding of the 'others'' specific conditions, problems, and struggles often leads to misunderstandings and resentments, impeding trustful solidary relationships.

The academic debate, however, fails to deal with a recent development that could be of crucial importance for the future of labour, and its possibilities to internationalize: transnational migration. In a context of increasing transnational economic and social interconnections, enhanced transport and communication technologies, as well as global media bringing people together around the globe, workforces are also becoming more transnational.[1] With economic restructuring causing the layoff of millions of workers and destroying livelihoods in many, especially Southern, countries, migration flows are growing. In the main, migration-receiving countries, migrants make up an increasing share of the work-force—and, albeit with some delay, union memberships. At the same time, many migrants today are what can be called transmigrants: migrants with a feeling of belonging to both their 'home' and 'host' countries, and who maintain strong personal relationships to, and concern for, families and communities 'back home'.

This chapter argues that transnational migration needs to be considered in our thinking about international labour solidarity, as the cross-border ties and emotional bonds many migrant union members maintain may help overcome one major obstacle to functioning solidarity relationships: the lack of an emotional foundation of solidarity, or 'felt solidarity', which is often the consequence of a limited solidarity at the grassroots level, and of direct contact between rank and file workers. Given the bureaucratic character of international solidarity, which is generally located at unions' leadership level, workers usually have few possibilities for interacting across borders. Solidarity thus often has no practical meaning to them—it is not a 'lived solidarity'. Based on exploratory research in a US labour union and its solidarity work with a Mexican partner union, it is argued here that migrant union members' social and emotional ties to their countries of origin can strengthen a sense of togetherness with partners in these countries. They can do so in three ways: (1) migrants' transnational identities, or 'ways of belonging' (Levitt and Schiller 2004), constitute an emotional basis for their engagement in the solidarity work; (2) the cultural capital migrants dispose of facilitates the establishment of close personal cross-border relationships that promote a sense of community among workers; and (3) these relationships can enable a communication at the grassroots level that promotes a lived solidarity involving the rank and file, local-level staff, and officers.

THE CURRENT ERA OF TRANSNATIONAL MIGRATION

The world is today increasingly transnational, while the deregulation of commodities, services, and financial markets on the one hand, and enhanced transport and communication technologies on the other, have led to the extreme growth of global commodity and financial flows. Workers seem to be the only factor not allowed to move as freely. Nevertheless, today's world is also one of increasing global migration flows, with more people than ever before living abroad. While most flows still consist of internal migration, also cross-border migration is increasing. The number of persons leaving their country of origin has risen to 3.2 per cent of the world's population in 2013, reaching 232 million people (up from 154 million in 1990), South-North migration making up half of them (United Nations 2013).

At the same time, migration is becoming more transnational[2]: As transnational studies have been showing since the 1990s, many (though not all) migrants today maintain close ties with their origin countries. Also in previous migration waves, migrants maintained, sometimes for long periods, contact with relatives and friends 'back home'. But such connections have arguably increased in scale and intensity in recent decades: due to modern long-distance transport and communication technologies—the 'time-space compression' (Harvey 1990), as well as the spread of global media and cultural globalization, many migrants are today more easily able to travel back and forth, and to maintain relationships with relatives and home communities (Vertovec 2001).[3] In 1994, Basch, Schiller, and Szanton Blanc (2005), in their seminal contribution *Nations Unbound*, showed that many contemporary immigrants no longer fit the traditional conception of migrants as 'coming to stay', uprooted from their old home country and adopting a new one. Instead, 'transnational social fields' (Levitt and Schiller 2004) develop, in which many of today's migrants 'develop networks, activities, patterns of living, and ideologies that span their home and the host society' (Basch, Schiller, and Szanton Blanc 2005: 4).

An important conceptual concretization of migrants' transnational lives has been made by Levitt and Schiller: In distinguishing between 'ways of belonging' and 'ways of being', they introduce a differentiation between migrants' transnational consciousness and practice. Concrete transnational practices such as engaging in transnational relationships and communication, or celebrating festivities of their community of origin, represent ways of being. The authors define these as 'the actual social relations and practices that individuals engage in rather than . . . the identities associated with their actions' (Levitt and Schiller 2004: 1010). They also include migrants' traveling back and forth and the exchange of material and nonmaterial goods, as well as financial remittances across borders.

On the other hand, 'ways of belonging' are not necessarily linked to transnational ways of being and refer to 'practices that signal or enact an identity which demonstrates a conscious connection to a particular group' (Levitt and Schiller 2004: 1010). Migrants' identities and loyalties

are today often transnational: Instead of leaving their home country behind, they identify, often even after having lived in another country for
decades, with both their (or their parents') country or community of origin and of residence (Basch, Schiller, and Szanton Blanc 2005; Pries 2010;
Vertovec 2001).

Within transnational social fields, also 'social remittances' circulate
across borders, consisting of, among others, ideas, behaviours, identities,
and social capital (Levitt 1998). The ideas and norms that migrants adopt
in receiving societies on such issues as cultural values, gender relations,
and democracy can influence social, cultural, political, and economic
practices and institutions in origin countries (Dannecker 2005; Hondagneu-Sotelo 1992). But social remittances are not unidirectional. They also
move in the opposite direction: Migrants bring ideas, norms, and practices, as well as specific skills and knowledge such as language and other
cultural skills—what others have called 'cultural capital'—to the societies
they settle in (Erel 2010; Nohl et al. 2006). '[T]hese experiences shape their
encounters with other immigrant communities as well as their interactions with the native-born' and can impact on host societies (Levitt and
Lamba-Nieves 2010: 9).

As a consequence of their persisting transnational ties, many migrants
remain economically, politically, or socially engaged in their origin country. Most prominently, the concern many migrants maintain for their
families 'back home' has led to impressive amounts of financial remittances being transferred to origin countries. Many migrants maintain a
concern for their countries and communities of origin extending beyond
their families, often involving a commitment to improving conditions
'back home' (Levitt and Lamba-Nieves 2010; Portes, Escobar, and Radford 2007). Political, social, and economic activities are among the ways
migrants engage in their countries of origin. Their involvement in party
politics and lobby groups serve to exert political influence. Also, a variety
of transnational migrant organizations, such as charity groups, and the
US-based Mexican Hometown Associations, promote social, cultural, and
economic development in their communities of origin (Escala-Rabaldán,
Bada, and Rivera-Salgado 2006; Orozco 2004).

INTERNATIONAL SOLIDARITY THEORY: LACK OF A FELT
SOLIDARITY AT THE GRASSROOTS LEVEL

Most of the theoretical and empirical literature dealing with international
labour solidarity agrees that international solidarity (and solidarity more
generally) is based on more than a mere community of interests. Evidently, the fundamental basis of international labour solidarity is a shared
interest, or a goal of workers in different countries: Solidarity in labour
unions, in contrast to other types of solidary groups such as families or

societies, is fundamentally based on a commonality of interests vis-à-vis a common opponent, the employer (Bayertz 1999; Fantasia 1988; Hyman 1975). This labour solidarity, national and international, is thus always, to a significant degree, strategic. Nevertheless, some sort of mutual identification, or sense of togetherness, is indispensable for stable solidary relationships (Hyman 2002; Zeuner 2004; for a historical perspective, see van der Linden 2003). In fact, what distinguishes solidarity from an exclusively strategic collaboration to attain a specific goal is that it involves a willingness to assist others, either for the sake of a long-term goal, based on a shared vision or belief, or because of a sentiment of being in the same boat—even without an immediate return for oneself. Hence, stable solidary relationships between unions, which go beyond the short-term attainment of concrete goals, presuppose, as a minimum, a sense of togetherness, or 'felt solidarity' among those involved. In fact, even highly strategic campaigns conducted by union leaderships, in practice, often do rely on a mutual identification of those in charge.[4] While a felt solidarity is generally based on having a common employer, or working in the same sector, other factors can also create a sense of togetherness, such as sharing the same political vision, having similar experiences, or even sharing sex or ethnicity (Hanagan 1980; Zeuner 2004; Zoll 2000). Broadly speaking, the stronger the identification with the 'brothers and sisters abroad', the higher the willingness of union members, and leaders, to assign resources to international solidarity, and personally support international activities, thereby creating a more stable solidary relationship.

In practice, unions often struggle to establish stable international relationships. While not the only impediment, the lack of a felt solidarity often constitutes a serious obstacle to the formation of stable international solidarity relationships.[5] Provided that a shared goal exists in the first place,[6] the lack of a mutual identification among workers often plays an important role in hindering functioning solidary relationships, as neither union members nor leaders are willing to commit to the continuous and dedicated support of their partners, and assign resources to them.

The lack of a felt solidarity often results from several factors: The responsibility for international solidarity is generally located at the higher levels of unions' bureaucracy. Most solidarity activities consist of official declarations and high-level conferences. Entailing few concrete activities involving the rank and file, international solidarity often has no relevance for members' everyday practice: it is not a 'lived solidarity', but, at best, a solidarity existing on paper. Members are frequently not even aware of their unions' international alliances and activities. This lack of embeddedness in unions' everyday work has been considered a major reason for the ephemerality of international union alliances (Bronfenbrenner 2007; Moody 1997; Waterman 1998). Furthermore, resulting from this, as well as the language barrier separating most workers in different countries, possibilities for direct contact and communication between workers are limited. Direct contact and personal relationships, however, are the basis for developing a sense of togetherness, and a felt solidarity: Only through communicating across borders can workers learn about each other and develop an understanding of shared challenges and goals, and hence, develop a relationship of trust and partnership (Gajewska 2008; Hoffmann 2004; Lindberg 2011). Given the huge differences in national historical developments and politico-institutional contexts that shape unions' logics of action, without developing an understanding of the partners' industrial relations systems and their concrete problems and struggles, misunderstandings and distrust are inevitable (Brecher, Costello, and Smith 2006; Greven and Schwetz 2011). In fact, the perception of workers abroad is in practice often dominated by ignorance and prejudices, especially in North-South contexts (Kay 2011). US unions, for instance, have a long history of protectionism and chauvinism against Mexican (and other) workers, often promoting 'Buy American' campaigns and advocating protectionist policies (Frank 1989; Milkman 2006). Without direct personal relationships and communication across borders at the grassroots level, that enable learning about each other's concrete conditions, such perceptions are hard to overcome—and a felt solidarity is unlikely to develop.

INTERNATIONAL LABOUR SOLIDARITY IN AN ERA OF TRANSNATIONAL MIGRATION: STRENGTHENING A FELT SOLIDARITY AND PROMOTING GRASSROOTS SOLIDARITY

With migrants constituting an ever larger share of workforces in many countries, union memberships are becoming more transnational. While most unions have traditionally viewed migrants as competitors to their existing membership, given their assumed willingness to accept bad working conditions and low wages, the sheer size of migrant workforces has forced unions in many countries to organize them. In the United States, for instance, the national federation of labour unions American Federation of Labor and Congress of Industrial Organizations reversed its historic anti-immigrant stance, and since the late 1980s, a number of unions began actively organizing low-wage migrant workers and collaborating with the immigrant rights movement. In many unions, migrants now constitute a large share of the membership, particularly in some geographic areas and high 'migrant' sectors of the economy. Migrants'—as other minorities'—political influence within unions is arguably still limited, given unions' mostly hierarchical structure and limited rank and file participation in decision-making (Fine 2006; Ness 2005). Their presence, nevertheless, has an important impact on unions. Hence, the basic assumption of this research is that the above-described developments can play a significant role in unions' solidarity with migration-origin countries: The social ties and emotional bonds that migrants maintain with, and the concern for, their countries of origin might help overcome the lack of a felt solidarity and promote a lived solidarity at the rank and file level.

Data and Research Methodology

Empirical research was conducted in a US labour union with a large share of Mexican-origin members. The United States is, in absolute numbers, the world's largest migration-destination country (United Nations 2013). Foreign-born workers represented 16.3 per cent of the workforce in 2013, many of whom maintain close transnational social ties to their countries and communities of origin (Bureau of Labor Statistics 2014). Mexican migrants constitute by far the largest group.

The researched case is the alliance between the United Steelworkers (USW) union and the Mexican mineworkers union Sindicato Nacional de Trabajadores Mineros, Metalúrgicos, Siderúrgicos y Similares ('los mineros'). Recently, the USW has been strongly engaged in forging international alliances. In 2008, they signed an agreement to merge with Unite in the UK and Ireland, forming a new union, Workers Uniting, of which also the mineros are intended to eventually form part of. The research was conducted in a union district and its locals, as the role of migrant members most likely manifests itself at the local and regional rather than at the national union level. The region chosen comprises the area of Northern Indiana and Northern Illinois, as this area has a decades-long history of Mexican migration into the steel industry, with Mexican-origin workers representing about 15 to 20 per cent of the union district's membership. Also, the former district director invested much effort in creating awareness for international connections and began organizing regular worker-to-worker exchanges. The district is strongly involved in solidarity work with the mineros.

The research conducted had an exploratory character: Given the virtually inexistent research on migrants' influence on unions' international solidarity work, the analysis was conducted in an open manner, instead of testing hypotheses defined in advance. Rather than providing definite and representative results, the intention was thus to discover possible ways in which migrants influence unions' international solidarity activities. Starting from the above-mentioned assumptions, the research empirically examined the concrete roles Mexican-origin migrants and their ties to Mexico played in the district's work with the mineros. Besides a review of written material and secondary literature on the two unions, the research consisted of sixteen interviews, conducted in January and February 2014, with elected union officers, staff and active members on the district and local level. They comprised both first- and second-generation migrants (the latter constituting the majority), as the children of migrants also frequently maintain transnational ties (Levitt and Schiller 2004). The strength of migrants' transnational ties varied. Particularly recent migrants had strong emotional bonds to Mexico, frequently visited and communicated with relatives and friends in their communities of origin, or even were engaged in Mexico-related charity organizations. Also, all second-generation migrants grew up speaking Spanish at home and celebrating Mexican festivities. Some strongly emphasized their Mexican identity, raised their children as 'Mexicans', and frequently visited relatives in Mexico. Others had a rather latent transnational identity, only having a vague feeling of belonging to Mexico and visiting and communicating with relatives only occasionally. But, as will be discussed below, also in the cases with limited transnational ties, the relationship to Mexico did play a role in migrants' involvement in the solidarity work.

Besides migrants, four nonmigrant staff persons in charge of the international work were interviewed. Topics discussed in the interviews were migrants' transnational ties to their communities and country of origin; members' motivation for, and involvement in, the activities with the mineros; and their relationships to the partners in Mexico.

Results suggest that transnational migrants can promote a felt solidarity at the grassroots level in three ways:

1. First, due to migrants' transnational 'ways of belonging', or transnational identities, their commitment to the solidarity work is at least partly based on a personal emotional bond to that country.
2. Second, their cultural capital—especially language and other cultural skills, as well as, at the very least, a basic knowledge of their country of origin—enables them to more easily relate to the partners and to build personal relationships, thus overcoming the notorious lack of direct cross-border contact and strengthening a personal connectedness among workers.
3. Furthermore, the relationships migrant union members maintain with the partners enables a low-threshold communication and information exchange that gives practical meaning to the international work, promotes the involvement of locals, low-level staff, and the rank and file, strengthening a mutual identification among workers.

Transnational 'Ways of Belonging': Migrants' Bonds to Their Country of Origin as an Emotional Basis for International Solidarity

While it cannot be argued that migrant union members in general have a particular concern for their origin countries, let alone for unions there, the findings suggest that migrants' transnational 'ways of belonging' can constitute an emotional foundation for their engagement in solidarity work. Migrants were among the strongest supporters of the work with the mineros, and those dedicating most energy and time to it. More importantly, the majority of migrants that were engaged in it did so, at least in part, based on a personal connectedness to their (or their parents') country of origin. Thus, the feeling of belonging to Mexico constituted an emotional basis for their engagement, that is, for a felt solidarity. The awareness of 'being in the same boat' and of being stronger together, especially when employed by the same multinational company, had been actively promoted by the former district director, and was very strong among members who had been engaged with the solidarity work. It would therefore be wrong to assume that migrants' transnational identities constituted the sole motivation for their engagement. Only in very few cases was the emotional commitment to the 'home country', or communities, the principal cause of migrants' engagement. This was the case of a recent migrant who was actively engaged in a charity organization linked to his state of origin. His concern for improving conditions 'back home' extended to the work in the union and to the work with the mineros.

Besides this case, first- and second-generation migrants' motivation to engage in solidarity was often principally based on the cognitive insight of its importance, but significantly strengthened by their bonds to Mexico, arising from a general sense of personal relatedness to the country and an interest in learning more about workers and the labour movement there. Sometimes, the engagement went along with a commitment to improving conditions in Mexico more generally. Some migrants were involved in altruistic organizations, providing food baskets and basic school supplies to elementary school pupils, or doing missionary work in Mexico. While this emotional commitment was especially felt by recent migrants, and those maintaining close personal ties to Mexico (making frequent visits), it also applied to second-generation migrants. Generally, how migrants related to Mexico, and whether they feel a particular commitment, depended on their specific migration histories and the way second-generation migrants were raised in the United States. Migrants who came to the United States in adolescence or adult age mostly maintained close emotional bonds to Mexico, and often had a strong interest in contributing to the improvement of conditions 'back home'. Migrants who migrated as children and second-generation migrants often did less. However, this was not true in all cases: As transnationalism studies explain, many children of migrants are raised with a strong awareness of their 'roots', meaning that second-generation migrants often do indeed have a strong emotional bond to their parents' country of origin. In fact, some of the second-generation migrants interviewed were particularly strongly committed to the solidarity work with the mineros, which was related to their personal background: It gave them the opportunity to learn more about their parents' country of origin, their own roots, and made them feel like 'real Mexicans', as the assistant to the district director explained:

> When I go there, . . . I feel like a true Mexican, and to me that means a lot. Because it would have meant a lot to my Dad and my Mom. . . . I just feel proud. . . . When I go to Mexico, I feel like I am a Mexican born in Mexico. Because [the mineros] . . . won't treat you any different than they do another Mexican. . . . I am a Mexican here, but there is Mexican and Mexican. And [a first-generation migrant member] don't understand it because he is from Mexico. But for me . . . it means a lot.[7]

Thus, while variation between migrants and their histories exists, for those migrants involved in the solidarity work with the mineros, their personal bonds to Mexico generally represented an important emotional factor in their engagement.

Building on Migrants' Cultural Capital: Strengthening the Emotional Foundation of Solidarity through the Cross-Border Relationships Migrants Establish

Even more importantly, migrants' background allowed them to establish personal relationships with mineras more easily than their nonmigrant colleagues, thereby overcoming the notorious lack of personal relationships across borders. While the establishment of such direct cross-border contact between workers and local-level staff, especially at the level of 'sister plants' sharing the same employer, was actively promoted by the district director through the realization of regular worker-to-worker exchanges, it was mostly the presence of migrants that made the establishment of close personal relationships possible. Almost all of the numerous cross-border relationships at the level of elected local officers, staff, and regular members were maintained, on the USW side, by Mexican migrants. In fact, many developed friendships with mineros and stayed in touch even after their return from visits to Mexico. Nonmigrant participants in the exchanges, with almost no exception, did not: While they, as a large part of the membership more broadly, supported the solidarity with the mineros, they did not maintain contact with Mexican colleagues upon their return. In contrast, many of the interviewed migrant members and staff communicated on a regular basis with the Mexican partners through email, social networks, such as Facebook, and some of them by phone. Topics communicated about varied from questions directly related to the union and solidarity work, to personal issues such as the Mexicans asking their colleagues to bring them mobile phones, books, or other objects from the United States.

In a large part, this was due to the fact that migrants can actually communicate with the mineros: Given that the language barrier is, in many international solidarity relationships, one of the most important practical obstacles to the establishment of close relationships, the fact that migrants could talk with their partners in Spanish is a significant advantage.[8] Being able to communicate without depending on translators allows for an easier and more informal exchange—especially beyond the official work-related communication and on personal topics—which is the basis for the establishment of friendships. Also, as migrant members and staff were usually the only ones to speak Spanish, they were employed by the union leadership as translators in the solidarity work. Consequently, many of them repeatedly participated in the exchanges to Mexico, which gave them the opportunity to strengthen relationships.

However, beyond the language factor, it was also a lower cultural barrier that seemed to allow migrants to relate more easily to the partners: Migrant-origin members and staff often stated that their background (i.e., being from Mexico) 'broke the ice' in the initial communication and that it created an immediate sense of mutual understanding:

> (I went to Mexico) last year . . . we just became friends. . . . And basically that's . . . because my family is from Mexico . . . my Dad is from Guadalajara Jalisco, and it's about three hours away from where they're at. . . . That's the thing, it just kind of broke the ice with that topic, and then we just started talking and then went from there . . . I told them (that my parents are from Mexico) cause they ask, you know, how do you know Spanish?[9]

Even when compared to the few nonmigrants who spoke Spanish, the relationships migrants built were generally stronger and, importantly, less formal. In the case of most first- and some second-generation migrants, this is partly due to their ability to communicate in a colloquial manner, allowing them to 'jump right in' to informal conversations with the mineros. As one first-generation migrant explained:

> it is a little different because . . . I can fit right in, because if they start joking around, or whatever, I got it. And even [the district director] . . . he speaks Spanish, . . . but if you're joking around, it's a little different, and he misses a lot. . . . So I can relate a lot easier with them. . . . Even [the second-generation migrant assistant to the district director], he was born and raised in the [United States], so really he misses a lot of things, even though he speaks Spanish . . . so yeah, it's a little easier for me, and . . . I believe, for . . . the guys in Mexico, too, because . . . like, they wanna relate certain messages to [the district director] or to the Steelworkers . . . I think they feel comfortable relating their message to me more than relating it to (them) . . . in the translation, they miss a lot of things.[10]

A further factor is that many migrants have at least an implicit knowledge of Mexico, an understanding of Mexican culture and habits, and an understanding of 'how things work there' in general and in politics in particular. This makes it easier for them to situate issues discussed, enables a communication in which not every topic needs to be explained from scratch, and provides a basis for further communication via email or on the phone. In fact, most of the migrants involved in the solidarity work had a broader interest in the political and economic situation in Mexico: Many said they were keeping themselves up to date on developments in Mexico, mostly through reading Mexican newspapers and watching Mexican news, as well as through communicating with friends and relatives in Mexico. This was true also for second-generation migrants, as one of them explained about his understanding of the Pasta de Conchos tragedy[11] and Mexican politics:

> I had seen some information on the news about what was going in Mexico, I frequently watch the Spanish channels for news. . . . It's very, very limited what they were showing here. . . . I would keep up to date what's going on. [And speaking to] my Mom, she's like, did you hear what happened over there? . . . The [Mexican] government switched the information around to cover the eyes of the people. . . . Which I understood, because I had gone to Mexico . . . I understood what the politics are over there . . . friends that I've had over there, they're still my friends, they've been involved in politics there, small local politics. . . . I have a lot of friends that are from Mexico, so . . . we talk and . . . they go over there and . . . they have family that still live there, they come back with information.[12]

Many migrants also stated that after returning from visiting the mineros, they could not, as many nonmigrant members, 'disconnect', but felt the need to be further involved and informed about the developments in Mexico.

While this may not be true for all union members and staff of Mexican origin, where it is, it makes relating and maintaining relationships to partners abroad easier. In some cases, the solidarity work and migrants' transnational identity mutually reinforced each other, as for some second-generation migrants who were previously not strongly involved in transnational practices, the experience of working with the mineros seemed to strengthen their emotional bonds to Mexico, as they were now in closer contact with, and learned new things about the country.

Altogether, migrants' language and cultural skills, as well as their knowledge of and interest in Mexico, allows them to more easily establish and maintain close personal relationships with their partners, and thus to develop a mutual identification as a basis for the solidarity relationships. It is important to note that the personal relationships migrants established with colleagues in Mexico did not lead to a perception among the rest of union members of a merely 'inter-Mexican' solidarity. On the contrary, given the former district director's efforts at creating a consciousness for international solidarity, the strategic importance of the alliance was widely accepted among the membership.

Migrants' Personal Relationships Promoting a Lived Solidarity at the
Grassroots Level

Importantly, the development of these cross-border relationships be-tween workers and local-level staff and officers can contribute to 'bring-ing down' international solidarity from the official relationships at the leadership level, to establishing a practical solidarity at the grassroots level. In particular, the relationships migrants established led to a low-threshold communication and information exchange relevant to the soli-darity work that frequently escaped the national or district leadership level, thereby strengthening, to a certain degree, the involvement of low-level officers, staff, and regular members in the international work.

While in the USW, as in other unions, the communication with part-ners abroad is generally carried out at the national and district leadership levels, here a significant direct cross-border communication about topics related to the solidarity work took place between regular members, as well as local officers and staff. While made possible, in the first place, through the district director's commitment to building such relation-ships, it was mostly through migrants' cross-border relationships that a communication and informal information exchange at lower levels of the union hierarchy effectively took place. And in the few cases where non-migrants communicated on topics related to the solidarity work—as in the case of collaboration at the sister-plant level, where some of the locals' presidents maintained cross-border communication—they usually de-pended on migrant staff's language skills if migrants themselves were not in charge of the communication altogether.

The topics that migrant members and staff talked about with mineros varied from personal issues to political topics and information directly related to the union and the solidarity work. Among the information that they exchanged on a regular basis was general information on the situa-tion in Mexico, such as the security situation in the country, the war on drugs, the political situation, and particularly topics related to the labour movement, such as the huge 2013 teachers' strike and the Mexican government's attack on the labour movement. Also, they frequently talked about the situations and current struggles of their respective un-ions, especially the Mexican one. Finally, they communicated about more specific issues, such as current contract negotiations and the conduct of concrete union activities. Besides direct personal communication, they also often exchanged newspaper articles on the general political and eco-nomic situation in Mexico, and on topics more closely linked to union issues, such as politics concerning unions and workers.

For those involved, this low-threshold communication transformed the solidarity work into a lived solidarity: Through regular information exchange on developments concerning their partners, the workers, staff, and officers involved had a better understanding of their situation, cur-

rent struggles, and needs. Being involved in and understanding the current developments concerning the Mexican union, and discussing them
with their partners, thus lent practical meaning to the solidarity work.
Also, such information exchange provides the basis for a mutual identification and a sense of togetherness. In particular, it enhances an understanding of shared challenges, needs, and common goals, especially by
uncovering employers' strategies of pitting workers against each other.
Workers talked to were, for instance, aware of employers' tactics of
threatening to relocate production to Mexico and the United States, respectively. Also, they knew that employers in the United States often
kept to the safety and work standards established in a Global Safety
Agreement, while not keeping to them in Mexico. Those maintaining a
close cross-border communication thus generally identified strongly with
their partners and their struggles, usually stressing the goals uniting
them.

Beyond that, the information exchanged was partly directly relevant
to the international work, thereby strengthening the involvement of the
rank and file in it, and contributing to solidarity relationships below the
district and national union level. In a number of cases, relevant information reached the district director or local presidents through migrants'
relationships to the Mexican partners. In fact, in several cases, mineros
workers and leaders directly addressed their colleagues in USW locals
with specific information or requests, who then forwarded it to the district or national level. These included requests for specific support activities, such as trainings, or for information on safety standards concerning
common employers. In one case, a mineros member contacted her friend,
a USW member, asking for USW support in freeing her father, a union
leader, who had been kidnapped by drug cartels. This is probably related
to the above-mentioned fact that workers in Mexico felt more comfortable contacting their coworkers, rather than officially addressing the district or national leadership, due both to the more informal character of
the relationships and to the desire to make sure that the entire information was correctly understood. Also, regarding solidarity on the sister
plant level, such low-threshold communication made collaboration easier. In the local studies that had a Mexican sister plant, many migrant
members and staff maintained a cross-border communication and information exchange that ensured a constant information flow. And although
the president himself was nonmigrant and had poor Spanish skills, regular communication with the mineros took place at the local leadership
level, made possible by the presence of migrant staff and members: It was
one of the Mexican-origin staff persons who not only translated the communication, but was in charge, more generally, of maintaining the information exchange with the mineros, and this ensured regular communication on the solidarity work. Beyond communicating, he was also responsible for other tasks, such as reviewing and translating reports, organiz-

ing visits to Mexico, and, occasionally, travelling to Mexico for meetings with the counterparts. Through his personal background, he felt a special commitment to the work with the mineros and easily interacted with and related to them. Furthermore, in the repeated trips to the Mexican sister plant, the president always took a number of Mexican-origin staff and members as translators and supporters in organizational issues. Thus, while in this case it was not mainly migrants' personal relationships with the mineros through which most relevant communication took place, migrant-origin staff and members played an important role in enabling a close local-to-local solidarity.

CONCLUSION

Informed by insights from transnational migration studies and international labour theory, and based on empirical research in a US union with a large migrant membership, I argue that transnational migration can strengthen a felt solidarity between labour unions and promote a grassroots solidarity involving the rank and file—the lack of which often constitutes major problems in international labour solidarity. The results suggest that it can do so in three ways. First, migrants' transnational 'ways of belonging' constituted an emotional basis for their solidarity with the partners. Second, due to their language and cultural skills, and a basic knowledge of Mexico, migrants could easily relate to the partners, thereby overcoming the notorious lack of personal cross-border relationships. Third, the relationships migrants built enabled a low-threshold communication across borders that contributed to a lived solidarity and promoted the involvement of local-level staff and members in the international work.

However, the intention is not to argue that migrants necessarily play the role described above. Rather, I am arguing that their presence in unions can potentially have these effects: Evidently, it depends on a union's willingness (and ability) to build on migrants' contribution, and on the migrants' scope for action in their respective unions. In the cases studied, migrant union members encountered a district director supportive of their cross-border relationships and communication, and of rank and file involvement in international solidarity. Given the hierarchical structure of most unions and, especially, their international solidarity work, this may not always be the case. Also, migrants are still often viewed by unions as a problem rather than contributing skills and knowledge potentially enriching them.

Also, the findings merely give initial insights on the role migration can play in international labour solidarity: Given the exploratory character of the study, which only involved one union, one migrant group, and a small number of interviews, further research is needed to deepen and specify the gained insights. First of all, the results presented need to be verified through research with larger samples, and in cases whose characteristics differ from the one studied here: For instance, do migrant groups from other countries of origin differ from the Mexican-origin migrants in the way they relate to their country of origin and how they are involved in solidarity work? Are findings different in cases where migrant members are mostly first generation? Also, what role do migrants play in international solidarity in unions where the structural conditions are different—for instance, when the leadership is less supportive of rank and file involvement and cross-border contact? Beyond that, further questions not addressed here should be examined. For instance, while the focus here lay on migrants themselves, it is worth investigating to what degree migrants influence other members' attitude towards international solidarity: Do migrants' cross-border relationships at the rank and file level contribute to a solidarity also felt by nonmigrant members? Also, how do migrant groups view and engage in the solidarity with a country that is not their own? Would, for instance, the language and cultural skills that other Latin American migrants have also lead to the establishment of cross-border relationships, although not with their own country of origin? Many areas for further research therefore remain.

NOTES

1. However, nation-states remain important actors in political, social, and economic processes. But many of these are today not anymore solely defined by the 'container' of the nation-state, but cross national boundaries (Pries 2010).

2. Despite differences, most definitions of the term 'transnational' agree on some basic characteristics. Portes, Guarnizo, and Landolt (1999) suggest that in order for the term 'transnational migrant' not merely to be a substitute for the older term 'immigrant', 'transnationalism' should refer to 'occupations and activities that require *regular and sustained* social contacts *over time* across national borders for their implementation' (219, emphasis added).

3. Transnational migration should not be misunderstood, however, as a completely new phenomenon, or transnational migration studies as a 'theory' explaining all of today's migration processes. Rather, it is a research perspective that draws attention to transnational phenomena that had been disregarded before and intends to take transnational connections into account in the social sciences.

4. This is not to say that no successful cases of merely rational, strategic cross-border collaboration between unions, such as strategic corporate campaigns, exist. However, such alliances are mostly directed at the attainment of short- or medium-term goals and seldom result in stable, long-term relationships.

5. Evidently, many fundamental obstacles to international solidarity relationships exist. Among them are the national politico-institutional contexts that unions are embedded in, as well as conflicting interests arising from workers' position in the global economy.

6. Workers in different parts of the world do not necessarily share the same interests but can, at least on a short-term level, have opposite interests. Especially in a context of employers playing workers off against each other, the pursuit of local strategies can be more rational than international solidarity in defending workers' 'spatial' (as opposed to 'class') interests (Herod 2003).

7. Interview with staff person 1, Chicago, 29 January 2014.

8. In fact, migrants' language skills allowed for a large share of the communication in the alliance to be carried out in Spanish, which is remarkable given that most international work involving US unions takes place in English.

9. Interview with USW member 4, Hammond, 5 February 2014.

10. Interview with USW member 1, Chicago, 24 January 2014.

11. In 2006, about sixty-five miners were buried through a gas explosion in a coal mine in Northern Mexico, owned by Grupo México. In view of their previous strikes for improved health and safety measures, reported gas leaks prior to the explosion, and the company's half-hearted rescue attempts, the mineros began a years-long protest and accused the company of 'industrial homicide'.

12. Interview with USW member 2, Chicago, 10 February 2014.

FOURTEEN

Towards a 'Cosmopolitan' Labour Movement?

Managerial and Mobilizing Dynamics in International Trade Unionism

Charles Umney

INTRODUCTION

Through the concept of 'cosmopolitanism' (Beck 2002, 2012; Beck and Sznaider 2006; Delanty 2012), sociological literature has explored how actors orient towards new identifications that transcend national boundaries. Among the most pressing questions in this widely debated terrain has been the interconnection between cosmopolitanism and international economic integration (Pichler 2008; Skrbis and Woodward 2007). The links between the two are somewhat unclear. Does greater economic interdependence further the development of cosmopolitan identities? Among which actors, and under what circumstances, is cosmopolitanism more likely to emerge? In contrast to depictions of it as primarily an elite activity, sociologists have been keen to emphasize how people can be thrown into 'cosmopolitan' states in the course of working life under globalisation (Werbner 1999). Given this, it is striking that there has been so little cross-fertilization between literatures on cosmopolitanism and organized labour.

This conceptual chapter places ideas surrounding cosmopolitanism alongside scholarship on international trade unionism. It considers first what the study of international trade unionism reveals about cosmopolitanism before integrating the notion of cosmopolitanism into a tentative theorization of international trade unionism. Approaching these subjects from a Marxian perspective, the article argues that despite the empirical heterogeneity of international trade unionism, two main dynamics can be distinguished, referred to as 'managerial' and 'mobilizing' internationalisms. These orientations have material determinants; Managerial internationalism is rooted in labour market 'normality', and mobilizing internationalism in labour market 'tension'. In each case, cosmopolitan norms and material interest interact differently. In 'managerial' forms, the normative priorities of union officials are the dominant force in developing (or disrupting) cosmopolitanism. In 'mobilizing' forms, international solidarity is likely to develop in a disjointed manner, constrained temporally and spatially by the same material conditions which give rise to it.

The structure of the chapter is intended to reflect the Marxian spirit of 'rubbing conceptual blocks together to make a fire' (Mulhern 2011: 237). In its first half, it juxtaposes sociological literature on cosmopolitanism with Marxian materialist thought, highlighting a productive tension between the inherently 'cosmopolitan' concept of class consciousness, and the material impediments that obstruct solidarity. The resulting theoretical framework is then applied to a review of empirical literature on international trade unionism. This chapter considers the determinants of 'managerial' and 'mobilizing' modes of international activity, and the extent to which they enable cosmopolitan union orientations.

COSMOPOLITANISM AND THE MARXIAN TRADITION

There are obvious differences between sociological literature on cosmopolitanism and Marxian thought. Most broadly, cosmopolitanism denotes 'the primacy of world citizenship over all national, religious, cultural, ethnic and other parochial affiliations' (Beck and Sznaider 2006: 6). Certainly, the idea of 'world citizenship' parallels Marx and Engels's countryless proletarian as invoked in the *Communist Manifesto*. However, whereas the latter was the product of material forces—the dialectical antithesis of capitalist expansion—sociologists have more usually interpreted cosmopolitanism as an ethical or cultural orientation. To be 'cosmopolitan' signifies an intellectual or cultural openness (Roudometof 2005; Skrbis and Woodward 2007) or a belief in the legitimacy of global governance (Mau, Mewes, and Zimmermann 2008). Nonetheless, this article will argue that Marxian perspectives can interact constructively with the concept of cosmopolitanism, providing a useful theoretical framework for international trade unionism.

Here, 'cosmopolitanism' is understood as the de-emphasis of local reference points and a corresponding belief that social action should be global in scope—more abstractly, a 'universal' rather than a 'particular' outlook (Cheah 2006). 'Cosmopolitanism' might therefore be seen as the end of a continuum, which ranges from total absorption in one's immediate surroundings to complete disregard for borders and local particularities. These two extremes are of course ideal types, with a myriad of in-between points, as examined below. Moreover, to be 'cosmopolitan' must surely imply some kind of sustained, rather than transitory, commitment to this kind of normativity.

Cosmopolitanism is distinct from 'transnationalism', the latter denoting the objective extent to which actors are intertwined in cross-border economic interconnections (Roudometof 2005). Certainly, one might suppose that where transnationalism is greater, cosmopolitan orientations are more likely to emerge, but in fact cosmopolitanism is a 'fragile commitment' (Skrbis and Woodward 2007: 744), which can equally be threatened by transnational integration. The competition for resources implied by transnationalization may lead to antagonism rather than identification—indeed we might expect this effect to be sharpest among those outside wealthy elites (Pichler 2008). Hence, Beck (2012: 11) observes that the 'epochal facts' of increased global interconnection have expanded, rather than reduced, competition between different groups of workers.

One of the most important questions surrounding cosmopolitan, then, is the interaction between objective structural interconnection and human subjectivity. As Beck and Sznaider (2006) ask: Under what circumstances does objective transnationalism lead to normative cosmopolitanism? And under what conditions is the reverse true? As Weenink (2008: 1103) argues, cosmopolitanism should be considered an expression of agency, but one which is exercised under structurally given conditions. When the material upheaval of globalization impinges upon people's daily lives, they are forced to make normative decisions about how they react to it. But what forms does this impingement take, and how do these forms shape the possible responses?

Marxian thought is underpinned by the idea of class as a social relation rooted in production. Their view of ever-expanding class conflict—destroying illusory national boundaries and sentimental cultural ties as capitalism proliferates—renders Marx and Engels the consummate 'cosmopolites' (Lowy 1984). Despite the repeatedly dashed hopes of a borderless workers' movement—which have cast considerable doubt over the cosmopolitan potential of class categories (Hyman 2005; Logue 1980)—there remains much value in highlighting a class dimension to cosmopolitanism. Perhaps, however, this dimension is only revealed after 'turning the Marxian argument on its head' (Beck 2002). Rather than cosmopolitanism as the destiny of the working class, Beck (2002: 33) claims that it is 'the activists of capital, who have made globalisation their profession, [that] have no nation, while the workers and workers' movements . . . call on "their" state for help, to protect them from the adventures of globalisation'. The real value of the Marxian approach is to address cosmopolitanism as a question of the interaction between material structures and human consciousness, which I hope to do here.

Social histories of class formation emphasize how working class movements 'make themselves' in response to the material world around them, and emergent cosmopolitan norms have often been important in this process. Linebaugh and Rediker (2000: 352) record how the connections developed between highly mobile proletarians in the late eighteenth century evolved into 'egalitarian, multi-ethnic conceptions of humanity'. Similarly, Thompson (1963) identified internationalism as central to the early working class movement in England, particularly following the French Revolution. Werbner (1999) highlights more recent instances of 'working class cosmopolitans' among migrant workforces, showing that the latter are equally capable of 'opening up to the world' as elites. This paper argues that analysis of international trade unionism must recognize both the potential for solidarity to develop through the efforts of workers, but also understand why the latter face stronger structural barriers to cosmopolitanism than managerial elites. The next section will consider theoretically why this might be the case.

Towards a Theoretical Framework

Marxian theory is concerned with contradictions in capitalist development and so is well placed to consider why transnationalism can, far from furthering cosmopolitanism, have the opposite effect. Harvey (2006a) argues that capital is impelled, on one hand, to 'annihilate space' as it conquers new markets. On the other hand, it simultaneously creates new boundaries. As new economic geographies emerge in the search for greater profitability, existing cultural, political, and infrastructural environments are undermined. Hence, for Harvey (2006: 419–20), class conflict is distorted by territorial fragmentation. 'Encrusted traditions' and 'local prejudices' become blurred with the economic claims workers demand of governments and local employers. Consequently, two opposing conceptions of space are juxtaposed. At critical junctures where capital reshapes economic space to find more profitable configurations, the universalizing force of capitalist class power is brought into sharp relief. The empirical consequences, however, are immediate pressures to preserve existing arrangements upon which living standards depend. Hence, the local and the cosmopolitan are sharply polarized at points of 'tension' — where capital's reconfiguration of space threatens the material well-being of particular groups at particular times.

For Haworth and Ramsay (1986), workers' responses to these 'tensions' cannot be understood without recognizing that labour and capital have qualitatively different 'starting points'. The latter is likely to view workplace relations in 'abstract' terms, as 'calculated, objectified, impersonal aggregates' (Haworth and Ramsay 1986: 60). By contrast, workers experience these relations 'concretely', as networks of social relation-ships, within which solidarities develop. For Haworth and Ramsay (1986), this 'concrete' rather than 'abstract' experience confers an inher-ently *reactive* character on union action. Capital is impelled to transcend existing arrangements in pursuit of greater profitability, and workers must respond. Nonetheless, they do not view this 'reactive' character as inevitable, suggesting that proactive construction of *political* conscious-ness among workers—rather than reacting to material threats—could po-tentially overcome it. But rather than sharply dividing between material and political rationales for action, they suggest that the development of political norms shapes how material interest is interpreted and pursued. The two are interrelated, and analysis can seek to untangle them.

My theoretical framework synthesizes the notion of spatial contradic-tion under capitalism with an understanding of the generally reactive character of union action. As Harvey (2006a) argues, capital is impelled to seek new spatial configurations. As Haworth and Ramsay (1986) suggest, workers are impelled to react to these reconfigurations. Given the contra-dictory spatial horizons involved in this process—between the abstract 'space' of multinational capital and the concrete threat to 'place'—it fol-lows that at moments of 'tension', potential responses are polarized be-tween the local and the cosmopolitan. This polarization may manifest in a sharply posed choice between challenging the scope of capital through expanded solidarity or efforts to preserve local conditions. The ambiva-lence inevitably underpinning cosmopolitanism—between opportunity for new solidarities and hostility to potential threats—comes to a head in these moments of tension.

Of course, in practice union responses assume an array of forms which cannot be satisfactorily encapsulated in this bipolar way. Howev-er, as Hyman (1975) argues, unions perpetually list between 'exclusive' and 'inclusive' tendencies, and empirical diversity reflects the different actions these logics produce in different circumstances. The argument here is that moments of tension become points of decision between the particular logic of 'place' preservation and the cosmopolitan logic of class solidarity. As suggested below, cases of 'mobilizing internationalism' are the disjointed and constrained empirical syntheses of these two things.

This framework recalls Marxism's dialectical emphasis on the quanti-tative and qualitative dynamics of social change. Qualitative changes in empirical life should be interpreted by considering changes in the under-lying dynamics of existing factors, rather than first seeking new variables. The relevant dynamic here is the balance of power between employer and employee. Developments that expand capital's spatial power, like the opening of new labour markets, alter this balance. From the perspec-tive of union members such changes may be abstract, but if and when they are manifested as concrete threats to employment security, then workers must make qualitative decisions about their reaction. Expressed most abstractly, this means that changes in the nature of trade union solidarity emerge disjointedly, through responses to particular tensions which become visible as the balance of class power shifts.

For Mandel (cited in Post 1999), because unions generally engage in struggle only reactively, there is an inherent discontinuity in which the origins of labour bureaucracy can be located. It is in response to tensions that mobilization can occur. But because tensions are manifestations of underlying material dynamics, the latter's parameters shape the terms under which the former are experienced, and therefore the possible reactions to them. While political and normative factors may have substantial autonomy in catalyzing class solidarities, they do so under anterior conditions: 'the necessary starting point for new generations of practice' (Hall 1985: 95). It is in response to such tensions that cosmopolitan and local logics clash, and consequently through which international solidarity can emerge. But whether a genuine cosmopolitanism can be the outcome of these clashes will be discussed further below.

The preceding discussion considered the relationship between cosmopolitanism and transnationalism, examining the connections between them through a Marxian lens. I juxtaposed the notion of a cosmopolitan class identity with the localizing pressures exerted by capitalist reconfiguration of economic space, and argued that this distinction becomes sharply polarized at particular points of 'tension'. Next, I will argue that, through union responses to these tensions, a 'mobilizing' internationalism may emerge, but one which is constrained by the anterior conditions giving rise to it. By contrast in times of 'normality', a 'managerial' model of internationalism is likely to prevail, more reflective of the normative priorities of union elites.

INTERNATIONAL TRADE UNIONISM

International Trade Unionism as the Interaction of Cosmopolitan Norms and Material Interest

The last section noted the importance of cosmopolitan norms among insurgent proletarians, particularly in the labour movement's early, 'defining' period before the mid-nineteenth century (Van der Linden 2008; see also Hobsbawm 1962). While cosmopolitan currents among politically engaged working class activists are therefore historically evident, identifying such a tradition among unions themselves is considerably harder. As bargaining actors, unions make demands of the institutions capable of meeting these claims—frequently the state. Consequently, the same movements are likely to 'make peace with the nation' (Linebaugh and Rediker 2000: 352) when those claims are recognized. Accordingly, Logue (1980: 51) confines the strongest instances of international workers' activity, for example the eight-hour day movement, to 'the period of initial organisation'.

Consequently, industrial relations throughout the twentieth century and beyond have remained dominated by national actors, with the international environment—from the perspective of union members—a remote extra layer (Gumbrell-McCormick 2008). Early twentieth century trade unionists, such as Edo Fimmen, sought to avoid this. Fearing that confederations of national centres would remain little more than forums for negotiating particular interests with all the rivalries that entailed, Fimmen directed his energy towards the sectorally organized international trade secretariats (today renamed global union federations). Because these were able to directly mirror multinational corporation structures, they could ostensibly work as a means towards directly coordinated multinational collective bargaining (Levinson 1972). This 'evolutionary optimism' (Ramsay 1999) ties transnationalism and cosmopolitanism together, anticipating that the increasing interlinking of workers through multinational corporations will normalize global solidarity as a response to economic necessity.

While Levinson's vision of widespread multinational bargaining generally remains unrealized, some international trade secretariats/global union federations have indeed achieved striking advances. For example, the International Transport Workers' Federation's 'Flag of Convenience' (FOC) campaign establishes internationally recognized wages on ships registered to less-regulated countries. These conditions can be enforced through international union action—where dockers in different countries may refuse to unload ships violating international agreements. The International Transport Workers' Federation has sought to counter conflicts of interest between capital and labour supply countries by emphasizing the normative value of a universal minimum wage for seafarers (Koch-Baumgarten 1998; Lillie 2004). Hence, while the FOC campaign is ostensibly about improving economic conditions, it also capitalizes on internationalist ideology among port unions. Moreover, while dockers have 'no consistent structural interest' (Lillie 2004: 58–59) in the campaign, they are threatened by wider deregulation of sea transport. In this sense, the campaign is best understood via the dynamic *interaction* between cosmopolitan norms and material interest. The former can catalyse a wider reformulation of the latter.

Such cases challenge more pessimistic visions of international unionism. Logue's (1980: 10) theorization suggests the very purpose of unions—to 'pursue the *short-term* economic interests of their members' (emphasis added)—excludes international solidarity. Cosmopolitan norms are, for Logue, merely 'ideological residues', and international activity remains the preserve of rarefied elites. Certainly, complex and contradictory short-term economic interests have beset the history of international union organizations (Carew et al. 2000), and consequently some writers (e.g., Gumbrell-McCormick 2008) posit a clear distinction between 'economic' and 'political' rationales for international activity. For Logue, the latter is the weaker force, confined to officials with the time for such pursuits, and the former provides little reliable motivation for solidarity.

An economic rationale has been invoked to justify both Levinson's optimism and Logue's pessimism. A productive synthesis may be to follow Van der Linden (2008) in distinguishing a more nuanced typology of rationales for international cooperation, ranging from short-term economic interest to normative support for international solidarity. Two categories are situated in between: Longer-term economic interests and indirect interests (the belief that improving others' working conditions will help preserve one's own). Hence, normative orientations, rather than being separate from material motivations, are manifested in different ways of interpreting material interest. The idea of cosmopolitanism as a continuum might be converted into the following diagram, which shows increasingly 'cosmopolitan' ways of pursuing interest.

As argued previously, perpetual antagonism between 'exclusive' and 'inclusive' orientations underpins the historical development of trade unionism, and the adoption of different orientations in response to specific material tensions pushes union strategies in different directions along Figure 14.1. The previous section argued that the 'tensions' which enable mobilization occur against a backdrop of sharply polarized spatial logics, and this both generates and seals off collective constituencies. These tensions therefore simultaneously push unions towards expanded cooperation and present obstacles to more cosmopolitan forms of solidarity. This contradiction is explored in the following section.

'Tension' and Mobilizing Internationalism

By examining contemporary empirical scholarship on international trade unionism, this section argues that cases of international mobilization tend to be reactions to specific material tensions. For our purposes, 'mobilizing internationalism' means internationally coordinated grassroots activity (primarily strikes or other industrial action) targeted at policymaking elites—as in Turnbull's (2006) case study—or shared multinational employers. Erne's (2008) *European Unions* voices this ambition forcefully, arguing for a more democratic (i.e., grassroots-led) pan-Euro-

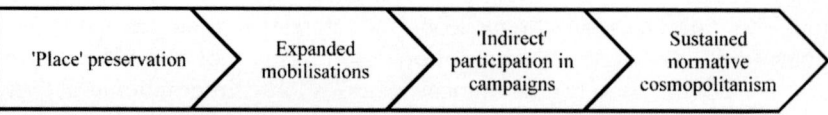

Figure 14.1. Degrees of cosmopolitanism.
Source: adapted from Van der Linden (2008).

pean union engagement. This section argues that such mobilizations are possible, but also suggests that their reactive character confers temporal and spatial limitations on 'mobilizing internationalism', generally limiting its progress along the diagram in Figure 14.1.

Turnbull (2006: 311–12) highlights the reactive nature of recent international mobilizations in the European docks sector, tracing the development of pan-European solidarity against liberalizing legislation to the International Transport Workers' Federation's decision to 'mobilise big actions *against specific issues*' (emphasis added). In Erne's case, critics (see Phelan et al. 2009) have pursued similar lines of argument. Phelan suggests that mobilizations are sporadic interruptions of the normally 'technocratic' character of international trade unionism. Hancké (in Phelan et al. 2009; see also Hancké 2000) characterizes mobilizations as 'defensive coalitions' rather than proactive efforts to build a cosmopolitan labour identity. Hancké (Phelan et al. 2009: 203) acknowledges the possibility for solidaristic norms, but argues that these norms 'work best when infused with a healthy dose of self-interest'. So interpreted, mobilizing internationalism is not about whether unions follow economic or political rationales, but the spatial and temporal horizons of their reactions to tensions. In other words, whether they react to material threats through 'place' preservation or through expanded cooperation over particular grievances.

Meardi (2012) and Greer and Hauptmeier's (2008) depictions of intra-European trade union cooperation resonate with this notion of tensions. Meardi (2012: 104) argues that disinterest in international solidarity may reflect a lack of scope for 'coercive comparisons' (i.e., direct labour market competition) between workers in different countries. Where coercive comparisons do exist, international solidarity is 'needed, but uneasy': A rationale for solidarity coexists with a material basis for rivalry. Finally, Meardi suggests that where capital successfully stabilizes new international divisions of labour, the contradictory rationale for solidarity again weakens. 'Tension' has been followed by release. Greer and Hauptmeier (2008) argue that where employers pursue coercive comparisons, and where a lack of access to 'co-management resources' impedes the ability of union elites to influence employers, the key actor becomes the 'political entrepreneur'—activists or leaders that inject principles of solidarity to frame particular tensions as necessitating international, rather than local, collective action. In their study, such mobilizations—as opposed to elite bargaining—were confined to the European level, a fact which will be examined further below.

What Greer and Hauptmeier term 'political entrepreneurship' is integral to trade union mobilization more broadly. Kelly's (1998: 29) application of mobilization theory to trade unionism highlights the importance of normative framing in industrial relations disputes. He points towards the use of 'emotionally loaded categories'—such as class solidarity—in defining expanded constituencies for collective action. Carew et al.'s (2000: 526) history repeatedly illustrates the need for international solidarity to be 'achieved time and time again' by looking beyond short-term interest in response to economic challenges. Mobilization progresses through the 'framing' of spatially and temporally expanded models of solidarity. However, as Kelly (1998) shows, a necessary condition for this process is *specific* grievances, which can be reacted against and reframed. Inherently 'cosmopolitan' concepts, such as class solidarity, can be used to frame specific disputes and push mobilizing responses into the second stage shown in Figure 14.1. In this way, as Weenink (2008) has suggested, cosmopolitanism emerges through the utilization of agency (in this case by union activists), in response to specific impingements of transnationalism into daily life. Where there are exceptional pockets of militant ideology, as among docker participants in the FOC campaign, mobilization may progress some way along Figure 14.1. The 'anterior conditions' of these tensions, however, push perpetually back in the other direction. I argue here that these constraining conditions take two specific forms.

The first constraint is spatial. Because mobilizing constituencies form in reaction to specific grievances, they generally encompass only those workers who are directly threatened by 'tensions'. It was previously theorized that tensions reflect capital's search for more profitable arrangements. This process must also have actual or potential 'beneficiaries'—whose material well-being is embedded in prospective new 'place' configurations—and the existence of these 'beneficiaries' imposes limits to the scope of solidarity. Even an exceptional case reflecting substantial normative commitment, such as the FOC campaign, reveals interest antagonisms between unions from 'labour supply' (i.e., developing) and 'capital supply' (i.e., developed) countries embodied in tensions over FOC minimum rates.

These barriers are clearest within Europe. European unions' decisions to expand solidarity in response to Europe-wide restructuring initiatives have also depended on a 'shared European vulnerability' relative to the rest of the world (Fetzer 2008: 295). In other words, expanded mobilization between European unions against shared employers was catalysed by the existence of potential beneficiaries of new spatial configurations beyond Europe. Indeed, the continuing development of international union institutions within Europe may enhance the sense of the non-European world as a threat (Ghighliani 2005). More broadly, other writers observe barriers to solidarity between workers whose existing 'places' are undermined, and workers whose 'places' are in creation (Silver 2003). In these contexts, mobilizing internationalism may be an attempt to define a larger, but still exclusive, conception of 'place' and to expand the constituencies mobilizing in its defence. Hence, the potential use of cosmopolitan class categories to mobilize nonetheless falls short of an actual cosmopolitanism. Mobilizing solidarities expand disjointedly within the contours of uneven capitalist development, simultaneously creating and limiting constituencies for collective action.

Moreover, because of its reactive nature, mobilizing internationalism is also constrained temporally. As Meardi (2012) observes, where tensions produced by coercive comparisons are eventually diminished, the rationale (however uneasy) for solidarity weakens. Hyman (2005) identifies an historical 'agitator' internationalism—a 'bottom-up' response to employer internationalisation—which is inherently reactive, enduring only while particular mobilizing struggles continue unresolved. In the next section, I will consider more precisely how these temporal dynamics are sharply different in 'managerial' models of internationalism.

In these senses, the reactive character of mobilizing internationalism means it is unlikely to be fully 'cosmopolitan' insofar as, in practice, any embrace of universalist principles cannot be separated from the disruptive pressures of interest representation. Because it reacts to specific threats to material security in specific places, instances of mobilization are inherently finite. Additionally, because expanded solidarities formed in response to capital's reconfiguration of economic space are catalysed by the 'shared vulnerability' (Fetzer 2008) of a particular constituency, they are liable to exclude the 'beneficiaries' of new spatial arrangements. The framing of particular tensions can use 'emotionally loaded categories' (Kelly 1998: 29) such as class solidarity to catalyse expanded mobilizations rather than place preservation, but this cosmopolitan thrust collides with the abovementioned limits, giving mobilizing internationalism a disjointed character.

'Normality' and Managerial Internationalism

The term 'managerial internationalism' may take on pejorative, elitist overtones (Martinez-Lucio 2010), with some writers drawing a clear link between bureaucratic conservatism and labour parochialism (most forcefully Moody 1997). For Logue (1980), the international activity of full-time officials is often parasitical and irrelevant to members' interests. While acknowledging the potentially conservative role of bureaucracy, this section offers an ambivalent portrayal of managerial internationalism. It suggests the normative activity of officials is the most likely route to a sustained cosmopolitanism within unions, albeit at the expense of grassroots agency. In particular, it emphasizes how the development of international interpersonal contacts at elite levels facilitates sustained normative commitment to international activity among international union officials.

As Hyman (2005) has argued, while mobilizations disrupt the bureaucratic division of labour, the status quo of international trade unionism is usually the deferral of international affairs 'upwards' to union elites. This may be because the agency of managerial elites is less constrained by specific structural configurations than that of workers. Logue (1980) argues that, where officials undertake international activity, they do so liberated from imperatives of interest representation. Gumbrell-McCormick (2008) argues that political commitments to internationalism among unions primarily reflect the normative positions of union officials. Accordingly, the more optimistic accounts of union cooperation through institutions, such as European Work Councils, emphasize personal agency and developing interconnections between union officials at the elite level. Such interconnections stabilize the 'inner life' of institutions (Banyuls, Haipeter, and Neumann 2008), and catalyse an 'evolution in the attitude' of key actors (Da Costa and Rehfeldt 2007: 315). Contra reactive mobilizations, these developing interpersonal solidarities may provide more scope for a sustained cosmopolitan commitment to grow steadily. As Waddington (2006) argues, key 'office holders' within European Work Councils are most likely to de-emphasize local reference points in their activities, enabling more developed communication and information.

Despite its elitism, this organizational dynamic may also be more adapted to international 'social movement' campaigning. This assertion appears counterintuitive, given associations between 'social movement unionism' and grassroots initiative (e.g., Moody 1997). More nuance therefore needs to be added to the central distinction. Managerial and mobilizing internationalisms should be understood not as rigid empirical categories, but rather as 'directions'. Mobilizing internationalism sees active agency transferred 'downwards', as unions stimulate expanded solidarity between members in reaction to tensions. Managerial internationalism sees agency transferred 'upwards' to full-time officials. This does not mean the issues it addresses are necessarily irrelevant to members. For example, members may express normative commitment towards causes such as human rights campaigning, which go on to become part of a cosmopolitan 'rights'-oriented unionism.

However, while such campaigns may indeed reflect cosmopolitan norms shared at the grassroots level, their driving agency often gravitates away from member mobilization and towards managerial coordination. Frank's (2003) historical study infers a 'hierarchical dynamic' to 'social movement' campaigning. Because normativity, rather than material interest, is prominent union activity that increasingly prioritizes influencing the consumer, or voting choices of the public at large—inevitably weakening the primacy of member self-representation (Ross 2008). 'Managerial internationalism', as discussed here, cannot therefore be caricatured as simply insular bureaucracy, but may also facilitate innovative forms, such as social movement unionism.

If managerial internationalism catalyses ongoing interpersonal contact and reflects the normative orientations of key officials, it is also therefore less confined by the temporal and spatial barriers inherent in the mobilizing model. Managerial internationalism is the 'normality' of international trade unionism, sporadically disrupted by the eruption of underlying material antagonisms into visible 'tensions'. The latter, by definition, are disjointed and finite, and it is in the gaps between them that managerial agency consolidates. Hence, even accounts of celebrated instances of international solidarity, like the 1990s Liverpool dock lockouts, suggest that following initial surges in solidarity the preeminent actors in maintaining and coordinating communications on a day-to-day basis were increasingly officials (Kennedy and Lavalette 2004). Even in sustained international campaigns, which emphasize militant industrial solidarity, mobilizations tend to be reactive, with full-time officials tasked with fostering contacts between tensions (Umney 2012). Thus, different unions are not divided into 'mobilizing' or 'managerial' brackets. Instead, wherever it occurs, the former temporarily disrupts the latter. This suggests an oscillation between 'directions' within unions depending on material circumstances.

Cosmopolitanism is therefore hardly alien to union rank and file, but its development assumes radically different forms at different organizational levels. In mobilizing internationalism, it is disjointed, and continually runs up against countervailing forces. In managerial internationalism, it is often (though not always) isolated from grassroots concerns, and thus able to develop more independently. Union officials may thus resemble the 'voluntary cosmopolitans' highlighted by Pichler (2008), whose relatively sheltered economic position affords them the liberty to cultivate a 'personal involvement' in cosmopolitanism. Following Haworth and Ramsay (1986), like the capitalist, full-time union officials have different 'starting points' from their members. In their relative removal from workplace pressures, they can consider the role of the union in more abstract terms. Thus, their action can more easily extend beyond reacting to threats to 'place', loosening the constraints of anterior material conditions that obstruct progress along Figure 14.1. One might also hypothesize that, because by definition cosmopolitan norms are aspatial and atemporal, they may even legitimate a managerial division of labour within unions. If mobilizations are inherently 'particular', then they cannot be used to further a sustained normative cosmopolitanism. Therefore, the two types identified here may, in fact, be complementary. The contacts forged by officialdom in times of 'normality' may be invaluable tools to draw on in times of 'tension', comparable to the idea of a 'ratchet' in Levinson's (1972) work (Ramsay 1999). This is not to suggest managerial internationalism is inherently cosmopolitan. Rather, the normativity of official agency has greater autonomy in managerial models. 'Cosmopolitan' officials are critical conditions for sustained international solidarity, and parochial officials are a major barrier. Where officials do assume 'cosmopolitan' outlooks, in order to translate into international mobilization, this must interact with, and in the process give a new meaning to, existing expectations about interest representation.

CONCLUSION

This contribution has sought to bring together the hitherto distant bodies of literature on cosmopolitanism and transnational industrial relations. In doing so, it has suggested two points for consideration in the ongoing debate over cosmopolitanism. First, it has sought to show how cosmopolitanism develops according to different dynamics at elite and grassroots levels within unions. Secondly, it has suggested that the ambivalence of economic transnationalism, simultaneously a driver of cosmopolitanism and its opposite, is heightened for workers at points of 'tension', at which these competing logics clash and find new form.

The chapter has also sought to build the notion of cosmopolitanism into a theorization of international trade unionism. It has pointed towards contradictions in the spatial dynamics of capitalism, reflecting the juxtaposition between a universalizing class antagonism and the material pressures to preserve 'place'. These contradictions both produce and constrain instances of 'mobilizing internationalism', which can most abstractly be described as qualitative manifestations of underlying power shifts between labour and capital. The kernel of truth in the suggestion that cosmopolitanism is confined to managerial elites lies in the fact that 'managerial internationalism' does not face the temporal and spatial constraints exerted on mobilizing internationalism to the same degree, if at all.

Of course, the concrete empirical forms taken by international trade unionism will remain heterogeneous. Nonetheless, despite this practical diversity, this article argues that the core of these two different 'directions' will always be discernible. International trade unionism's 'normality' is likely to remain dominated by full-time international officials, and increasingly cosmopolitan union orientations are possible depending on their own preferences. At times of 'tension', the potential exists for the limited expansion of solidarity to create a constrained and disjointed mobilizing model. It is mistaken to look for an undiluted normative cosmopolitanism as the driving force behind working class opposition to globalization. Rather, focus should be on the ways in which inherently cosmopolitan concepts, such as class solidarity, catalyse the expansion of the scope of material conflicts between employer and employee. It is only through this kind of class analysis that an emancipatory element to cosmopolitanism can be discerned.

Questions for the Future

Towards an Analytical Framework

Knut Kjeldstadli, Andreas Bieler, Roland Erne, Darragh Golden, Idar Helle, Tiago Matos, and Sabina Stan

To what extent is transnational trade union action possible? And if possible, what are the conditions enabling and promoting such action? The contributors to this book have approached these themes from several analytical angles and levels. Obviously, it is not possible to cover all angles in one discussion. Yet, it may be useful to have a notion about the location of one's own contribution in relation to others. What does a text say, and what is ignored? Without an understanding of how your own approach is located within an overarching analytical framework, a student of trade unionism may choose her/his research design in a somewhat haphazard way. We have to know: Do contributions differ by opposite claims in the same field? Or do they differ simply by not working in the same field? We are under no illusion that this summary or this volume offers a complete and comprehensive analysis, if that was even possible. But we do think that it provides first steps towards a more complex understanding. Hence, in this conclusion we will critically engage with the various contributions to this volume by moving systematically through various levels of analysis before discussing in more detail the new power resources available to workers. Drawing on historical materialism, we will start with the structure of the global political economy, before moving to various superstructural levels. This approach equips us well to address the question of structure; it shall have to be complemented with analyses concerning agency.

LEVELS OF ANALYSIS

In relation to the structural dynamics underlying the global political economy, Andreas Bieler stresses the growth imperative of capitalism, producing both internal pressure for capitalization and an outwards thrust. This expansion links various national economies, sectors, and economic units in 'uneven and combined development'. This relatively abstract category may be filled with more specific analyses of 'varieties of capitalism' (Crouch and Streeck 1997) in a move towards a more concrete level of analysis. Malayan and Swiss economies *do* differ, to put it bluntly. However, the varieties cannot be understood by being ordered along a hierarchical scale, where some 'national models' perform 'better' than others. Instead, they shall be placed within the international division of labour; the development between varieties is uneven, which is the result of their specific combination. Thus, workers in different parts of the world may be placed in different circumstances. They may be 'intertwined in cross-border economic interconnections' to different degrees, as Charles Umney points out. And their location may convince them that they have, or claim to have, different or opposing interests, at least in the short run. Nevertheless, the insistence on bringing the economy in does not mean that unions' political positioning and agency can be taken as given. One cannot read 'a trade union's strategies simply off the economic structure' (Bieler, this volume).

Building on an understanding of economic structure, the next level that is activated may be called the *social level* or class structure. Marcel van der Linden is concerned with changes in the global working class, its size, changing composition, and its (re)location — meaning a differently composed class, where the classical skilled worker is no longer the de facto standard worker and huge sectors of the working class being located in the Global South. These changes are not followed up with an adequate reorganization of trade unions. On the contrary, union density is shrinking and labour parties have lost ground. The difficult, if not impossible, task is a radical reformation of trade unions on the premises of the new global working class — which is in precarious work, performs service tasks, and is also recruited from categories previously considered as being from the 'core' of the proletariat. Analyses of class structure also include a spatial dimension. Bieler does not stress the differences between the working classes in the North and South; he endorses the notion of a transnational 'class-in-itself', an 'emerging global proletariat [which] is not yet a class-for-itself'. In his discussion of militant mass strikes that took place, more or less, simultaneously in South Africa, Brazil, and India, Jörg Nowak finds some striking similarities. Although there were neither acts of solidarity or communication nor copying between the three countries, there is a connection: All three strikes were triggered by a working class who worked in a growth sector while they only experienced the downside of this development. Such similar structural positioning may perhaps be a step towards transitional solidarity, in the same way these mass strikes spread geographically within the three countries. Moreover, Ingo Schmidt sees the possibility of a reformative phase, in which today's new working class, 'a motley crew', develops into a more coherent European working class — as did the early British working class described by E. P. Thompson—but now on a European level. After a period of integration after World War II, a period of radicalization in the 1970s, and neoliberal dominance since, he foresees a possible new militancy in Europe. And yet, he also points to the possibility of a split in the class along racist and nationalist divisions. Like Bieler and van der Linden, he sees no simple, direct link from class position to politics. Nevertheless, he does consider transnational solidarity to be a possibility. One component of this composite new working class is labour migrants or transmigrants. While migrants are often seen as a weak link, a category at a distance to unions, Jenny Jungehülsing shows that Mexican migrants to the United States function as a bridge between unions in their old and new country. Tiago Matos tells how Spanish posted workers and a Norwegian union were able to combine forces. Also Knut Kjeldstadli deals with migrants—or more precisely, the way a dominant union in Oslo, Norway, developed a policy of integration.

Moving 'upwards' from the social level, from the issue of class composition, there is the *ideational* level, the ideological, psychological, and cultural dimensions. A very simple approach is to deduct the existence of a certain attitude from the given class composition. The problem is, of course, that unionists do not always behave in accordance with these expectations. In fact, they often act in the opposite way, supporting national corporations rather than fellow workers abroad. One effort to deal with this discrepancy is the notion of 'false consciousness': Workers do not understand what is good for them. However, as Bieler comments, this is an unsatisfactory conclusion. One answer, which is probably closer to the truth, may be reached by looking at time horizons: They may see that in the long run transnational solidarity is preferable, yet support other policy choices in the short run. Another approach relies on the notions of Antonio Gramsci about 'hegemony' and 'common sense', but also the possibility of a space where 'good sense' may develop counter to hegemony (Robinson 2006). Theories about this ideological and psychological level, trying to explain why workers go against what radicals consider their best interest, are probably among the ones in most need of development.

Moreover, there is the *political* level to be discussed. One may conceive political action as organizing and participating in power struggles. Jörg Nowak's chapter underlines that the contents and meaning of mass strikes may develop and shift in the process over time. Seemingly 'economic' demands may become political and affect society at large. Politics may also be more precisely understood as practices concerning the state and actors such as political parties as well as transnational bodies such as the European Economic Community, dealt with by Darragh Golden. An analysis should not be restricted to being 'a glimpse of the present'. Time has to be taken into consideration. Sometimes the importance of *history* is best understood in terms of tradition, trajectories, or path dependence.

The importance of different historical national contexts comes out in Darragh Golden's text. The Italian pattern has been dominated by the global power struggles linked to the Cold War logic, by the conflicts between the communist, the social democratic, and the Catholic labour movement. The Irish were more concerned with 'the national question', and their stance on internationalism was subordinated to this nationalism. The force of history, or path dependence, has its limits though. The Italian General Confederation of Labour, the Italian confederation linked to the Communist party, swung from resistance against the European Economic Community to a more positive position around 1960.

Finally, we need to consider the individual level. For practical transnational solidarity to develop, there have to be people with a transnational consciousness or attitude, someone who identifies with 'foreigners'. We may dub this *the personal factor*. In the words of Bianca Föhrer in this volume: 'Workers' representatives need to identify transnationally, both as a person and as representative body.' There is here clearly an emotional element, a feeling of identification. As Jenny Jungehülsing puts it, transnational solidarity has to be 'felt' or 'lived', a theme often overlooked in theories of transnational movements. In the case of the American union with Mexican members or Oslo construction workers, the importance of a radical leadership core comes out as decisive. In a way, this only begs a new question: *Why* do particular individuals fill this initiating role? This may perhaps be approached best by individual psychology, but a more sociological take on the matter could be to look for collective memories, as mentioned in the Oslo case, be it through trade union education (Föhrer), ethnic ties (Jungehülsing), fight and learning cycles (Kjeldstadli), or cycles of contestation (Webster). Both previous experiences and new learning processes should be investigated.

When reflecting on the possibility of trade union agency, a premise for trade union efficacy is power. Looking for *sources of power*, resources on various dimensions that may open up such action, is therefore central in a study of transnational union action, and of unions in general. The next section will draw out the related findings, explored in various contributions to this volume.

TRADE UNION AGENCY, POWER RESOURCES, AND STRATEGY

Starting from Eric Olin Wright's (2000) distinction between *structural* power and *associational* power, Beverly Silver (2003) developed this distinction further in relation to labour movements. Associational power depends on collective organizations such as trade unions and political parties. In her contribution to this book, Marissa Brookes suggests a more precise formulation: 'the capacity of workers to mobilize themselves to act collectively'. One example is the mass strikes in India, Brazil, and

South Africa analysed by Jörg Nowak. Structural power, in turn, can be divided into two subtypes. 'The first subtype of structural power (which we shall call marketplace bargaining power) is the power that results directly from tight labor markets. The second subtype of structural power (which we shall call workplace bargaining power) is the power that results from the strategic location of a particular group of workers within a key industrial sector' (Silver 2003: 13). While strike action is more narrowly focused on the workplace, association power also relates to broader mobilizations of alliances between trade unions and social movements in resisting exploitation in the sphere of social reproduction. An additional power resource of secondary character is institutional power. *Institutional* power, Marissa Brookes points out in this volume, is 'the capacity to hold an employer accountable by invoking the formal or informal rules that structure the employment relationship'. In laws, regulations, practices, and procedures, power is embedded. Institutions 'function as substitutes for those social compromises agreed upon in the past' (Brinkman and Nachtwey 2013: 8). This power hinges on the adversary's willingness—or feeling of being pressured—to abide by rules and norms. It is the way in which associational and structural power is incorporated in societal institutions including, for example, labour law or the welfare state. Importantly, institutional power can continue even if the underlying structural and associational power resources for trade unions are dwindling. Societal institutions fix basic compromises and sometimes even enshrine them in law beyond economic developments and short-term changes in power relations between capital and labour (Dörre 2011: 277). However, it also needs to be remembered that 'in the long term institutional power cannot work without the substantiation of structural and organisational power' (Brinkman and Nachtwey 2013: 8). Since the early 1970s, institutional power has increasingly been undermined as a result of global restructuring and capital renouncing national class compromises in industrialized countries.

Nevertheless, while global restructuring has undermined institutional power resources, it has also provided new types of power. The scholarly literature has identified an almost plethoric number of sources. Webster, Lambert, and Bezuidenhout identify symbolic/moral power and logistical power as new sources of strength for labour in this respect. Symbolic, or moral, power 'involves the struggle of "right" against "wrong", providing the basis for an appeal both to the public and politicians, as well as to allies in civil society' (Webster, Lambert, and Bezuidenhout 2008: 12). It is part of associational power, 'since it draws on forms of social organization. But it draws its strength from taking moral claims in the workplace and articulating them as general social claims' (Webster, Lambert, and Bezuidenhout 2008: 12). Making public the abuse of worker and human rights in shareholder meetings, on the basis of having acquired a few shares, is an example of what this new power source consists of and what its potential is (Webster, Lambert, and Bezuidenhout 2008: 197). In this volume, Webster also mentions *logistical* power, a variety of structural power, where 'disruptive politics are drawn from the workplace into the public arena', for instance by physically blocking access.

Normative power is at the heart of Jamie K. McCallum's plea for 'governance' as a nongovernmental field where new 'rules of engagement' may be developed, rules that may open the opportunity for workers to exercise power. Examples are neutrality agreements, social clauses, codes of conduct, and global framework agreements. McCallum argues against obtaining 'rights' for workers as a basic strategy. Rights make workers dependent on court decisions. Rules tell how a certain engagement is to be played out, yet the workers themselves and other actors have to enact the play. How far is this normative source of power really binding? In the terminology of Webster, is there strong *discursive* or *symbolic* or *moral* power? How far does moral power have to rest on mutual interest? Will such considerations be abandoned if interests on the side of capital are redefined? Can adversaries be publicly shamed? In this volume, Sabrina Zajak's focus on transnational labour rights activism represents a case in which appeals are made to moral claims of social justice.

Brookes also mentions *coalitional* power, the ability to mobilize additional resources, from actors with sympathy and solidarity for the union's cause. A pertinent question then is the role of mass media: The way they work to mould public opinion, as shown by Matos in his report on the Spanish plumbers in Norway. Webster also sees *cooperative* power: Built more on an equal alliance, of shared interest, for instance between social movements and unions. Such alliances may also be struck between unions, social movements, and political parties, as has been the case in Ireland, Italy, and Norway, with various political orientations. Democratic political systems have allowed labour to shift class conflict from the marketplace to the political arena. In Matos' analysis of the Spanish plumbers, the efforts by the Norwegian 'Red-Green' government (2005–2013) to equip unions with legal tools to combat social dumping are mentioned. The power springing from such cooperation is one example of *political mobilisation and exchange power* (Erne 2008: 30), an entity too often neglected in trade union studies. Resulting from our CAS international workshop in Oslo in 2014 we have, therefore, devoted two conference special journal issues to this topic. Whereas (contentious) labour politics is at the centre of our *Transfer* issue on 'European Collective Action in Times of Crisis' (Erne et. al 2015), our *Labor History* issue assesses the contribution of 'politicization' processes to transnational trade union action (Erne, Helle, and Stan 2015).

These analyses of sources of power lead to a new look at the old pair of structure and agency. While several types of power spring from structure, associational power is intimately linked to agency; so is coalitional power. Unions may draw on existing moral power; they may also produce such power, for instance by the way they choose to frame conflicts. Some are able to produce societal power, in which broader societal issues beyond the workplace are at stake. Hence, in analyses of power resources, sharp dichotomies should be avoided. In a way, the analysis of power resources indicates the internal relationship between structure and agency, in which the former constrains and enables agency, while the latter in turn may transform the structural setting.

Clearly, work on typologies of power resources will remain of interest. However, just as important is the question raised by Brookes and Matos: In which context is a particular type of power appropriate? It depends on the core interest. For instance, is structural power most effective 'because employers have a core interest in the smooth and profitable functioning of business and depend fundamentally on workers performing their assigned tasks' (Brookes)? Institutional power works well when there is an interest in perpetuating a certain arrangement that may secure profits. This leads to the question of choice of *strategies*. These may be analysed from a number of angles. One perspective is to study the repertoire of action according to degree of *militancy*. While McCallum's contribution to this volume suggests strategies which involve elements of cooperation with capital, Webster reports from a field with much deeper class conflicts. And Nowak's account of mass strikes speaks of tensions between established unions and wildcat strikes also involving acts of violence. Linked to militancy is also the question of who are the *subjects* in such action, captured in Charles Umney's conceptual pair, managerial or mobilizing transnationalism, the leadership or the rank and file?

Strategy, furthermore, contains an idea about the *venue* for action, about space. Some unions genuinely work cross-national or bilocal, such as the Mexican immigrants in the United States (Jungehülsing). Others concentrate on the national scene, such as the Oslo construction workers (Kjeldstadli). This national frame also pertains to the strikes, analysed by Nowak, which do not go beyond borders. Venue is also relevant when Sabrina Zajak argues for the concept of 'multiple transnational pathways of influence'. Campaigners may target international organizations or direct their efforts towards other states or regions or, finally, support civil society organizations—and they may shift between or combine pathways.

In sum, as the contributions to this volume make clear, transnational solidarity is always the result of concrete actions, concrete moments of struggle. And while it is not automatic, and while global restructuring has undermined trade union possibilities, labour movements, defined broadly, have also gained new opportunities. The struggle for transnational solidarity clearly continues.

Bibliography

Agarwala, R. (2013). *Informal Labor, Formal Politics, and Dignified Discontent in India.* New York: Cambridge University Press.

Alexander, P. (2012). 'A Massive Rebellion of the Poor', *Mail & Guardian*, 13 April.

Alexander, P. (2013). 'Marikana, Turning Point in South African History', *Review of African Political Economy*, 40(138): 605–19.

Allen, K. (1997). *Fianna Fail and Irish Labour: 1926 to the Present.* Dublin: Pluto Press.

Alsos, K., & Eldring, L. (2008). 'Labour Mobility and Wage Dumping: The Case of Norway', *European Journal of Industrial Relations*, 14(4): 441–59.

Alternative Trade Mandate Alliance. (2013). 'Trade: Time for a New Vision. The Alternative Trade Mandate'. Available at http://www.alternativetrademandate.org/wp-content/uploads/2014/02/Trade-time_for_a_new_vision-JAN14-PRINT.pdf. Accessed 1 October 2014.

Alzaga, V. (2011). 'Justice for Janitors Campaign: Open-Sourcing Labour Conflicts against Global Neo-Liberalism'. Open Democracy. Available at https://www.opendemocracy.net/valery-alzaga/justice-for-janitors-campaign-open-sourcing-labour-conflicts-against-global-neo-libera. Accessed 30 January 2013.

Amin, S. (1976). *Unequal Development: An Essay on the Social Formations of Peripheral Capitalism*, trans. B. Pearce. New York: Monthly Review Press.

Amin, S. (2010). *The Law of Worldwide Value* (2nd ed.). New York: Monthly Review Press.

Aminzade, R. R., & McAdam, D. (2001). 'Emotions and Contentious Politics', in R. R. Amininzade, J. A. Goldstone, D. McAdam, E. J. Perry, W. H. Sewell, S. Tarrow, & C. Tilly (Eds.). *Silence and Voice in the Study of Contentious Politics*. Cambridge: Cambridge University Press, 14–50.

Anderson, B. (2006). *Imagined Communities: Reflections on the Origin and Spread of Nationalism*. London/New York: Verso.

Anderson, J., Hamilton, P., & Wills, J. (2010). 'The Multi-Scalarity of Trade Union Practice', in S. McGrath-Champ, A. Herod, & A. Rainnie (Eds.). *Handbook of Employment and Society: Working Space*. Northampton: Edward Elgar Publishing, 383–97.

Anner, M. (2011). *Solidarity Transformed: Labor Responses to Globalization and Crisis in Latin America*. Ithaca: Cornell University Press.

Anner, M., Bair, J., & Blasi, J. (2012). 'Buyer Power, Pricing Practices, and Labor Outcomes in Global Supply Chains', Institutions Program Working Paper Series INST2012-11. Available at http://www.colorado.edu/ibs/pubs/pec/inst2012-0011.pdf. Accessed 8 December 2012.

Anner, M., & Evans, P. (2004). 'Building Bridges across a Double Divide: Alliances Between US and Latin American Labour and NGOs', *Development in Practice* 14(1): 34–47.

Antunes, R. (2013). *The Meanings of Work: Essay on the Affirmation and Negation of Work*. Leiden: Brill.

Armbruster, R. (1995). 'Cross-National Labor Organizing Strategies', *Critical Sociology*, 21(2): 75–89.

Armbruster-Sandoval, R. (2004). *Globalization and Cross-Border Labor Solidarity in the Americas: The Anti- Sweatshop Movement and the Struggle for Social Justice*. New York: Routledge.

Armbruster-Sandoval, R. (2005). 'Workers of the World Unite? The Contemporary Anti-Sweatshop Movement and the Struggle for Social Justice in the Americas', *Work and Occupations*, 32(4): 464–85.

Asia-Europe People's Forum. (1998). 'A People's Vision Towards a More Just Equal and Sustainable World'. Available at http://www.tni.org/archives/asem-watch_asem24. Accessed 30 September 2012.

Bai, R. (2012). 'The Role of the All China Federation of Trade Unions: Implications for Workers Today', in A. L. Yu (Ed.). *China's Rise: Strength and Fragility*. London: Merlin Press, 199–224.

Bailey, D., De Waele, J. M., Escalona, F., & Viera, M. (Eds.). (2014). *European Social Democracy during the Global Economic Crisis – Renovation or Resignation?* Manchester: Manchester University Press.

Ball, M. (2003). 'Considering Trade Union Education as a Community of Practice', *International Journal of Lifelong Education*, 22(3): 297–310.

Bakker and Gill. (2003). 'Global Political Economy and Social Reproduction' in I. Baker and S. G. H. (Eds.). *Power, Production, and Social Reproduction*. Basinstoke: Palgrave MacMillan, 3–12.]

Banks, A., & Russo, J. (1998). 'Development of International Campaign-Based Network Structures: A Case Study of the IBT and ITF World Council of UPS Unions', *Comparative Labour Law and Policy Journal*, 20(4): 543–68.

Banyuls J., Haipeter T., & Neumann L. (2008). 'European Works Councils at General Motors Europe: Bargaining Efficiency in Regime Competition?', *Industrial Relations Journal*, 39(6): 532–47.

Barnouin, B. (1986). *The European Labour Movement and European Integration*. London: Frances Pinter.

Baron, D. P. (2003). 'Private Politics', *Journal of Economics & Management Strategy* 12(1): 31–66.

Barratt Brown, M. (1972). 'Imperialism and Working Class Interests in the Developed Countries', in M. Barratt Brown (Ed.). *Essays on Imperialism*. Nottingham: Spokesman Books, 79–135.

Bartley, T. (2011), 'Mapping the Hard and Soft Law Terrain: Labor Rights and Environmental Protection. Transnational Governance as the Layering of Rules: Intersections of Public and Private Standards', *Theoretical Inquiries in Law* 12(1): 517–665.

Bartley, T., & Zhang, L. (2012). 'Opening the "Black Box": Transnational Private Certification of Labor Standards in China'. Indiana University Research Center for Chinese Politics and Business, RCCPB Working Paper 18.

Barrientos, S., & Smith, S. (2007). 'Do Workers Benefit from Ethical Trade? Assessing Codes of Labour Practice in Global Production Systems', *Third World Quarterly*, 28(4): 713–29.

Basch, L. G., Schiller, N. G., & Szanton Blanc, C. (2005 [1994]) *Nations Unbound: Transnational Projects, Postcolonial Predicaments, and Deterritorialized Nation-States*. London & New York: Taylor & Francis.

Bayertz, K. (Ed.). (1999). *Solidarity*. Dordrecht: Kluwer Academic Publishers.

Beck, U. (2002). 'The Cosmopolitan Society and its Enemies', *Theory, Culture & Society*, 19(2): 17–44.

Beck, U. (2008). 'The Cosmopolitan Perspective: Sociology of the Second Age of Modernity', in S. Khagram & P. Levitt (Eds.). *The Transnational Studies Reader: Intersections and Innovations*. New York: Routledge, 222–30.

Beck, U. (2012), 'Redefining the Sociological Project: The Cosmopolitan Challenge', *Sociology*, 46(1): 7–12.

Beck, U., & Sznaider, N. (2006). 'Unpacking Cosmopolitanism for the Social Sciences: A Research Agenda', *British Journal of Sociology*, 57(1): 1–22.

Beinin, J. (2011). 'Workers and Egypt's January 25 Revolution', *International Labor and Working Class History*, 80: 189–96.

Bendiner, B. (1987). *International Labour Affairs: The World Trade Unions and the Multinational Companies*. Oxford: Clarendon Press.

Bergh, T. (2009). *Kollektiv Fornuft. Bind 3, LOs Historie 1969-2009*. Oslo: Pax Forlag.

Bernaciak, M. (2010). 'West–East European Labour Transnationalism(s): Rivalry or Joint Mobilisation?' in A. Bieler & I. Lindberg (Eds.). *Global Restructuring, Labour and the Challenges for Transnational Solidarity*. London: Routledge, 33–47.

Bernstein, S., & Cashore, B. (2000). 'Globalization, Four Paths of Internationalization and Domestic Policy Change: The Case of Ecoforestry in British Columbia, Canada', *Canadian Journal of Political Science/Revue Canadienne de Science Politique*, 33(1): 67–99.

Bew, P., Hazelkorn, E., & Patterson, H. (1989). *The Dynamics of Irish Politics*. London: Lawrence and Wishart.

Bezuidenhout, A., & Buhlungu, S. (2011). 'From Compounded to Fragmented Labour: Mineworkers and the Demise of Compounds in South Africa', *Antipode*, 43(2): 237–63.

Bhagat, R. B., & Mohanty, S. (2009). 'Emerging Pattern of Urbanization and the Contribution of Migration in Urban Growth in India', *Asian Population Studies*, 5(1): 5–20.

Bieler, A. (2006). *The Struggle for a Social Europe: Trade Unions and EMU in Times of Global Restructuring*. Manchester: Manchester University Press.

Bieler, A. (2013). 'The EU, Global Europe and Processes of Uneven and Combined Development: The Problem of Transnational Labour Solidarity', *Review of International Studies*, 39(1): 161–83.

Bieler, A. (2015). 'Mobilising for Change: The First Successful European Citizens' Initiative "Water Is a Human Right"', paper presented at the *ETUI Monthly Forum*, Brussels/Belgium, 22 January.

Bieler, A., Hilary, J., & Lindberg, I. (2014). 'Trade Unions, "Free Trade" and the Problem of Transnational Solidarity: An Introduction', *Globalizations*, 11(1): 1–9.

Bieler, A., & Lindberg, I. (Eds.). (2010). *Global Restructuring, Labour and the Challenges for Transnational Solidarity*. London: Routledge.

Bieler, A., Lindberg, I., & Pillay D. (Eds.). (2008a). *Labour and the Challenges of Globalization: What Prospects for Transnational Solidarity?* London: Pluto Press.

Bieler, A., Lindberg, I., & Pillay, D. (2008b). 'What Future Strategy for the Global Working Class? The Need for a New Historical Subject', in A. Bieler, I. Lindberg & D. Pillay (Eds.). *Labour and the Challenges of Globalization: What Prospects for Transnational Solidarity?* London: Pluto Press, 264–85.

Bieler, A., Lindberg, I., & Sauerborn, W. (2010). 'After Thirty Years of Deadlock: Labour's Possible Strategies in the New Global Order', *Globalizations*, 7/1-2: 247–60.

Birchfield, V., & Freyberg-Inan, A. (2004). 'Constructing Opposition in the Age of Globalization: The potential of ATTAC', *Globalizations*, 1(1): 278–304.

Blanford, K., & Cummings, D. (2013). 'Construction in Brazil: PAC 2 – Paving the Way for the Future', *World Cement*, June: 36–41.

Boltanski, L., & Chiapello, E. (2007). *The New Spirit of Capitalism*. London: Verso.

Bond, P., & Mottiar, S. (2013). 'Movements, Protest and Massacre in South Africa', *Journal of Contemporary African Studies*, 31(2): 283–302.

Borgers, F. (1996). 'The Challenges of Economic Globalization for U.S. Labor', *Critical Sociology*, 22(2): 67–88.

Bowles, P. (2010). 'Globalization's Problematic for Labor: Three Paradigms', *Global Labour Journal*, 1(1): 12–31.

Bratton, J., Sawchuk, P., Forshaw, C., Callinan, M., & Corbett, M. (2010). *Work and Organizational Behaviour* (2nd ed.). Basingstoke: Palgrave Macmillan.

Brecher, J., Costello, T., & Smith, B. (2006). 'International Labor Solidarity: The New Frontier', *New Labor Forum*, 15(1): 9–18.

Breman, J., & van der Linden, M. (2014). 'Informalizing the Economy: The Return of the Social Question at a Global Level', *Development and Change*, 45(5): 920–40.

Bridgford, J., & Stirling, J. (2000). 'European Systems of Trade Union Education', in J. Bridgford & J. Stirling (Eds.). *Trade Union Education in Europe*. Brussels: European Trade Union College, 7–28.

Bridgman, T., & McLaughlin, C. (2013). 'The Battle for Middle Earth: New Zealand's Bid to Save *The Hobbit'*, in P. Fatien Diochon, E. Raufflet, & A. J. Mills (Eds.). *The Dark Side 2: Critical Cases on the Downside of Business* Leeds: Greenleaf, 127–36.

Brinkman, U., Choi, H., Detje, R., Dörre, K., Holst, H., Karakayali, S., & Schmalstieg, C. (2008). *Strategic Unionism: Aus der Krise zur Eineuerung*. Wiesbaden: Springer.

Brinkman, U., & Nachtwey, O. (2013). 'Industrial Relations, Trade Unions and Social Conflict in German Capitalism', *La Nouvelle Revue du Travail*, 3.

Brochmann, G., & Kjeldstadli, K. (2008). *A History of Immigration: The Case of Norway 1900-2000*. Oslo: Universitetsforlaget.

Bronfenbrenner, K. (Ed.). (2007). *Global Unions: Challenging Transnational Capital through Cross-Border Campaigns*. Ithaca: Cornell University Press.

Brookes, M. (2013). 'Varieties of Power in Transnational Labour Alliances: An Analysis of Workers' Structural, Institutional, and Coalitional Power in the Global Economy', *Labour Studies Journal*, 38(3): 181–200.

Buhlungu, S. (2010). *A Paradox of Victory: COSATU and the Democratic Transformation in South Africa*. Pietermaritzburg: UKZN Press.

Bukharin, N. (1915/1929). *Imperialism and World Economy*. New York: International Publishers.

Bureau of Labor Statistics. (2014). 'Foreign-Born Workers: Labour Force Characteristics—2013'. Available at http://www.bls.gov/news.release/pdf/forbrn.pdf. Accessed 28 September 2014.

Buschak, W. (2003). 'The European Trade Union Confederation and the European Industry Federations', in U. Optenhögel, M. Schneider, & R. Zimmermann (Eds.). *European Trade Union Organisations Inventory of the Archive of Social Democracy and the Library of the Friedrich-Ebert-Stiftung*. Available at http://library.fes.de/pdf-files/id/01622txt.pdf. Accessed 18 January 2014.

Büthe, T., & Mattli, W. (2011). *The New Global Rulers: The Privatization of Regulation in The World Economy*. Princeton: Princeton University Press.

Butollo, F., & Brink, T. T. (2012). 'Challenging the Atomization of Discontent', *Critical Asian Studies*, 44(3): 419–40.

Callinicos, A. (2009). *Imperialism and Global Political Economy*. Cambridge: Polity Press.

Capps, G. (2012). 'Victim of its Own Success? The Platinum Mining Industry and the Apartheid Mineral Property System in South Africa's Political Transition', *Review of African Political Economy*, 39(131): 63–84.

Caraway, T. L. (2006). 'Political Openness and Transnational Activism: Comparative Insights from Labor Activism', *Politics Society* 34(2): 277–304.

Carew, A. (1987). *Labour under the Marshall Plan: The Politics of Productivity and the Marketing of Management Science*. Detroit: Wayne State University Press.

Carew, A. (2000). 'Towards a Free Trade Union Centre: The International Confederation of Free Trade Unions (1949 – 1972)', in A. Carew, M. Dreyfus, G. van Goethem, R. Gumbrell-McCormick, & M. van der Linden (Eds.). *The International Confederation of Free Trade Unions*. Bern: Peter Lang, 268–291.

Carew, A., Dreyfus, M., Van Goethem, G., Gumbrell-McCormick, R., & van der Linden, M. (Eds.). (2000). *The International Confederation of Free Trade Unions*. Bern: Peter Lang.

Carr, B. (1999). 'Globalization from Below: Labour Internationalism under NAFTA', *International Social Science Journal*, 51(159): 49–59.

Castells. M. (1996). *The Rise of the Network Society. The Information Age: Economy, Society and Culture*. Oxford: Blackwell.

Castells, M. (2012). *Networks of Outrage and Hope: Social Movements in the Internet Age*. Cambridge: Polity Press.

Caster, M. (2014). 'Yue Yuen: wildcat strikes and labor struggles in China'. Available athttp://roarmag.org/2014/05/yue-yuen-strike-workers-struggle-china/. Accessed 30 October 2014.

Castree, N. (2000). 'Geographic Scale and Grass-Roots Internationalism: The Liverpool Dock Dispute, 1995–1998', *Economic Geography*, 76(3): 272–92.

Celik, E. (2014). 'Circulation of the Social Movement Unionism Concept as a Case of Intellectual South-South and North-South Dialogue', Joint Session, XV111 ISA World Congress of Sociology, Yokohama, Japan.

Cella, G. P. (2012). 'The Representation of Non-standard Workers. Theory and Culture of Collective Bargaining', *Transfer: European Review of Labour and Research*, 18(2): 171–84.

Chan, C. K. (2013). 'Community-based organizations for migrant workers' rights: the emergence of labour NGOs in China', *Community Development Journal*, 48(1): 6–22.

Chan, C. K., & Hui, E. (2012). 'The Dynamics and Dilemma of Workplace Trade Union Reform in China: The Case of the Honda Workers' Strike', *Journal of Industrial Relations*, 54(5): 653–68.

Chan, J., Pun, N., & Selden, M. (2013). 'The Politics of Global Production: Apple, Foxconn and China's New Working Class', *New Technology, Work and Employment* 28(2): 100–15.

Chaney, E. M. (1979). 'The World Economy and Contemporary Migration', *The International Migration Review*, 13(2): 204–12.

Chayko, M. (2002). *Connecting: How We Form Social Bonds and Communities in the Internet Age*. Albany, NY: State University of New York Press.

Cheah, P. (2006). 'Cosmopolitanism', *Theory, Culture & Society*, 23(2): 486–96.

Chen, C. J. (2013). 'Die Zunahme von Arbeitskonflikten in China: Ein Vergleich von ArbeiterInnenprotesten in verschiedenen Sektoren', in G. Egger, D. Fuchs, T. Immervoll, & L. Steinmass (Eds.). Arbeitskämpfe in China. Berichte von *d* er Werkbank *d* er Welt . Wien: Promedia, 78–105.

Chen, F., & Tang, M. (2013). 'Labor Conflicts in China: Typologies and Their Implications', *Asian Survey*, 53(3): 559–83.

China Labour Bulletin. (n.d.). 'Strike map'. Available at http://www.numble.com/PHP/mysql/clbmape.html. Accessed 30 October 2014.

China Labour Bulletin. (2012). 'A Decade of Change: The Workers' Movement in China 2000-2010', *China Labour Bulletin Research Report*, March.

China Labour Bulletin. (2014). 'Searching for the Union: The Workers' Movement in China 2011-13', *China Labour Bulletin Research Report*, February.

Chinguno, C. (2013a). 'Marikana Massacre and Strike Violence Post-Apartheid', *Global Labour Journal*, 4(2): 160–66.

Chinguno, C. (2013b). 'Marikana: Fragmentation, Precariousness, Strike Violence, and Solidarity', *Review of African Political Economy*, 40(138): 639–46.

Chun, J. (2005). 'Public Dramas and the Politics of Justice', *Work and Occupations*, 32(4): 486–503.

Chun, J. (2009). *Organizing at the Margins: The Symbolic Politics of Labor in South Korea and the United States*. Ithaca, NY: Cornell University Press.

Ciampani, A. (1999). 'La Storia del Movimento Sindacale Italiano e l'Europa: Oltre la Diplomazia Sindacale, in A. Vasori (Ed.). *Storia delle Relazioni Internazionali dal 1943 al 1992*. Rome: Laterza, 215–34.

Ciampani, A. (2000). *La CISL: Tra Integrazione Europea e Mondializzazione*. Roma: Edizioni Lavoro.

Ciccaglione, B. (2009). *Free Trade and Trade Unions of the Americas: Strategies, Practices, Struggles, Achievements*. Vienna: Chamber of Labour.

Cleaver, H. (2000). *Reading Capital Politically* (2nd ed.). Leeds: Anti/Theses.

Coates, D. (2000). *Models of Capitalism: Growth and Stagnation in the Modern Era*. Cambridge: Polity.

Cobble, D. (1992). *Dishing it Out: Waitresses and their Unions in the Twentieth Century*. Urbana: University of Illinois Press.

Cobble, D., & Vosko, L. F. (2000). 'Historical Perspectives on Representing Nonstandard Workers', in F. Carré, M. A. Ferber, L. Golden, & S. A. Herzenberg (Eds.). *Nonstandard Work. The Nature and Challenges of Changing Employment Arrangements*. Ithaca: ILR Press, 291–312.

Compa, L. (2004), 'Trade Unions, NGOs, and Corporate Codes of Conduct', *ILR Collection*. Available at http://digitalcommonsilrcornelledu/articles/379. Accessed 1 February 2014.

Congress of South African Trade Unions. (2008). 'COSATU CEC Statement', Statement of the COSATU Central Executive Committee held on 1–3 September, Johannesburg. Available at http://www.cosatu.org.za/show.php?ID=1693. Accessed 17 January 2014.

Connor, T., & Phelan, L. (2013). 'Antenarrative and Transnational Labour Rights Activism. Making Sense of Complexity and Ambiguity in the Interaction between Global Social Movements and Global Corporations', *Globalizations*, 12(2): 1–15.

Cooke, F. L., & Wood, G. (2011). 'Introduction to a Symposium on Employment Relations and New Actors in Emerging Economies', *Industrial Relations*, 66(1): 3–33.

Cox, R. W. (1983). 'Gramsci, Hegemony and International Relations: An Essay on Method', *Millennium: Journal of International Studies*, 12(2): 162–75.

Cox, K. R. (1998). 'Spaces of Dependence, Spaces of Engagement and the Politics of Scale, or, Looking for Local Politics', *Political Geography*, 17(1): 1–23.

Crouch, C., & W. Streeck (Eds.). (1997). *Political Economy of Modern Capitalism*. New York: Sage.

Croucher, R. (2004). 'The Impact of Trade Union Education - A Study of Three Countries in Eastern Europe', *European Journal of Industrial Relations*, 10(1): 90–109.

Croucher, R., & Cotton, E. (2009). *Global Unions, Global Business*. London: Middlesex University Press.

Cyrus, B., & Davis, C. (1993). 'Transnational Capital, the Global Labor Process, and the International Labor Movement', in B. Berberoglu (Ed.). *The Labor Process and Control of Labor: The Changing Nature of Work Relations in the Late Twentieth Century*. Westport, CT: Praeger, 152–70.

Da Costa, I., & Rehfeldt, U. (2007). 'European Works Councils and Transnational Bargaining about Restructuring in the Auto Industry', *Transfer: European Review of Labour and Research*, 13(2): 313–16.

Dahl, R. (1961). *Who Governs?: Democracy and Power in an American City*. New York: Yale University Press.

Daiber, B., Hildebrandt, C., & Streithorst, A. (Eds.). (2010). *From Revolution to Coalition – Radical Left Parties in Europe*. Berlin: Rosa-Luxemburg-Stiftung.

Dannecker, P. (2005). 'Transnational Migration and the Transformation of Gender Relations: The Case of Bangladeshi Labour Migrants', *Current Sociology*, 53(4): 655–74.

Deaux, K., & Martin, D. (2003). 'Interpersonal Networks and Social Categories: Specifying Levels of Context in Identity Processes', *Social Psychology Quarterly*, 66(2): 101–17.

Degryse, C. (2013). *1973 – 2013: 40 Years of History of the European Trade Union Confederation*. Brussels: European Trade Union Institute.

Del Biondo, I. (2007). *L'Europa Possibile: La CGT e la CGIL di Fronte al Processo di Integrazione Europea (1957-1973)*. Roma: Ediesse.

Delanty, C. (2012). 'A Cosmopolitan Approach to the Explanation of Social Change: Social Mechanisms, Processes, Modernity', *The Sociological Review*, 60(2): 333–54.

Departamento Intersindical de Estatística e Estudos Socioeconômicos. (2013). *Estudo Setorial da Construçã o 2012*, Estudos pesquisa No. 65, May 2013. Sao Paulo: Departamento Intersindical de Estatística e Estudos Socioeconômicos.

Doogan, K. (2009). *New Capitalism?: The Transformation of Work*. Cambridge, Malden: Polity Press.

Dörre, K. (2010). 'Social Classes in the Process of Capitalist Landnahme. On the Relevance of Secondary Exploitation', *Socialist Studies*, 6(2): 43–74.

Dörre, K. (2011). 'Funktionswandel der Gewerkschaften. Von der intermediären zur fraktalen Organisation', in T. Haipeter & K. Dörre (Eds.). *Gewerkschaftliche Modernisierung*. Wiesbaden: VS Verlag, 267–301.

Dörre, K., Holst, H., & Nachtwey, O. (2009). 'Organizing—A Strategic Option for Trade Union Renewal?' *International Journal of Action Research*, 5(1): 33–67.

Duchene, F. (1994). *Jean Monnet: The First Statesman of Interdependence*. New York: W. W. Norton & Co. Inc.

Duménil, G., & Lévy, D. (2011). *The Crisis of Neoliberalism*. Cambridge: Harvard University Press.

Dunphy, R. (2004). *Contesting Capitalism?: Left Parties and European Integration*. Manchester: Manchester University Press.

Egels-Zandén, N. (2013). 'Revisiting Supplier Compliance with MNC Codes of Conduct: Recoupling Policy and Practice at Chinese Toy Suppliers', *Journal of Business Ethics* 119(1): 1–17.

Eldring, L., Fitzgerald, I., & Arnholtz, J. (2012). 'Post-accession Migration in Construction and Trade Union Responses in Denmark, Norway and the UK', *European Journal of Industrial Relations*, 18(1): 21–36.

Ellem, B. (2006). 'Scaling Labour, Australian Unions and Global Mining', *Work Employment Society*, 20(2): 369–87.

Engels, F. (1893). 'Marx-Engels Correspondence 1893 - Engels to Franz Mehring, 14/07/1893'. Available at https://www.marxists.org/archive/marx/works/1893/.htm. Accessed 2 October 2014.

Erel, U. (2010). 'Migrating Cultural Capital: Bourdieu in Migration Studies', *Sociology*, 44(4): 642–60.

Erne, R. (2008). *European Unions: Labor's Quest for a Transnational Democracy*. Ithaca: Cornell University Press.

Erne, R. (2014). 'Explaining Transnational Union Action: Lessons from the EU Integration Process'. Paper presented at workshop 'Labour and Transnational Action in Times of Crisis: From Case Studies to Theory', 27–28 February 2014, Centre for Advanced Study, Oslo.

Erne, R., Bieler, A., Golden, D., Helle, I., Kjeldstadli, K., Matos, T. M., & Stan, S. (2015). 'Politicising the Transnational', *Labor History*, vol. 56.3, forthcoming.

Esbenshade, J. (2004). 'Codes of Conduct: Challenges and Opportunities for Workers' Rights', *Social Justice*, 31(3): 40–59.

Escala-Rabadán, L., Bada, X.. & Rivera-Salgado, G. (2006). 'Mexican Migrant Civic and Political Participation in the U.S.: The Case of Hometown Associations in Los Angeles and Chicago', *Norteamérica. Revista Académica del CISAN-UNAM*, 1(2): 127–72.

Eurofound. (2006). 'European Restructuring Monitor'. Available at http://www.eurofound.europa.eu/emcc/erm/annualreports.htm. Accessed 23 June 2014.

European Trade Union Institute. (2013). *ETUI Trainers' Guide - Design and Implement Effective Learning and Training Events*. Brussels: European Trade Union Institute/International Training Centre International Labour Organization.

European Automobile Manufacturers' Association–European Metalworkers' Federation. (2008a). 'European Metalworkers and Auto Manufacturers Urge EU to Better Balance Trade Negotiations' (22 May 2008). Available at http://www.acea.be/index. php/news/news_detail/european_metalworkers_and_auto_manufacturers_urge_ eu_to_better_balance_trad. Accessed 1 April 2010.

European Automobile Manufacturers' Association–European Metalworkers' Federation. (2008b). 'European Metal Workers and Auto Industry Warn That Pending Doha Deal Puts EU Manufacturing at Risk' (29 July 2008). Available at http://www. acea.be/index.php/news/news_detail/european_metal_workers_and_auto_ industry_warn_that_pending_doha_deal_puts_e. Accessed 1 April 2010.

European Commission. (2013). *Standard Eurobarometer 80 – Public Opinion in the European Union*. Brussels: European Commission.

Eurostat. (2014). 'Recent Developments in Unemployment at a European and Member State Level'. Available at http://epp.eurostat.ec.europa.eu/statistics_explained/index.php/Unemployment_statistics. Accessed 2 October 2014.

Evans, B., & Schmidt, I. (Eds.). (2012). *Social Democracy after the Cold War*. Athabasca: Athabasca University Press.

Evans, P. (2010). 'Is it Labour's Turn to Globalize? Twenty-first Century Opportunities and Strategic Reponses', *Global Labour Journal*, 1(3): 352–79.

Fantasia, R. (1988). *Cultures of Solidarity: Consciousness, Action, and Contemporary American Workers.* Berkeley: University of California Press.

Featherstone, L. (2002). *Students against Sweatshops: The Making of a Movement.* New York: Verso.

Feld, W. (1968). 'Communists and the Common Market', *Journal of Common Market Studies*, 6(3): 250–66.

Fetzer, T. (2008). 'European Works Councils as Risk Communities: The Case of General Motors', *European Journal of Industrial Relations*, 14(3): 289–308.

Fichter, M., & Helfen, M. (2011). 'Going Local with Global Policies: Implementing International Framework Agreements in Brazil and the United States', in K. Papadakis (Ed.) *Shaping Global Industrial Relations. The Impact of International Framework Agreements.* New York: Palgrave Macmillan. Co- published with International Labour Office, 73–97.

Filippelli, R. L. (1989). *American Labor and Post-War Italy 1943 – 1953.* Stanford: Stanford University Press.

Fine, J. (2006). *Worker Centers: Organizing Communities at the Edge of the Dream.* Ithaca: ILR Press.

Fleay, C. (2006). 'Human Rights, Transnational Actors and the Chinese Government: Another Look at the Spiral Model', *Journal of Global Ethics* 2(1): 43–65.

Frank, D. (1999). *Buy American: The Untold Story of Economic Nationalism.* Boston: Beacon Press.

Frank, D. (2003). 'Where are the Workers in Consumer-Worker Alliances? Class Dynamics and the History of Consumer-Labor Campaigns', *Politics & Society*, 31(3): 363–79.

Fransen, L., & Burgoon, B. (2013). 'Global Labour-Standards Advocacy by European Civil Society Organizations. Trends and Developments', *British Journal of Industrial Relations*.

Freeman, R. (2010). 'What Really Ails Europe (and America): The Doubling of the Global Labor Force', *The Globalist*, March 5. Available at http://www.theglobalist.com/what-really-ails-europe-and-america-the-doubling-of-the-global-workforce/. Accessed 16 December 2012.

Friberg, J. H. (2013). 'The Polish Worker in Norway: Emerging Patterns of Migration, Employment and Incorporation after EU's Eastern Enlargement', unpublished PhD Thesis, University of Oslo.

Friberg, J. H., & Guri, T. (Eds.). (2007). 'Polonia i Oslo: En Studie av Arbeids- og Levekår Blant Polakker i Hovedstadsområdet', FAFO-rapport No. 6/2013, Oslo.

Friedman, E. (2009). 'US and Chinese Labor at a Changing Moment in the Global Neoliberal Economy', *WorkingUSA*, 12(2): 219–34.

Friedman, E. (2012). 'Getting Through the Hard Times Together? Chinese Workers and Unions Respond to the Economic Crisis', *Journal of Industrial Relations*, 54(4): 459–75.

Gajewska, K. (2008). 'The Emergence of a European Labour Protest Movement?' *European Journal of Industrial Relations*, 14(1): 104–21.

Gall, G. (2012). 'Quiescence Continued? Recent Strike Activity in Nine Western European Economies', *Economic and Industrial Democracy*, 34(4): 667–91.

Gallas, A., Nowak, J., & Wilde, F. (Eds.). (2012). *Politische Streiks im Europa der Krise.* Hamburg: VSA-Verlag.

Gallin, D. (2001). 'Propositions on Trade Unions and Informal Employment in Times of Globalisation', in P. Waterman & J. Wills (Eds.). *Place, Space and the New Labour Internationalisms.* Oxford: Blackwell, 227–45.

Gamson, W. A. (1991). 'Commitment and Agency in Social Movements', *Sociological Forum*, 6(1): 27–50.

Garvin, T. (2004). *Preventing the Future: Why was Ireland so Poor for so Long?* Dublin: Gill & Macmillan.

Geiger, T. (2000). 'Why Ireland Needed the Marshall Plan but Did Not Want It: Ireland, the Sterling Area and the European Recovery Program, 1947–1948', *Irish Studies in International Affairs*, 11: 193–215.

Gentile, A. (2015). 'The Hegemonic Breaking of Intra-European Labour Solidarity: How the AFL's "Free" Trade Unionism and Labour INGOs' National Sovereignty Clause Skew EU Docker Solidarity Today', *Mobilizations: An International Journal*.

Gereffi, G., Spener, D., & Bair, J. (Eds.). (2002). *Free Trade and Uneven Development: The North American Apparel Industry after NAFTA*. Philadephia: Temple University Press.

Ghigliani, P. (2005). 'International Trade Unionism in a Globalizing World: A Case Study of New Labour Internationalism', *Economic and Industrial Democracy*, 26(3): 359–82.

Glyn, A. (2006). *Capitalism Unleashed: Finance, Globalization, and Welfare*. Oxford: Oxford University Press.

Gramsci, A. (1971). *Selections from the Prison Notebooks*, ed. and trans. Q. Hoare & G. Nowell Smith. London: Lawrence and Wishart.

Gravel, E., Duplessis, I., & Gernigon, B. (2001). *The Committee on Freedom of Association: Its Impact over 50 Years*. Geneva: International Labour Organization.

Green, M. E., & Ives, P. (2009). 'Subalternity and Language: Overcoming the Fragmentation of Common Sense', *Historical Materialism*, 17(1): 3–30.

Greenfield, G. (1998). 'The ICFTU and the Politics of Compromise', in E. Meiksins Wood, P. Meiksins, & M. Yates (Eds.), *Rising from the Ashes? Labor in the Age of 'Global' Capitalism*. New York: Monthly Review Press, 180–89.

Greenhouse, S. (2009). 'Labor Fight Ends in Win for Students', *New York Times*, Nov. 17.

Greer, I., Ciupijus, Z., & Lillie, N. (2013). 'The European Migrant Workers' Union: Union Organizing Through Labour Transnationalism', *European Journal of Industrial Relations*, 19(1): 5–20.

Greer, I., & Hauptmeier, M. (2008). 'Political Entrepreneurs and Co-Managers: Labour Transnationalism at Four Multinational Auto Companies', *British Journal of Industrial Relations*, 46(1): 76–97.

Greer, I., & Hauptmeier, M. (2012). 'Identity Work: Sustaining Transnational Collective Action at General Motors Europe', *Industrial Relations*, 51(2): 275–99.

Greven, T., & Schwetz, T. (2011). 'Neue Instrumente für Gewerkschaften. Die transnationalen strategischen Kampagnen der United Steelworkers of America gegen die Continental AG', in F. Gerlach, T. Greven, U. Mückenberger, & E. Schmidt (Eds.). *Solidarität über Grenzen: Gewerkschaften vor neuer Standortkonkurrenz*. Berlin: Edition Sigma, 131–48.

Guigni, M. (2001). 'Modern Protest Politics', in P. N. Stearns (Ed.). *Encyclopedia of European Social History from 1350 to 2000 Volume 1*. New York: Charles Scribners & Sons, 311–31.

Gumbrell-McCormick. (2000). 'Facing New Challenges', in A. Carew, M. Dreyfus, G. van Goethem, R. Gumbrell-McCormick, & M. van der Linden (Eds.). *The International Confederation of Free Trade Unions*. Bern: Peter Lang.

Gumbrell-McCormick. (2008). 'International Actors in International Regulation', in P. Blython, N. Bacon, J. Fiorito, & E. Heery (Eds.). *Handbook of Industrial Relations*. London: Sage, 325–45.

Habermas, J. (1987). *The Theory of Communicative Action, Vol. II*. Boston: Beacon Press.

Habermas, J., & Derrida, J. (2003). 'February 15, or What Binds Europeans Together: A Plea for a Common Foreign Policy, Beginning in the Core of Europe', *Constellations*, 10(3): 291–97.

Haggard, S., & Kaufman, R. (2008). *Development, Democracy, and Welfare States–Latin America, East Asia, and Eastern Europe*. Princeton: Princeton University Press.

Hall, P. (1986). *Governing the Economy: The Politics of State Intervention in Britain and France*. Oxford: Oxford University Press.

Hall, S. (1985). 'Significance, Representation, Ideology: Althusser and the Post-Structuralist Debates', *Critical Studies in Mass Communication*, 2(2): 91–114.

Hall, S. (1996). 'The Problem of Ideology: Marxism without Guarantees', in D. Morley & K. H. Chen (Eds.). *Stuart Hall: Critical Dialogues in Cultural Studies*. London: Routledge, 25–46.

Hamamovitch, C. (2003). 'Creating Perfect Immigrant: Guestworkers of the World in Historical Perspective', *Labor History*, 44(1): 69–94.

Hanagan, M. P. (1980). *The Logic of Solidarity: Artisans and Industrial Workers in Three French Towns, 1871-1914*. Urbana: University of Illinois Press.

Hancké , B. (2000). 'European Works Councils and Industrial Restructuring in the European Motor Industry', *European Journal of Industrial Relations*, 6(1): 35–59.

Hardiman, N. (1988). *Pay, Politics and Economic Performance in the Republic of Ireland*. Oxford: Clarendon Press.

Hardy, J., Calveley, M., Kubisa, J., & Shelley, S. (2014). 'Labour Strategies, Cross-Border Solidarity and the Mobility of Health Workers: Evidence From Five New Member States', *European Journal of Industrial Relations*, 20(4): 1–19.

Hardy, J., Eldring, L., & Schulten, T. (2012). 'Trade Union Responses to Migrant Workers from the "New Europe": A Three Sector Comparison in the UK, Norway and Germany', *European Journal of Industrial Relations*, 18(4): 347–63.

Harrod, J. (2014). 'Patterns of Power Relations: Sabotage, Organisation, Conformity and Adjustment', *Global Labour Journal*, 5(2): 134–52.

Harrod, J., & O'Brien, R. (2002). 'Organized Labour and the Global Political Economy', in J. Harrod & R. O'Brien (Eds.). *Global Unions?: Theories and Strategies of Organized Labour in the Global Political Economy*. London: Routledge, 3–28.

Hart-Landsberg, M. (2013). *Capitalist Globalization: Consequences, Resistance, and Alternatives*. New York: Monthly Review Press.

Harvey, D. (1985). 'The Geopolitics of Capitalism', in D. Gregory & J. Urry (Eds.). *Social Relations and Spatial Structures*. London: Macmillan, 128–63.

Harvey, D. (1990). *The Condition of Postmodernity: An Enquiry into the Origins of Cultural Change*. Oxford: Blackwell Publishing Ltd.

Harvey. (1996). *Justice, Nature, and the Geography of Difference*. Oxford: Blackwell Publishers.

Harvey, D. (2005). *A Brief History of Neoliberalism*. Oxford: Oxford University Press.

Harvey, D. (2006a). *The Limits to Capital*. London: Verso.

Harvey, D. (2006b). 'Neo-liberalism and the Restoration of Class Power', in D. Harvey (Ed.). *Spaces of Global Capitalism: Towards A Theory of Uneven Geographical Development*. London: Verso, 7–68.

Hassel, A. (2008). 'The Evolution of a Global Labor Governance Regime', *Governance*, 21(2): 231–51.

Haworth, N., & Ramsay, H. (1986). 'Matching the Multinationals: Obstacles to International Trade Unionism', *International Journal of Sociology and Social Policy*, 6(2): 55–82.

Hederman, M. (1983). *The Road to Europe: Irish Attitudes 1948 – 1961*. Dublin: Institute of Public Administration.

Hederman, M. (1988). 'The Beginning of the Discussion on European Integration in Ireland', in W. Lipgens & W. Loth (Eds.). *Documents on the History of European Integration: Volume 3. The Struggle for European Union by Political Parties and Pressure Groups in Western European Countries 1945 – 1950*. Berlin: de Gruyter, 763–800.

Helle, I., & Matos, T. (Forthcoming). 'Contention and Democracy in Norway after 1945', in F. Mikkelsen, Rene Karpanschof, & Stefan Nyzell (Eds.). *Contention and Democracy in the Nordic Countries 1750-2012*. London: Palgrave.

Hensman, R. (2001). 'Organizing against the Odds: Women in India's Informal Sector', *Socialist Register 2001*, 37: 249–57.

Herod, A. (1995). 'The Practice of International Labor Solidarity and the Geography of the Global Economy', *Economic Geography*, 71(4): 341–63.

Herod, A. (1997a). 'Labor as an Agent of Globalization and as a Global Agent', in K. R. Cox (Ed.). *Spaces of Globalization: Reasserting the Power of the Local*. New York: The Guilford Press, 167–200.

Herod, A. (1997b). 'From a Geography of Labor to a Labor Geography: Labor's Spatial Fix and the Geography of Capitalism', *Antipode*, 29(1): 1–31.

Herod, A. (2001). *Labour Geographies, Workers and the Landscapes of Capitalism*. New York: Guilford Press.

Herod, A. (2003). 'Geographies of Labor Internationalism', *Social Science History*, 27(4): 501–23.

Herod, A. (2006). 'Trotsky's Omission: Labour's Role in Combined and Uneven Development', in H. Radice & B. Dunn (Eds.). *100 Years of Permanent Revolution: Results and Prospects*. London: Pluto Press, 152–65.

Herod, A., Rainnie, A., & McGrath-Champ, S. (2007). 'Working Space: Why Incorporating the Geographical is Central to Theorizing Work and Employment Practices', *Work, Employment & Society*, 21(2): 247–64.

Higham, J. (1998). *Strangers in the Land. Patterns of American Nativism 1860-1925*. New Brunswick: Rutgers University Press.

Hilary, J. (2014). 'European Trade Unions and Free Trade: Between International Solidarity and Perceived Self-Interest', *Globalizations*, 11(1): 47–57.

Hitlin, S. (2003). 'Values as the Core of Personal Identity: Drawing Links between Two Theories of Self', *Social Psychology Quarterly*, 66(2): 118–37.

Hobsbawm, E. (1962). *Age of Revolution, 1789-1848*. New York: New American Library.

Hobsbawm, E. (1978). 'The Forward March of Labour Halted?' *Marxism Today*, September 1978: 279–86.

Hobsbawm, E. (1984). *Worlds of Labour: Further Studies in the History of Labour*. London: Weidenfeld & Nicholson.

Hoffmann, J. (2004). 'Jenseits des Mythos–"InternationaleSolidarität" als Herausforderung der Gewerkschaftspolitik im Zeitalter der Globalisierung und Europäisierung', in J. Beerhorst, A. Demirovic, & M. Guggemos (Eds.). *Kritische Theorie im Gesellschaftlichen Strukturwandel*. Frankfurt: Suhrkamp Verlag, 34–64.

Hogg, M. A., & Ridgeway, C. L. (2003). ,Social Identity: Sociological and Social Psychological Perspectives', *Social Psychology Quarterly*, 66(2): 97–100.

Holland, D., Fox, G., & Daro, V. (2008). 'Social Movements and Collective Identity: A Decentered, Dialogic View', *Anthropological Quarterly*, 81(1): 95–126.

Hondagneu-Sotelo, P. (1992). 'Overcoming Patriarchal Constraints: The Reconstruction of Gender Relations among Mexican Immigrant Women and Men', *Gender & Society*, 6(3): 393–415.

Horn, G.-R., & Kenney, P. (Eds.). (2004). *Transnational Moments of Change: Europe 1945, 1968, 1989*. Lanham: Rowman & Littlefield.

Humphrys, E. (2013). 'Organic Intellectuals in the Australian Global Justice Movement: The Weight of 9/11', in C. Barker, L. Cox, J. Krinsky, & A. Gunvald Nilsen (Eds.). *Marxism and Social Movements*. Leiden, Boston: Brill, 357–75.

Husson, M. (1999). 'Riding the Long Wave', *Historical Materialism*, 5(1):77–102.

Hyman, R. (1975). *Industrial Relations: A Marxist Introduction*. London: MacMillan.

Hyman, R. (1994). 'Trade Unions and the Disaggregation of the Working Class', in M. Regini (Ed.). *The Future of Labour Movements*. London: Sage Publications Ltd, 150–68.

Hyman, R. (2002). 'Where Does Solidarity End?' *Eurozine*, 17 September. Available at http://www.eurozine.com/. Accessed 28 September 2014.

Hyman, R. (2005). 'Shifting Dynamics in International Trade Unionism: Agitation, Organisation, Bureaucracy, Diplomacy', *Labor History*, 46(2): 137–54.

Hyman, R. (2010). 'Trade Unions, Global Competition and Options for Solidarity', in A. Bieler & I. Lindberg (Eds.). *Global Restructuring, Labour, and the Challenges for Transnational Solidarity*. New York: Routledge, 16–30.

Imig, D., & Tarrow, T. (2000). 'Political Contention in a Europeanising Polity', *West European Politics*, 23(4): 73–93.

Imig, D., & Tarrow, T. (Eds.). (2001). *Contentious Europeans. Protest and Politics in an Emerging Polity*. Boulder, CO: Rowman & Littlefield.

Inglehart, R., & Klingemann, H. D. (1976). 'Party Identification, Ideological Preference and the Right-Left Dimension among Western Mass Publics', in I. Budge, I. Crewe, & D. Farlie (Eds.). *Party Identification and Beyond*. London: John Wiley & Son, 243–73.

Integrerings- og mangfoldsdirektoratet. (2007). IMDI_rapport 9-2007: Intergrerings-kart. Arbeidsinnvandring – en kunnskapsstatus. Available at http://www.imdi.no/Documents/Rapporter/Imdi_rapport_9-2007_integreringskart_2007_Arbeidsinnvandring_en_kunnskapsstatus.pdf. Accessed 15 January 2014.

International Labour Organization. (2007). *The Role of Trade Unions in Workers' Education: The Key to Trade Union Capacity Building*. Geneva: International Workers' Symposium, 8–12 October 2007.

International Labour Organization. (2014). *Transitioning from the Informal to the Formal Economy*. Geneva: International Labour Organization. Available athttp://www.ilo.org/wcmsp5/groups/public/---ed_norm/---relconf/documents/meetingdocument/wcms_218128.pdf. Accessed 16 December 2014.

International Viewpoint, 2 March 2013. Available at http://www.internationalviewpoint.org/IMG/pdf/IV_458_MARCH_2013.pdf. Accessed 18 March 2013.

International Viewpoint, 4 November 2013. Available at http://www.internationalviewpoint.org/IMG/pdf/IV466November2013.pdf. Accessed 23 November 2013.

International Trade Union Confederation. (2002). 'ICFTU China Policy'. Available at http://www.icftu.org/displaydocument.asp?Index=991217172&Language=EN. Accessed 30 September 2013.

International Trade Union Confederation. (2008). 'Working for the Social Dimension of the Asia-Europe Meeting'. Background document to ASEM Trade Union Summit 2008. Trade unions' input to the 2nd ASEM Labour and Employment Ministers Meeting.

International Trade Union Confederation. (2010). 'Internationally Recognized Core Labour Standards in the People's Republic of China'. Report for the World Trade Organization General Council Review of the Trade Policies of the People's Republic of China.

International Trade Union Confederation. (2013). 'Global Poll', report prepared for the G20 Labour and Finance Ministers Meeting, Moscow (July 2013).

International Trade Union Confederation. (2014). *Building Workers' Power. Congress Statement*. Berlin: International Trade Union Confederation.

International Union of Food, Agricultural, Hotel, Restaurant, Catering, Tobacco, and Allied Workers' Associations. (2009). 'Unilever, IUF Settlement Resolves Conflict Over Precarious Work at Lipton Pakistan'. Available at http://www.iuf.org/casualtea/. Accessed 22 September 2014.

Italian Confederation of Workers' Trade Unions. (1955). *Il Congresso Nazionale, Roma 23 – 27 Aprile 1955: Relazione della Segreteria Confederale*. Roma: Abete.

Italian Confederation of Workers' Trade Unions. (1956). 'Rilancio dell'Unitá Europea e la Posizione della CISL', *Politica Sindacale*.

Italian General Confederation of Labour. (1961). *I Congressi della CGIL Vol. VI*. Roma: Sindacale Italiana.

Italian General Confederation of Labour. (1969). *Documenti Politici dall'XI al XII Congresso*. Roma: Editori Riuniti.

Italian General Confederation of Labour. (1977). *La CGIL dall'8° al 9° Congresso: Atti e Documenti CGIL e Documenti Unitari*. Roma: Editore Sindacale Italiana.

Jain, H. (2010). 'Community Protests in South Africa: Trends, Analysis and Explanations', Local Government Working Paper Series No. 1, Community Law Centre, University of the Western Cape.

Jakopovich, D. (2008). 'Revolution and the Party in Gramsci's Thought: A Modern Application', *International Viewpoint*. Available at http://www.internationalviewpoint.org/spip.php?article1555. Accessed 17 November 2008.

Johns, R., & Vural, L. (2000). 'Class, Geography, and the Consumerist Turn: UNITE and the Stop Sweatshops Campaign', *Environment and Planning*, 32(7): 1193–213.

Joynt, K., & Webster, E. (2013). 'Discordant Voices: The Hidden World of Johannesburg's Inner City Clothing Workers', *Journal of Workplace Rights*, 16(2): 149–69.

Juravich, T. (2007). 'Beating Global Capital: A Framework and Method for Union Strategic Corporate Research and Campaigns', in K. Bronfenbrenner (Ed.). *Global Unions: Challenging Global Capital through Cross-Border Campaigns*. Ithaca: Cornell University Press, 16–39.

Kalecki, M. (1943). 'Political Aspects of Full Employment', *Political Quarterly*, 14(4): 322–30.

Kan, W. (2011). 'Collective Awakening and Action of Chinese Workers: The 2010 Autoworkers Strike and Its Effects', *Sozial Geschichte Online* 6, 9–27.

Kapsos, S. (2007). *World and Regional Trends in Labour Force Participation: Methodologies and Key Results*. Geneva: International Labour Organisation.

Karaagac, B., & Yilmaz, G. (2013). 'Organized Labour in the Gezi process: Reflections on a popular Uprising and Weakened Organized Labour', *Socialist Project – The Bullet*. Available at http://www.socialistproject.ca/bullet/846.php. Accessed 23 June 2014.

Katsiaficas, G. (2006). *The Subversion of Politics – European Autonomous Social Movements and the Decolonization of Everyday Life*. Oakland: AK Press.

Katznelson, I., & Zolberg, A. (Eds.). (1986). *Working Class Formation – Nineteenth-Century Patterns in Western Europe and the United States*. Princeton: Princeton University Press.

Kay, T. (2005). 'Labor Transnationalism and Global Governance: The Impact of NAFTA on Transnational Labor Relationships in North America", *American Journal of Sociology*, 111(3): 715–56.

Kay, T. (2011). *NAFTA and the Politics of Labor Transnationalism*. New York and Cambridge: Cambridge University Press.

Kay, T. (2014). 'Economic Interests Versus Organizational Culture: Explaining Variation in the Emergence in Labor Transnationalism', Paper presented at workshop "Labour and Transnational Action in Times of Crisis: From Case Studies to Theory", 27–28 February 2014, Centre for Advanced Study, Oslo.

Keane, E. (2006). *An Irish Statesman and Revolutionary: The Nationalist and Internationalist Politics of Sean McBride*. London: I.B. Tauris & Co.

Keck, M. E., & Sikkink, L. (1998). *Activists beyond Borders: Advocacy Networks in International Politics*. Ithaca: Cornell University Press.

Keck, M. E., & Sikkink, L. (1999). 'Transnational Advocacy Networks in International and Regional Politics', *International Social Science Journal* 51(2): 89–101.

Kelly, J. (1998). *Rethinking Industrial Relations: Mobilisation, Collectivism and Long Waves*. London: Routledge.

Kennedy, J., & Lavalette, M. (2004). 'Globalisation, Trade Unionism and Solidarity: Further Reflections on the Liverpool Dock Lockout', in R. Munck (Ed.). *Labour and Globalisation: Results and Prospects*. Liverpool: Liverpool University Press, 206–26.

Kennedy, M., & O'Halpin, E. (2000). *Ireland and the Council of Europe: From Isolation towards Integration*. Strasbourg: Council of Europe Publishing.

Kent, A. (2001). 'States Monitoring States: The United States, Australia, and China's Human Rights, 1990-2001', *Human Rights Quarterly* 23(3): 583–624.

Kent, A. (2002). 'China's International Socialization: The Role of International Organizations', *Global Governance*, 8(3): 343–64.

Keogh, D. (1991). 'Ireland, the Vatican and the Cold War: the Case of Italy, 1948', *The Historical Journal*, 34(4): 931–52.

Kiely, R. (2007). *The New Political Economy of Development: Globalization, Imperialism, Hegemony*. London: Palgrave.

Kiely, R. (2010). *Rethinking Imperialism*. London: Palgrave.

Kings, L., Ålund, A., & Schierup, C. K. (2013). 'Revolt of the Urban Periphery: Sweden's Riots in Context', *New Left Project*. Available at http://www.newleftproject. org/index.php/site/article_comments/revolt_of_the_urban_periphery_swedens_ riots_in_context. Accessed 23 June 2014.

Kjeldstadli, K. (forthcoming). 'Reaching Out. The Polish Workers and the Oslo Construction Workers' Union'.

Klessmann, C. (1985). 'Polish Miners in the Ruhr District', in D. Hoerder (Ed.). *Labor Migration in the Atlantic Economies: The European and North American Working Classes During the Period of Industrialization*. Westport, CT: Greenwood Press, 253–76.

Knight, J. (1992). *Institutions and Social Conflict*. Cambridge: Cambridge University Press.

Knudsen, J. S. (2014). 'Bringing the State Back In? US and UK Government Regulation of Corporate Social Responsibility (CSR) in International Business'. Rochester, NY: Social Science Research Network. SSRN Scholarly Paper. Available at http://papers.ssrn.com/abstract=2541002. Accessed 13 September 2014.

Knudsen, H., Whittall, M., & Huijgen, F. (2007). 'European Works Councils and the Problem of Identity', in M. Whittal, H. Knudsen, & F. Huijgen (Eds.). *Towards a European Labour Identity: The Case of the European Works Council*. London: Routledge, 5–18.

Koch-Baumgarten, S. (1998). 'Trade Union Regime Formation under the Conditions of Globalization in the Transport Sector: Attempts at Transnational Trade Union Regulation of Flag-of-Convenience Shipping', *International Review of Social History*, 43(3): 369–402.

Kohler, K. (2006). *The World Social Forum and a Counter-Hegemonic Vision: Towards a Theory of Transnational Identity Formation*. San Diego: International Studies Association Annual Conference, 25 March.

Kotthoff, H. (2007). 'The European Works Council and the Feeling of Interdependence', in M. Whittal, H. Knudsen, & F. Huijgen (Eds.). *Towards a European Labour Identity: The Case of the European Works Council*. London & New York: Routledge, 169–81.

Kraushaar, W. (2012). *Der Aufruhr der Ausgebildeten: Vom Arabischen Frühling zur Occupy-Bewegung*. Hamburg: Hamburger Edition.

Kumar, A., & Mahoney, J. (2013). 'Stitching Together: How Workers Are Hemming Down Transnational Capital in the Hyper-Global Apparel Industry', *Working USA*, 17(2): 187–210.

Lambert, R., Webster, E., & Bezuidenhout, A. (2012). 'Global Labour Studies: The Crises and an Emerging Research Agenda', *Labour History*, 53(2): 291–98.

Lane, F. (2008). 'Envisaging Labour History: Some Reflections on Irish Historiography and the Working Class', in F. Devine, F. Lane, & N. Purseil (Eds.). *Essays in Irish Labour History: A Festschrift for Elizabeth and John W. Boyle*. Dublin: Irish Academic Press, 24–42.

Langenbacher, N., & Schellenberg, B. (Eds.). (2011). *Is Europe on the 'Right' Path? Right-Wing Extremism and Right-wing Populism in Europe*. Berlin: Friedrich-Ebert-Foundation.

Lee, E. (1997). *The Labour Movement and the Internet: The New Internationalism*. London: Pluto Press.

Lee J. (1979). 'Aspects of Corporatist Thought in Ireland: The Commission on Vocational Organisation 1939–1943', in A. Cosgrave & D. McCartney (Eds.). *Studies in Irish History*. Dublin: University College Dublin, 324–47.

Lenin, V. I. (1916). 'Imperialism and the Split in Socialism'. Available at http://www.marxists.org/archive/lenin/works/1916/oct/x01.htm. Accessed 6 February 2012.

Lerner, S. (2007). 'Global Corporations, Global Unions', *New Labour Forum*, 16(1): 23–37.

Lesley, G. (2009). 'The Limits of Solidarity: Labor and Transnational Organizing against Coca-Cola', *American Ethnologist*, 36(4): 667–80.

Lévesque, C., & Murray, G. (2010a). 'Understanding Union Power: Resources and Capabilities for Renewing Union Capacity', *Transfer: European Review of Labour and Research*, 16(3): 333–50.

Lévesque, C., & Murray, G. (2010b). 'Local Union Strategies in Cross-Border Alliances: From Defensive Isolation to Proactive Solidarity', *Labour Studies Journal*, 35(2): 222–45.

Lévesque, C., & Murray, G. (2013). 'Renewing Union Narrative Resources: How Union Capabilities Make a Difference', *British Journal of Industrial Relations*, 51(4): 777–96.

Levinson, C. (1972). *International Trade Unionism*. London: George Allen & Unwin.

Levitt, P. (1998). 'Social Remittances: Migration Driven Local-Level Forms of Cultural Diffusion', *International Migration Review*, 32(4): 926–48.

Levitt, P., & Lamba-Nieves, D. (2010). 'Social Remittances Revisited', *Journal of Ethnic and Migration Studies*, 37(1): 1–22.

Levitt, P., & Schiller, N. G. (2004). 'Conceptualizing Simultaneity: A Transnational Social Field Perspective on Society', *International Migration Review*, 38(3): 1002–39.

Lichtenstein, N. (2002). *State of the Union: A Century of American Labor*. Princeton University Press.

Lier, D. C. (2007). 'Places of Work, Scales of Organising: A Review of Labour Geography', *Geography Compass*, 1(4): 814–33.

Liguori, G. (2009). 'Common sense in Gramsci', in J. Francese (Ed.). *Perspectives on Gramsci: Politics, Culture and Social Theory*. London: Routledge. 122–33.

Lillie, N. (2004). 'Global Collective Bargaining on Flag of Convenience Shipping', *British Journal of Industrial Relations*, 42(1): 47–67.

Lillie, N. (2006). *A Global Union for Global Workers: Collective Bargaining and Regulatory Politics in Maritime Shipping*. New York: Routledge.

Lindberg, I. (2011). 'Varieties of Solidarity. An Analysis of Cases of Worker Action Across Borders', in A. Bieler & I. Lindberg (Eds.). *Global Restructuring, Labour, and the Challenges for Transnational Solidarity*. New York: Routledge, 206–19.

Linebaugh, P., & Rediker, M. (2000). *The Many-Headed Hydra: The Hidden History of the Revolutionary Atlantic*. London: Verso.

Lipsig-Mumme, C., & Webster, E. (2012). 'Reconnections: Labor Sociologies in a Globalizing Era', in A. Sales (Ed.). *Sociology Today: Social Transformations in a Globalizing World*. London: Sage, 230–44.

Locke, R. (2013). *The Promise and Limits of Private Power Promoting Labor Standards in a Global Economy*. Cambridge: Cambridge University Press.

Locke, R., Rissing, B. A., & Pal, T. (2013). 'Complements or Substitutes? Private Codes, State Regulation and the Enforcement of Labour Standards in Global Supply Chains', *British Journal of Industrial Relations*, 51(3): 519–52.

Logue, J. (1980). *Toward a Theory of Trade Union Internationalism*. Gothenburg: University of Gothenburg.

Lowy, M. (1984). 'Marx and Engels: Cosmopolites: The Future of Nations under Communism (1845-1848)', *Critiques: Journal of Socialist Theory*, 14(1): 5–12.

Ludwig, C., & Webster, E. (2014). *Contentious Politics: Framing the Cycles of Municipal Workers' Resistance in Johannesburg*. Johannesburg: Society, Work and Development Institute, University of the Witwatersrand.

Lukács, G. (1968/1971). *History and Class Consciousness. Studies in Marxist Dialectics*, trans. R. Livingstone. Cambridge, MA: The MIT Press.

Lukes, S. (1994). 'Power: A Radical View', in J. Scott (Ed.). *Power: Critical Concepts. Vol. II*. London: Routledge, 233–68.

Lukes, S. (2005 [1974]). *Power: A Radical View* (2nd ed). Hampshire: Palgrave Macmillan.

Luxemburg, R. (1906/2008). 'The Mass Strike, the Political Parties and the Trade Unions', in H. Scott (Ed.). *The Essential Rosa Luxemburg*. Chicago: Haymarket Books, 111–81.

Luxemburg, R. (1913/2003). *The Accumulation of Capital*, trans. A. Schwarzschild. London: Routledge.

Lyddon, D. (2003). 'History and Industrial Relations', in A. Ackers & A. Wilkinson (Eds.). *Understanding Work and Employment*. Oxford University Press, Oxford, 89–118.

MacCallum, J. K. (2013). *Global Unions, Local Power: The New Spirit of Transnational Labor Organizing*. Ithaca, NY: ILR Press.

Maggiorani, M. (1998). *L'Europa degli Altri : Comunisti Italiani e Integrazione Europea (1957–1969)*. Rome: Carocci.

Mahoney, J., & Thelen, K. (2010). *Explaining Institutional Change, Ambiguity, Agency, and Power*. New York: Cambridge University Press.

Mair, P. (1993). 'The Party System and Party Competition', in J. Coakley & M. Gallagher (Eds.). *Politics in the Republic of Ireland*. Dublin: PSAI/Folens, 29–53.

Mandel, E. (1975). *Late Capitalism*. London: New Left Books.

Manky, O. (2014). 'Negotiating at the Margins: The Trajectories of Subcontraction in the Chilian and Puruvian Mining Industry', draft paper for the *International Labour Process Conference 2014*.

Marcuse, H. (1964). *The One-Dimensional Man–Studies in the Ideology of Advanced Industrial Society*. Boston: Beacon Press.

Marino, S. (2012). 'Trade Union Inclusion of Migrant and Ethnic Minority Workers: Comparing Italy and the Netherlands', *European Journal of Industrial Relations* 18(1): 5–20.

Martinez-Lucio, M. (2010). 'Dimensions of Internationalism and the Politics of the Labour Movement: Understanding the Political and Organisational Aspects of Labour Networking and Coordination', Employee Relations , 32(6): 538–56.

Marx, K. (1852). 'The Eighteenth Brumaire of Louis Bonaparte'. Available athttp://www.marxists.org/archive/marx/works/1852/18th-brumaire/index.htm. Accessed 25 February 2014.

Marx, K. (1867/1990). *Capital, Volume 1*. London: Penguin.

Marx, K., & Engels, F. (1848/1998). 'Manifesto of the Communist Party', in M. Cowling (Ed.). *The Communist Manifesto: New Interpretations*. Edinburgh: Edinburgh University Press, 14–37.

Mason, P. (2013). *Why It's Still Kicking Off Everywhere*. London: Verso.

Mathers, A. (1999). 'Euromarch: The Struggle for a Social Europe', *Capital & Class*, No. 68: 15–19.

Mau, S., Mewes, J., & Zimmermann, A. (2006). 'Cosmopolitan Attitudes through Transnational Social Practices?' *Global Networks* 8(1): 1–24.

Maull, H. W. (2010). 'Das Asia-Europe Meeting (ASEM): Baustein effektiverer globaler Ordnungsstrukturen?' in D. Nabers (Ed.). *Multilaterale Institutionen in Ostasien-Pazifik*. Wiesbaden: VS Verlag für Sozialwissenschaften, 181–206.

McCarthy. (1973). *Decade of Upheaval: Irish Trade Unions in the 1960s*. Dublin: Institute of Public Administration.

McCarthy, C. (1974). 'From Division to Dissension: Irish Trade Unions in the Nineteen Thirties', *The Economic and Social Review*, 5(4): 353–84.

McCarthy, C. (1977). *Trade Unions in Ireland 1894 – 1960*. Dublin: Institute of Public Administration.

McDonald, K. (2002). 'From Solidarity to Fluidarity: Social Movements beyond "Collective Identity": The Case of Globalization Conflicts', *Social Movement Studies*, 1(2): 109–28.

McGuire, D. (2012). 'Global and Local Union Struggles against the GATS: An Assessment of the Opportunity and Capacity for Unions to Influence International Trade Policy', unpublished PhD Thesis, University of Kassel, Germany.

Meardi, G. (2012). 'Union Immobility? Trade Unions and the Freedoms of Movement in the Enlarged EU', *British Journal of Industrial Relations*, 50(1): 99–120.

Melucci, A. (1995). 'The Process of Collective Identity', in H. Johnston & B. Klandermans (Eds.). *Social Movements and Culture*. Minneapolis: University of Minnesota Press, 41–63.

Melucci, A. (1996). *Challenging Codes: Collective Action in the Information Age*. New York: Cambridge University Press.

Merk, J. (2009). 'Jumping Scale and Bridging Space in the Era of Corporate Social Responsibility: Cross-Border Labour Struggles in the Global Garment Industry', *Third World Quarterly*, 30(3): 599–615.

Milkman, R. (2006). *L.A. Story: Immigrant Workers and the Future of the U.S. Labor Movement.* New York: Russel Sage Foundation.

Miller, D., & Stirling, J. (1998). 'European Works Council Training: An Opportunity Missed?' *European Journal of Industrial Relations*, 4(1): 35–56.

Mohanty, C. T. (2003). *Feminism without Borders: Decolonizing Theory, Practicing Solidarity.* Durham: Duke University Press.

Moody, K. (1997). 'Towards an International Social Movement Unionism', *New Left Review*, 225: 52–75.

Moorhouse, H. F. (1978). 'The Marxist Theory of the Labour Aristocracy', *Social History*, 3(1): 61–82.

Morell, M. F. (2012). 'The Free Culture and 15M Movements in Spain: Composition, Social Networks and Synergies', *Social Movement Studies*, 11(3): 386–92.

Mudde, C. (2013). 'The Myth Of Weimar Europe', *Open Democracy*. Available at http://www.opendemocracy.net/can-europe-make-it/cas-mudde/myth-of-weimar-europe. Accessed 23 June 2014.

Mulhern, F. (2011). *Lives on the Left: A Group Portrait.* London: Verso.

Müller-Jentsch, W. (2004). 'Theoretical Approaches to Industrial Relations', in B. E. Kaufman (Ed.)/ *Theoretical Perspectives on Work and the Employment Relationship.* Champaign: Industrial Relations Research Association. 1–40.

Munck, R. (2002). *Globalisation and Labour: The New 'Great Transformation'.* London: Zed Books.

Murji, K., & Neal, S. (2012). 'Riot: Race and Politics in the 2011 Disorders', *Sociological Research Online*. Available at http://www.socresonline.org.uk/16/4/24.html. Accessed 23 June 2014.

Murphy, G. (1993). 'The Politics of Economic Realignment, Ireland 1948-1964', unpublished PhD thesis, Dublin City University.

Murray, J. (1998). 'Corporate Codes of Conduct and Labor Standards', *Corporate Codes of Conduct*. Available at http://digitalcommons.ilr.cornell.edu/codes/7. Accessed 5 March 2014.

Napierala, J., & Trevena, P. (2007). 'Motiver for å reise ut', in J. H. Friberg & T. Guri (Eds.). 'Polonia i Oslo: En Studie av Arbeids- og Levekår Blant Polakker i Hovedstadsområdet', FAFO-rapport No. 6/2013, Oslo.

Ness, I. (2005). *Immigrants, Unions, and the New U.S. Labor Market.* Philadelphia: Temple University Press.

Ngai, P., Shen, Y., Guo, Y., Lu, H., Chan, J., & Selden, M. (2014). 'Worker–Intellectual Unity: Trans-Border Sociological Intervention in Foxconn', *Current Sociology*.

Nielsen, N. J. (2013). 'Grænseløse Arbejdere: En Diskussion af Identitet og Selvbevidsthed med Udgangspunkt i Polske Migrantarbeidere', *Arbejderhistorie*, 2: 44–60.

Nohl, A.-M., Schittenhelm, K., Schmidtke, O., & Weiss, A. (2006). 'Cultural Capital during Migration: A Multi-level Approach for the Empirical Analysis of the Labor Market Integration of Highly Skilled Migrants', *Forum Qualitative Sozialforschung / Forum: Qualitative Social Research*, 7(3). Available at http://www.qualitative-research.net/index.php/fqs/article/view/142. Accessed 17 September 2014.

Novelli, M. (2011). 'Thinking through Transnational Solidarity: The Case of SINTRAEMCALI in Colombia', in A. Bieler & I. Lindberg (Eds.). *Global Restructuring, Labour and the Challenges for Transnational Solidarity.* London: Routledge, 141–61.

Novelli, M., & A. Ferus-Comelo (Eds.). (2009). *Globalization, Knowledge and Labour: Education For Solidarity within Spaces of Resistance.* London: Routledge.

Nowak, J., & Gallas A. (2014). 'Mass Strikes against Austerity: A Strategic Assessment', *Global Labour Journal*, 5(3): 306–21.

O'Connor, E. (1988). *Syndicalism in Ireland 1917 – 1923.* Cork: Cork University Press.

O'Connor, E. (2002). *James Larkin.* Cork: Cork University Press.

O'Connor, E. (2011). *A Labour History of Ireland 1824 – 2000*. Dublin: University College Dublin Press.

O'Hearn, D. (2001). *The Atlantic Economy: Britain, the US and Ireland*. Manchester: Manchester University Press.

Ødegård, A. M., Øyvind, B., & Alsos, A. (2012). 'A Case Study of Temporary Work Agencies in Norwegian Construction Sector: A Growing Informal Market Beyond Regulation.' *Transfer: European Review of Labour and Research*, 18(4): 461–70.

Olle, O., & Schoeller, W. (1987). 'World Market Competition and Restrictions upon International Trade Union Policies', in R. E. Boyd, R. Cohen, & P. C. W. Gutkind (Eds.). *International Labour and the Third World: The Making of a New Working Class*. Aldershot: Avebury, 26–47.

Orozco, M. (2004). 'Mexican Hometown Associations and Development Opportunities', *Journal of International Affairs*, 57(2): 1–21.

Papadakis, K. (Ed.). (2008). *Cross- Border Social Dialogue and Agreements: An Emerging Global Industrial Relations Framework?* Geneva: International Labour Office.

Papadakis, K. (Ed.). (2011). *Shaping Global Industrial Relations: The Impact of International Framework Agreements*. New York: Palgrave Macmillan. Co-published with International Labour Office.

Park, K. (2007). 'Constructing Transnational Identities without Leaving Home: Korean Immigrant Women's Cognitive Border-crossing., *Sociological Forum*, 22(2): 200–18.

Pasture, P. (2005). 'Introduction: Between Cross and Class. Christian Labour in Europe 1840–2000', in L. Heerma van Voss, P. Pasture, & J. de Maeyer (Eds.). *Between Cross and Class: Comparative Histories of Christian Labour in Europe 1840 – 2000*. Bern: Peter Lang, 9–48.

Pearson, R., & Seyfang, G. (2001). 'New Hope or False Dawn? Voluntary Codes of Conduct, Labour Regulation and Social Policy in a Globalizing World', *Global Social Policy*, 1(1): 49–78.

Penninx, R., & Roosblad, J. (Eds.). (2000). *Trade Unions, Immigration, and Immigrants in Europe 1960-1993: A Comparative Study of the Attitudes and Actions of Trade Unions in Seven West European Countries*. New York: Berghahn Books.

People's Union for Democratic Rights. (2013). 'Driving Force. Labour Struggles and Violation of Rights at Maruti Suzuki India Limited'. Available at http://www.pudr.org/?q=content/driving-force-labour-struggles-and-violation-rights-maruti-suzuki-india-limited. Accessed 13 February 2014.

Pernot, J. M. (2001). 'Dedans, Dehors, La Dimension Internationale dans le Syndicalisme Français, Vol I', unpublished PhD thesis, University of Paris X – Nanterre.

Phelan, C., Martin, A., "Hancké, B., Baccaro L., & Erne, R. (2009). 'Labour History Symposium on European Unions: Labour's Quest for a Transnational Democracy ', *Labor History* , 50(2): 187–216.

Pichler, F. (2008). 'How Real Is Cosmopolitanism in Europe?' *Sociology*, 42(6): 1107–26.

Pillay, D. (2008). 'Globalisation and the Informalisation of Labour: The Case of South Africa', in A. Bieler, I. Lindberg, & D. Pillay (Eds.). *Labour and the Challenges of Globalization: What Prospects for Transnational Solidarity?* London: Pluto Press, 45–64.

Pistone, S. (1988). 'Italian Political Parties and Pressure Groups in the Discussion on European Union', in W. Lipgens & W. Loth (Eds.). *Documents on the History of European Integration: Volume 3. The Struggle for European Union by Political Parties and Pressure Groups in Western European Countries 1945–1950*. Berlin: de Gruyter, 132–268.

Piven, F. F. (2000). 'Power Repertoires and Globalization', *Politics and Society*, 28(3): 413–30.

Piven, F. F. (2008a). 'Can Power from Below Change the World?' *American Sociological Review*, 73(1): 1–14.

Piven, F. F. (2008b). *Challenging Authority: How Ordinary People Change America*. Lanham, MD: Rowman & Littlefield.

Piven, F. F., & Cloward, R. A. (2000). 'Power Repertoires and Globalization', *Politics and Society*, 28(3): 413–30.

Polletta, F., & Jasper, J. M. (2001). 'Collective Identity and Social Movements', *Annual Review of Sociology*, 27(1): 283–305.

Portes, A., Escobar, C., & Radford, A. W. (2007). 'Immigrant Transnational Organizations and Development: A Comparative Study', *International Migration Review*, 41(1): 242–81.

Portes, A., Guarnizo, L. E., & Landolt, P. (1999). 'The Study of Transnationalism: Pitfalls and Promise of an Emergent Research Field', *Ethnic and Racial Studies*, 22(2): 217–37.

Post, C. (1999). 'Ernest Mandel and the Marxian Theory of Bureaucracy', in G. Achcar (Ed.). The Legacy of Ernest Mandel . London: Verso, 119–151.

Pries, L. (2010). *Transnationalisierung: Theorie und Empirie grenzüberschreitender Vergesellschaftung*. Wiesbaden: Springer.

Pries, L. (2013). 'Ambiguities of Global and Transnational Collective Identities', *Global Networks*, 13(1): 22–40.

Ramsay, H. (1999). 'In Search of International Union Theory', in J. Waddington (Ed.). *Globalization and Patterns of Labour Resistance*. London: Mansell, 192–220.

Robbins, A. (2013). 'The Future of the Student Anti-Sweatshop Movement: Providing Access to U.S. Courts for Garment Workers Worldwide', *Labor & Employment Law Forum*, 3(1): 120–51.

Robinson, A. (2006). 'Towards an Intellectual Reformation: The Critique of Common Sense and the Forgotten Revolutionary Project of Gramscian Theory', in A. Bieler & A. D. Morton (Eds.). *Images of Gramsci: Connections and Contentions in Political Theory and International Relations.* London: Routledge, 75–87.

Robinson, W. I. (2004). *A Theory of Global Capitalism: Production, Class, and State in a Transnational World.* Baltimore & London: John Hopkins University Press.

Robinson, W. I. (2008). *Latin America and Global Capitalism: A Critical Globalization Perspective.* Baltimore: Johns Hopkins University.

Rodal, A. B. (2013). 'Fagforeninger uten grenser – en studie av norske fagforeningers inkluderinfg av utenlandske arbeidstakere i bygingsbransj en', unpublished master's thesis, University of Bergen.

Rodriguez-Garavito, C. A. (2005). 'Global Governance and Labor Rights: Codes of Conduct and Anti-Sweatshop Struggles in Global Apparel Factories in Mexico and Guatemala', *Politics & Society*, 33(2): 203–33.

Rosenberg, J. (2006). 'Why is there no International Historical Sociology?' *European Journal of International Relations*, 12(3): 307–40.

Ross, A. (2008). 'The Quandaries of Consumer-Based Activism: A Low Wage Case Study', *Cultural Studies*, 22(5): 770–87.

Roudometof, V. (2005). 'Transnationalism, Cosmopolitanism and Globalization', *Current Sociology*, 53(1): 113–35.

Ruggie, J. G. (1982). 'International Regimes, Transactions, and Change: Embedded Liberalism in the Postwar Economic Order', *International Organization*, 36(2): 379–415.

Sadler, D. (2004). 'Trade Unions, Coalitions and Communities: Australia's Construction, Forestry, Mining and Energy Union and the International Stakeholder Campaign against Rio Tinto', *Geoforum*, 35(1): 35–46.

Scharpf, F. W. (2007). 'Reflections on Multilevel Legitimacy', Max-Planck-Institute-for-the-Study-of-Societies, Working Paper 07/3.

Schaumberg, W. (2014). 'General Motors Is Attacking European Workers. Is There No Resistance? The Example of Opel Bochum', *Interface: A Journal For and About Social Movements*, 6(1): 412–15.

Schmidt, I. (2009). 'New Institutions, Old Ideas: The Passing Moment of the European Social Model', *Studies in Political Economy*, 84: 7–28.

Schmidt, I. (2011). 'There Were Alternatives: Lessons from Efforts to Advance Beyond Keynesian and Neoliberal Economic Policies in the 1970s', *Working USA*, 14(4): 473–98.

Schmidt, I. (2013). 'Unmaking Neoliberal Europe and the Search for Alternatives', *Perspectives on Global Development and Technology*, 12(1): 41–62.

Schmidt, I. (2014) "The Downward March of Labor Halted? The Crisis of Neoliberal Capitalism and the Remaking of Working Classes", *Working USA*, 17(1): 5-22.

Scipes, K. (2014). 'Building Global Labor Solidarity Today: Learning from the KMU of the Philippines', *Class, Race and Corporate Power*, 2(2): 2–15.

Scoville, J. G. (1973). 'Some Determinants of the Structure of Labor Movements', in A. Sturmthal & J. G. Scoville (Eds.). *The International Labor Movement in Transition*. Urbana, IL: University of Illinois Press, 58–78.

Sefalafala, T., & Webster, E. (2013). 'Working as a Security Guard: The Limits of Professionalization in a Low Status Occupation', *South African Review of Sociology*, 44(2): 76–96.

Seidman, G. (2008). 'Transnational Labour Campaigns: Can the Logic of the Market Be Turned Against Itself?' *Development and Change*, 39(6): 991–1003.

Seidman, G. (2009). *Beyond the Boycott: Labor Rights, Human Rights, and Transnational Activism*. New York: Russel Sage Foundation.

Selwyn, B. (2007). 'Labour Process and Workers' Bargaining Power in Export Grape Production, North East Brazil', *Journal of Agrarian Change*, 7(4): 526–53.

Selwyn, B. (2011a). ' Trotsky, Gerschenkron and the Political Economy of Late Capitalist Development', *Economy and Society*, 40(3): 421–50.

Selwyn, B. (2011b). 'Beyond Firm-Centrism: Re-integrating Labour and Capitalism into Global Commodity Chain Analysis', *Journal of Economic Geography*, 12(1): 205–26.

Selwyn, B. (2012). *Workers, State and Development in Brazil: Powers of Labour, Chains of Value*. Manchester: Manchester University Press.

Sewell, W. H. (1992). 'A Theory of Structure: Duality, Agency, and Transformation', *American Journal of Sociology*, 98(1): 1–29.

Shelley, S. (2007). 'The Outcomes and Usefulness of Union Learning', in S. Shelley & M. Calveley (Eds.). *Learning with Trade Unions–A Contemporary Agenda in Employment Relations*. Aldershot/Burlington: Ashgate, 115–30.

Silver, B. J. (2003). *Forces of Labor: Workers' Movements and Globalization since 1870*. New York: Cambridge University Press.

Sinwell, L., & Mbatha, S. (2013). 'Commemorating Marikana: The Spirit of Ambush Lives On', *Amandla*, 32: 32–33.

Skjærvø, K. A. (2011). 'Et alternativ til dagens allmenngjøringsordning', Report to Fellesforbundet, Oslo, January 2011.

Skrbis, Z., & Woodward, I. (2007). 'The Ambivalence of Ordinary Cosmopolitanism: Investigating the Limits of Cosmopolitan Openness', *The Sociological Review*, 55(4): 730–47.

Spalding, H. A. (1992). 'The Two Latin American Foreign Policies of the U.S. Labor Movement: The AFL-CIO Top Brass vs. Rank-and-File', *Science and Society*, 56(4): 421–39.

Spencer, B. (2007). 'The Present and Future Challenges of Labour Education in The Global Economy', in *Strengthening the Trade Unions: The Key Role of Labour Education*. Labour Education 2007/1-2, No. 146-147. Available at http://library.fes.de/pdf-files/gurn/00346.pdf. Accessed 4 April 2012.

Stan, S., Helle, I., & R. Erne. (2015). 'European Collective Action in Times of Crisis', *Transfer. European Review of Labour and Research*, 21 (2), forthcoming.

Standing, G. (2010). *Work after Globalisation: Building Occupational Citizenship*. Cheltenham: Edward Elgar.

Standing, G. (2011). *The Precariat: The New Dangerous Class*. London: Bloomsbury Academic.

Stang, G. C. (2008). 'Kortvarig ansettelse – langvarig læring? En studie av sammenhengen mellom arbeidsinnvandring, organisasjonsendring og læring i to utvalgte entrprenørbedrifter', unpublished master's thesis, University of Oslo.

Statistics Norway. (2011). 'Arbeid. Stabil yrkesdeltakelse og ledighet', *Samfunnsspeilet*.

Stevis, D. (1998). 'International Labor Organizations, 1864-1997: The Weight of History and the Challenges of the Present', *Journal of World-Systems Research*, 4(1): 52–75.

Stevis, D., & Boswell, T. (2007). *Globalization & Labor: Democratizing Global Governance*. Lanham, MD: Rowman & Littlefield.

Stiglitz, J. E. (2012). *The Price of Inequality: How Today's Divided Society Endangers our Future*. New York: W.W. Norton & Company.

Stinchcombe, A. (1965). 'Social Structure and Organizations', in J. G. March (Ed.). *Handbook of Organizations*. Chicago: Rand McNally, 142–93.

Stirling, J. (2007). 'Globalisation and Trade Union Education', in S. Shelley & M. Calveley (Eds.). *Learning with Trade Unions: A Contemporary Agenda in Employment Relations*. Ashgate: Ashgate Publishing Ltd, 207–24.

Støstad, J. E. (2013). *Sosial Dumping: Trues den Norske Modellen*. Oslo: Gyldendal Arbeidsliv.

Streeck, W., & Thelen, K. (2005). *Beyond Continuity: Institutional Change in Advanced Political Economies*. Oxford: Oxford University Press.

Strikwerda, C. (1999). 'Tides of Migration, Currents of History: The State, Economy, and the Transatlantic Movement of Labor in the Nineteenth and Twentieth Centuries', *International Review of Social History*, 44(3): 367–94.

Sturmthal, A. (1973). 'Industrial Relations Strategies', in A. Sturmthal & J. G. Scoville (Eds.). *The International Labor Movement in Transition*. Urbana, IL: University of Illinois Press, 1–33.

Süddeutsche Zeitung, 8-9 September 2001. Available at http://www.sueddeutsche.de. Accessed 18 January 2012.

Suri, J. (2003). *Power and Protest—Global Revolution and the Rise of Détente*. Cambridge: Harvard University Press.

Suzuki, H. (2008). 'European Integration and Trade Unions: The Role of Interest Groups in Policy-Making of European Integration and its Impact on National Welfare States', paper presented at International Symposium 'Implications for State Sovereignty of EU Integration in a Transnational World' Tokyo.

Tarrow, S. (2011 [1998]). *Power in Movement. Social Movements and Contentious Politics* (3rd ed.). New York: Cambridge University Press.

Tattersall, A. (2010). *Power in Coalition, Strategies for Strong Unions and Social Change*. Ithaca: Cornell University Press.

Thelen, K. (1999). 'Historical Institutionalism in Comparative Politics', *Annual Review of Political Science*, 2(1): 369–404.

Thompson, E. P. (1963). *The Making of the English Working Class*. Southampton: The Camelot Press.

Thompson, E. P. (1978). 'Eighteenth-Century English Society: Class Struggle Without Class?' *Social History*, 3(2): 133–65.

Thompson, E. P. (1991). *Customs in Common*. London: The Merlin Press.

Tilly, C. (1995a). *Popular Contention in Great Britain*. Cambridge, MA: Harvard University Press.

Tilly, C. (1995b). 'Globalization Threatens Labor's Rights', *International Labor and Working- Class History*, 47: 1–23.

Timming, A. R., & Veersma, U. (2007). 'Living Apart Together? A Chorus of Multiple Identities', in M. Whittal, H. Knudsen, & F. Huijgen (Eds.). *Towards a European Labour Identity: The Case of the European Works Council*. London: Routledge, 41–54.

Traub-Werner, M. (2002). 'Sustaining the Student Antisweatshop Movement: Linking Workers' Struggles', in M. Prokosch & L. Raymond (Eds.). *The Global Activist's Manual: Local Ways to Change the World*. New York: Thunder's Mouth Press/Nation Books, 191–98.

Trotsky, L. (1906/2007). 'Results and Prospects', in *The Permanent Revolution and Results and Prospects*. London: Socialist Resistance, 24–100.

Trotsky, L. (1929/2007). 'The Permanent Revolution', in *The Permanent Revolution & Results and Prospects*. London: Socialist Resistance, 111–256.

Trotsky, L. (1932/2008). *History of the Russian Revolution*. Chicago: Haymarket Books.

Trubek, D. M., & Trubek, L. G. (2006). 'New Governance & Legal Regulation: Complementarity, Rivalry, and Transformation', *Columbia Journal of European Law* 13(1): 1–26.

Tudyka, K. P. (1986). 'Die Weltkonzernräte in der Krise', *WSI-Mitteilungen*, 39(4): 324–29.

Turnbull, P. (2006). 'The War on Europe's Waterfront: Repertoires of Power in the Port Transport Industry', *British Journal of Industrial Relations*, 44(2): 305–326.

Umney, C. (2012). 'Managerial and Mobilising Internationalism in the British Docks and Seafaring Sector', *European Journal of Industrial Relations*, 18(1): 71–87.

United Nations. (2013). *Trends in International Migrant Stock: The 2013 Revision*. Available at http://esa.un.org/unmigration/wallchart2013.htm. Accessed 3 January 2014.

United Nations Conference on Trade and Development. (2008). *World Investment Report 2008: Transnational Corporations and the Infrastructure Challenge*. Geneva/New York: United Nations. Available athttp://unctad.org/en/Docs/wir2008_en.pdf. Accessed 18 December 2014.

United Nations Conference on Trade and Development. (2013). *Global Value Chains: Investment and Trade for Development*. *World Investment Report 2013*. New York/Geneva: United Nations. Available at http://unctad.org/en/PublicationsLibrary/wir2013_en.pdf. Accessed 18 December 2014.

Urata, M. (2010). 'Building Rank and File Activism: A Study of the Global Action Day Campaign in the History of the International Transport Workers' Federation', in A. Bieler & I. Lindberg (Eds.). *Global Restructuring, Labour, and the Challenges for Transnational Solidarity*. New York: Routledge, 58–72.

Van der Linden, M. (2003). *Transnational Labour History: Explorations*. London: Ashgate Publishing.

Van der Linden, M. (2006). 'A Case of Lost Identity? A Long View on Social Democracy Worldwide', in J. Callaghan & I. Favretto (Eds.). *Transitions in Social Democracy. Cultural and Ideological Problems of the Golden Age*. Manchester: Manchester University Press, 35–41.

Van der Linden, M. (2007). 'The "Law" of Uneven and Combined Development: Some Underdeveloped Thoughts', *Historical Materialism*, 15(1): 145–65.

Van der Linden, M. (2008). *Workers of the World: Essays toward a Global Labor History*. Leiden: Brill.

Van der Linden, M. (2014), 'San Precario: A New Inspiration for Labor Historians', *Labor: Studies in Working-class History of the Americas*, 10(1): 9–21.

Van der Pijl, K. (1998). *Transnational Classes and International Relations*. London: Routledge.

Van Goethem, G., & Waters, R.A. (Eds.). (2013). *American Labor's Global Ambassadors: The International History of the AFL-CIO during the Cold War*. Basingstoke: Palgrave Macmillan.

Véras, R. (2013). 'Suape em Construcao, peões em luta: o novo desenvolvimento e os conflitos do trabalho', *Caderno CRH*, 26(68): 233–52.

Véras, R. (2014). 'Brasil em obras, peões em luta, sindicatos surpreendidos', *Revista Crítica de Ciências Sociais*, 103: 111–36.

Vertovec, S. (2001). 'Transnationalism and Identity', *Journal of Ethnic and Migration Studies*, 27(4): 573–82.

Vester, M. (1970). *Die Entstehung des Proletariats als Lernprozess*. Frankfurt: Europäische Verlagsanstalt.

Waddington, J. (2006). 'The Performance of European Works Councils in Engineering: Perspectives of the Employee Representatives', *Industrial Relations*, 45(4): 681–708.

Wallerstein, I. (1995). *After Liberalism*. New York: The New Press.

Water is a Human Right. (n.d.). Available at http://www.right2water.eu/. Accessed 12 December 2014.

Waterman, P. (1998). *Globalization, Social Movements, and the New Internationalisms*. London: Continuum.

Webster, E. (1985). *Cast in a Racial Mould: Labour Process and Trade Unions in the Foundries*. Johannesburg: Ravan.

Webster, E. (2013). 'The Promise and the Possibility: South Africa's Contested Industrial Relations Path', *Transformation: Critical Perspectives in Southern Africa*, 81(82): 208–35.

Webster, E., Lambert, R., & Bezuidenhout, A. (2008). *Grounding Globalisation: Labour in the Age of Insecurity*. Oxford: Blackwell.

Weenink, D. (2008). 'Cosmopolitanism as a Form of Capital: Parents Preparing Their Children for a Globalizing World', *Sociology*, 42(6): 1089–106.

Werbner, P. (1999). 'Global Pathways: Working Class Cosmopolitans and the Creation of Transnational Ethnic Worlds', *Social Anthropology*, 7(1): 17–35.

Whelan, B. (2006). 'Ireland, the Marshall Plan and U.S. Cold War Concerns', *Journal of Cold War Studies*, 8(1): 68–94.

Wilderman, J. (2014). 'Farm Worker Uprising in the Western Cape: A Case Study of Protest, Organising, and Collective Action',. Research report, Global Labour University, Kassel, & the University of the Witwatersrand, Johannesburg.

Wills, J. (2002). 'Bargaining for the Space to Organize in the Global Economy: A Review of the Accor-IUF Trade Union Rights Agreement', *Review of International Political Economy*, 9(4): 675–700.

Wills, J. (2009). 'Subcontracted Employment and its Challenge to Labor', *Labour Studies Journal*, 34(4): 441–60.

Woolfson, C. (2007). 'Labour Standards and Migration in the New Europe: Post-Communist Legacies and Perspectives', *European Journal of Industrial Relations*, 13(2): 199–218.

Woolfson, C., & Sommers, J. (2006). 'Labour Mobility in Construction: European Implications of the Laval un Partneri Dispute with Swedish Labour', *European Journal of Industrial Relations*, 12(1): 49–68.

Wright, E. O. (2000). 'Working Class Power, Capitalist-Class interests, and Class Compromise', *American Journal of Sociology*, 105(4): 957–1002.

Wright, E. O. (2002). 'The Shadows of Exploitation in Webster's Class Analysis', *American Sociological Review* vol. 67(4): 832–53.

Xiaomin, Y. (2008). 'Impacts of Corporate Code of Conduct on Labor Standards: A Case Study of Reebok's Athletic Footwear Supplier Factory in China', *Journal of Business Ethics* 81(4): 513–29.

Xu, Y. (2013). 'Labor Non-Governmental Organizations in China: Mobilizing Rural Migrant Workers', *Journal of Industrial Relations* 55(2): 243–59.

Yates, C. A. B. (2003). 'The Revival of Industrial Unions in Canada: The Extension and Adaptation of Industrial Union Practices to the New Economy', in P. Fairbrother & C. Yates (Eds.). *Trade Unions in Renewal, A Comparative Study*. London: Taylor & Francis, 1–31.

Zajak, S. (2013a). 'In the Shadow of The Dragon: Transnational Labor Activism between State and Private Politics: A Multi-Level Analysis of Labor Activism Targeting China'. Cologne: University of Cologne, Max Planck Institute for the Studies of Societies.

Zajak, S. (2013b). 'Transnational Private Regulation and the Transformation of Labour Rights Organizations in Emerging Markets: New Markets for Labour Support Work in China', *Journal of Asian Public Policy*, 6(2): 178–95.

Zajak, S. (2014a). 'Europe meets Asia: The Construction of Access and Voice from Below'. Cologne: Max Planck Institute for the Studies of Societies, Discussion Paper 1/14.

Zajak, S. (2014b). 'Pathways of Transnational Activism: A Conceptual Framework'. Cologne: Max Planck Institute for the Studies of Societies, Discussion Paper 5/14.

Zeuner, B. (2004). 'Widerspruch, Widerstand, Solidarität und Entgrenzung: Neue und alte Probleme der deutschen Gewerkschaften', in J. Beerhorst, A. Demirovic, & M. Guggemos (Eds.). *Kritische Theorie im gesellschaftlichen Strukturwandel*. Frankfurt: Suhrkamp Verlag, 318–53.

Zoll, R. (2000). *Was ist Solidarität heute?* Frankfurt: Suhrkamp Verlag.

Zysman, J., Doherty, E., & Schwartz, A. (1996). 'Tales from the "Global" Economy: Cross National Production Networks and the Re-organization of the European Economy', Berkeley Roundtable on the International Economy, Working Paper No. 83.

Index

Notes on Contributors

Andreas Bieler is professor of political economy and fellow of the Centre for the Study of Social and Global Justice in the School of Politics and International Relations at Nottingham University. He is author of *The Struggle for a Social Europe: Trade Unions and EMU in Times of Global Restructuring* (Manchester University Press, 2006) and co-editor (with Bruno Ciccaglione, John Hilary, and Ingemar Lindberg) of *Free Trade and Transnational Labour* (Routledge, 2014). He runs the blog Trade Unions and Global Restructuring at http://andreasbieler.blogspot.co.uk/.

Marissa Brookes is assistant professor of political science at the University of California, Riverside. She earned her PhD from Northwestern University in 2013. She is currently preparing a book manuscript on the causes of success and failure in labour transnationalism based on a matched-pair comparative analysis of six transnational campaigns.

Roland Erne teaches international and comparative employment relations at University College Dublin. His work centres on European governance and the social and political implications of transnational movements. He is interested in how interest associations and social movements—particularly unions—respond to processes of regional integration and globalisation. In his most important book, *European Unions: Labor's Quest for a Transnational Democracy* (Cornell University Press), Erne describes the emergence of a European trade union movement that crosses national boundaries and challenges the assertion that no realistic prospect exists for remedying the European Union's democratic deficit.

Bianca Föhrer is in her final year of the PhD programme in industrial relations and human resources at University College Dublin. Prior to her doctoral studies, she worked in recruitment with leading multinational companies in Berlin and Dublin. Upon completing her dissertation, Bianca is looking forward to advancing her career in learning and development. Dedicated to lifelong learning herself, she is on a personal journey towards Reiki master and aspires to become a professional coach in the future. ·

Darragh Golden is a PhD candidate at University College Dublin. His research is focused on explaining variation with regards to stances adopted by Irish and Italian trade unions vis-à-vis European integration across time.

Idar Helle is a researcher in the field of contemporary history, with a special focus on labour movements and industrial relations in Norway and Europe. His publications on industrial relations and social movements include *Utfordrerne. Verkstedklubben og arbeiderne på Aker Verdal 1969-2009* (The Challengers: The Union and the Metal Workers at Aker Verdal [2009]). Helle has just completed *The History of the General Workers Union* (Pax Forlag, forthcoming).

Jenny Jungehülsing is a PhD researcher at the University of Kassel and holds a scholarship by the Hans Böckler Foundation, the foundation of the German Trade Union Federation. Her research focuses on the role transnational migration plays in international labour solidarity. She is co-editor of a forthcoming book on the challenges and opportunities to international solidarity in the era of globalization (VSA, 2015).

Knut Kjeldstadli was the project leader for the *Globalization and the Possibility of Transnational Actors* group. Kjeldstadli is professor of modern history at the University of Oslo. He has published books on labour history, urban history, Norwegian societal history, theory, and method of history. He edited *Norwegian Immigration History Volume I-III* (2003). Other books include *A History of Immigration: The Case of Norway ca. 900-2000* (with Grete Brochmann, 2013), *Sammensatte samfunn. Innvandring. Inkludering* (Complex societies. Immigration. Inclusion; 2008), and *Akademisk kapitalisme* (Academic Capitalism; 2010).

Tiago Matos is a PhD candidate in history and civilization at the European University Institute in Florence, Italy. His project looks at the relationship between crowds and the labour movement. He is also co-editor of the Norwegian web-based journal *Bytopia*.

Jamie K. McCallum is assistant professor of sociology at Middlebury College. His book, *Global Unions, Local Power: The New Spirit of Transnational Labor Organizing*, won the best book from the American Sociological Association's section on labour. His research focuses on labour, global political economy, social movements, and the history of work.

Jörg Nowak holds a PhD in political science. He currently works on mass strikes in Brazil, Russia, India, and China, and on Marxist accounts of rupture and revolution. His recent publications are *Strikes and Workers Movements in the 21st Century* (co-editor with Immanuel Ness and Madhumita Dutta; Pluto Press, 2015) and *Louis Althusser: Die Reproduktion des Materialismus* (co-editor with Ekrem Ekici and Frieder Otto Wolf, 2015).

Ingo Schmidt is academic coordinator of the Labour Studies Program at Athabasca University, Canada. His research focuses on international political economy and labour movements. His recent books include *Social Democracy after the Cold War* (co-edited with Bryan Evans; Athabasca University Press, 2012), and *Rosa Luxemburg's Accumulation of Capital* (in German; VSA Verlag, 2013).

Sabina Stan is a lecturer in sociology in the School of Nursing and Human Sciences, Dublin City University, Ireland. Her research has dealt with the postsocialist transformation of Romanian agriculture, and more recently with healthcare reform in Central and Eastern Europe, European East-West migration, transnational healthcare practices in Europe, the rising European healthcare system, and collective action in response to healthcare privatization and mobility in Europe. She has published with CNRS Editions (Paris) and Routledge, as well as in journals such as *Labor History, Social Science and Medicine,* and *Journal of the Royal Anthropological Institute.*

Charles Umney is a lecturer in employment relations at the University of Leeds. His PhD was awarded in 2012, and his thesis looked at international trade unionism from a Marxist perspective. More recently, his work has focused the labour market for musicians in London and Paris, and on the marketization of health and social care services in France.

Marcel van der Linden is president of the International Social History Association (2005–2010; 2010–2015), former research director of the International Institute of Social History, and professor for social movement history at the University of Amsterdam. Recent publications include *Workers of the World: Essays toward a Global Labor History* (Leiden: Brill, 2008, 2010; Brazilian edition 2013) and *Beyond Marx* (Leiden: Brill, 2013, edited with Karl Heinz Roth; Chicago: Haymarket, 2014).

Edward Webster is research professor in the Society, Work and Development Institute at the University of the Witwatersrand. Among his publications are *Grounding Globalisation: Labour in the Age of Insecurity*, written with Rob Lambert and Andries Bezuidenhout, winner of the 2008 Distinguished Scholarly Monograph Prize, awarded by the American Sociological Association Labor and Labor Movements Section. He is currently completing a book titled *Labour after Globalization: Old and New Sources of Workers' Power.*

Sabrina Zajak is junior professor for globalization conflicts, social movements, and labour at the Ruhr-University Bochum. She works at the Institute for Social Movements mainly on issues of transnational movements and activism, trade unions and nongovernmental organizations, globalization, governance, and labour standards. She is head of the research group 'Transnational Alliances between Social Movements and Trade Unions in Europe'. Recent publications include 'A Political Economic View of Social Movements: New Perspectives and Open Questions' in *Moving the Social* (2013).

Lightning Source UK Ltd.
Milton Keynes UK
UKOW04n1945061115

262242UK00001B/60/P